JAPAN'S EARLY EXPERIENCE OF CONTRACT MANAGEMENT IN THE TREATY PORTS

Japan's Early Experience of Contract Management in the Treaty Ports

YUKI ALLYSON HONJO

Routledge
Taylor & Francis Group

LONDON AND NEW YORK

First published 2003 by JAPAN LIBRARY

2 Park Square, Milton Park, Abingdon, Oxon OX14 4RN
711 Third Avenue, New York, NY 10017, USA

Routledge is an imprint of the Taylor & Francis Group, an informa business

First issued in paperback 2016

MEIJI JAPAN SERIES: 10

JAPAN'S EARLY EXPERIENCE OF CONTRACT MANAGEMENT
IN THE TREATY PORTS

British Library Cataloguing in Publication Data
A CIP catalogue entry for this book is available from the British Library

ISBN 978-1-903350-08-9 (hbk)
ISBN 978-1-138-97355-8 (pbk)

*To my parents who have always
supported me in all my endeavours*

CONTENTS

ABBREVIATIONS
& CONVENTIONS

All Japanese names in the text are listed with the last (family) name first and personal name second. For example, in the case of Itō Hachibei, Itō is the family name and Hachibei is the first name. To minimize confusion in the footnotes, a Japanese author's first name will be abbreviated and placed first; Ishii Kanji will be denoted as K. Ishii.

When referring to litigants in court cases, Japanese names are reproduced exactly as they appear in the publication. The modern transliteration will be noted in the text or footnotes. The original (mis)spelling was retained to aid any future non-Japanese speaker examining the original papers. Because the nineteenth-century transliteration of Japanese and Chinese was idiosyncratic, it was, at times, impossible to discern the original word.

All dollar figures are in Mexican silver dollars unless otherwise specified.

Western words and places in Japanese book and journal article titles are transliterated from the katakana syllabary. For example in K. Ishii's book, *Kindai Nihon Igirisu Shihon: Jyarudin Maseson shyōkai o chushin ni*, Jardine Matheson is 'Jyarudin Maseson'.

A reference is cited in full the first time it appears in each chapter.

THE FOLLOWING ABBREVIATIONS ARE USED IN THE REFERENCES:

Transactions of the Asiatic Society of Japan	TASJ
Foreign Office	FO
The Japan Weekly Mail	JWM
The Japan Herald	JH
The Japan Times	JT

(Note that *The Japan Times* and *The Japan Times Overland Mail* are separate publications.)

ACKNOWLEDGEMENTS

THIS STUDY could not have been finished without the input, guidance, inspiration, and assistance of many, particularly my supervisers Avner Offer and Ann Waswo who were instrumental in every stage and every aspect of this work. They were both a source of advice and vision. At the University of Tokyo, Professors K. Ishii and H. Takeda were extremely helpful in locating sources and S. Yoko of the International Students Office of the Department of Economics was also a constant source of support. Two people from my undergraduate days must also be thanked. A. Iriye, who was my undergraduate superviser for my senior honours thesis at Harvard University, was one of the first people to encourage my interest in the treaty ports. Y. Kira, as well as the rest of the staff of the Yokohama Archives of History, has continued to this day to be a source of information and ideas.

I would particularly like to thank the librarians at Oxford University, Tokyo University, Harvard University, and the Yokohama Archives of History. They were a most understanding and forgiving group. Also, the publicist at the Welsh National Opera was most helpful in providing me with information on *Madame Butterfly*. J. E. Hoare of the British Foreign Office was most kind in responding to my many queries. Without his expertise this book would not have been published. C. Woodruff and F. G. Notehelfer also gave many useful suggestions.

I owe a debt of gratitude to my friends and colleagues who have given me assistance and understanding. They are many, but

I particularly would like to mention A. Villanueva, P. Scalise, K. Okamura, M. Brown, D. Jeater, I. Tamm, J. Silversmith, J. Chessman, K. Fung, M. Nakabayashi, C. Gugenheim, and D. Brown. In Tokyo, I would like to thank the Furuta family; without their support, I surely would not have finished this work. The staff of Japan Library have demonstrated great patience with this manuscript.

I would also like to thank my parents, who maintained remarkably good humour through this protracted process.

My research was supported by grants from St Antony's, Oxford, the Japanese Ministry of Education and the Overseas Research Scheme.

The responsibility for all errors and omissions is mine and mine alone.

YUKI ALLYSON HONJO
May 2003

INTRODUCTION

Sono in quest paese
elastici del par, case e contratti. . .
Cosi mi sposo all'uso giapponese
per novecento novantanove
assi. Salvo a prosciogliermi ogni mese.
    Lt. B. F. Pinkerton in *Madame Butterfly*[1]

Tutto questo avverrà, te lo prometto
Tienti la tua paura – io son sicura
fede l'aspetto.
    Butterfly in *Madame Butterfly*[2]

THE TALE of the opera *Madame Butterfly* has been traditionally seen as a love story gone wrong; the American lieutenant betrays the love of the Japanese maid, and left with a child, she is driven to suicide. Puccini's opera, completed in 1900, was also about how a contract, albeit intimate, was misunderstood, and how that misunderstanding precipitated a disaster.

The opera's primary conflict centred on a misinterpretation of the terms of a marriage contract. The first act depicted the union of Butterfly, otherwise known as Cio-Cio San, and one Benjamin Franklin Pinkerton, a lieutenant in the United States Navy, in Nagasaki in 1889. Puccini depicted Pinkerton in the original production as a boorish, cruel creature who takes up a 'Japanese marriage' so he could enjoy all the benefits of being a married man. Pinkerton toasts, not his new 'bride' Cio-Cio San, but his future American wife and 'real' marriage. He also remarks that the marriage, like the house that he rents, is a contract for nine hundred and ninety-nine years that could be annulled with one month's notice. In this way, Pinkerton equates his commitment to the beautiful Butterfly to the lease on his house. The contract on the house and contract for Butterfly become conflated. Butterfly, on the other hand, is led to believe that this marriage is real and for perpetuity. She renounces her 'pagan' faith and insists that she be called 'Mrs B. F. Pinkerton'. Three years later in Act II, she tells Consul Sharpless that she believes that Pinkerton had married her under American law in which divorce is difficult. Pinkerton later leaves his 'wife' with his small child and returns to the United States, promising her that he will return. Butterfly eventually realizes that the tender words spoken by her 'husband' were false. Pinkerton's return to Nagasaki was not a happy event for Butterfly: he appears in Nagasaki with an American bride and demands Butterfly's son. Faced with a life without love and the loss of her child, Butterfly kills herself.

Yet, a contract was signed by both parties under no duress. In Act I, the Commissioner reads a contract aloud to the assembled guests and members of the wedding. Butterfly and Pinkerton sign the document, each taking the pen in turn under the Commissioner's guidance. The assembled guests, Butterfly's relations, are the witnesses. In the opera, the contract was valid under Western law. An American official, Consul Sharpless, was present and raised no objection. It was also valid under Japanese law as the Imperial Commissioner and Registrar conducted the contractual proceedings.

Clearly, the contract did not prevent the ensuing disaster as the expectations of Pinkerton and Butterfly remained disparate. Whereas Pinkerton believed that he was entering into a marriage in which he was to *play* the part of a husband and lover, Butterfly believed that she had actually entered into a real marriage. Pinkerton entered into the marriage precisely because of the convenient divorce procedures of Japanese law, and Butterfly believed that she could not be divorced as she had married an American subject to American law. Even within this intimate space between a man and a woman, the fundamental basis for their marriage was misunderstood and presumably undisclosed. One could imagine a rather far-fetched counter-factual scenario in which Butterfly is made to understand that the marriage is one of a temporary sort and that she could be divorced with one month's notice. Butterfly would have the choice of accepting that her marriage was more of a service agreement, or refusing the terms to await real love. In either case, it would be safe to say, Puccini's plot would lose its pathos and tragedy.[3]

Of course, *Madame Butterfly* is a fictional story which has been filtered through the Western consciousness of various authors.[4] The opera was as much a vehicle of that period's taste for exoticism and japonism as it was a story about late nineteenth-century Japan. And yet, as romantic, exotic, and often inaccurate as Puccini's Nagasaki may have been, the opera nonetheless highlights one of the problems that Japanese and Westerners faced in the treaty ports. Westerners and Japanese merchants were eager to trade not only their services, as perhaps in Butterfly's case, but also their goods. In order to trade, the Japanese and Western merchants had to conclude contracts which both sides understood and agreed upon. Both Japanese and Western merchants were eager to trade and pursue profit. Japanese merchants left their cities, towns, and villages and travelled to the treaty ports to trade with the Westerners. In turn, Western merchants sailed great distances from Europe, the United States, and Australia to trade in Japan. In 1861, Yokohama had 126 permanent foreign residents with about 10,000 seamen passing through the port. By 1885, the number of permanent Western residents in Japan had increased to 2,500, and in 1896, the number climbed to 4,700.

Yet the obstacles to trade were many. Until the arrival of Commodore Matthew Calbraith Perry's 'Black Ships' in 1853/4, the West had been largely inaccessible to Japanese merchants for trade except on a very limited basis with the Dutch living on Dejima island, Nagasaki. One obvious impediment was the language barrier. Initially, the Japanese did not speak any Western languages except Dutch, and the Westerners and their compradors (Chinese clerks) did not speak Japanese. To the Western merchants, Japan was an exotic 'fairyland' of which they had little knowledge. Both the Japanese and Western merchants were faced with unfamiliar business cultures with differing norms and practices. Many of the contracts made between the merchants were long-term open-ended contracts. Even when acting with good faith, the expectations could differ widely. For example, in the early 1860s when the ports first opened, there was no agreed procedure for who would pay the extra portage and storage costs incurred when ships were late coming into port.

Compounding these difficulties was the fact that there were plenty of opportunities for misunderstanding. Shipments of goods to and from Japan took time and were often late. In the interim, prices and demand could fluctuate widely. The trustworthiness of potential partners was not predictable, nor was there formalized redress for non-compliance with a contract through a court system. In this newly established community of merchants in the treaty ports, not only were the Japanese and Westerners unable to trust one another, the Westerners did not trust one another either. Law, the most obvious of instruments to ensure contractual compliance, was unclear at this time. Under extraterritoriality treaties between Japan and the West, Western residents were tried by Western law. Although the Western treaty ports superficially shared the same broad legal foundations, the American legal system was functionally different from the British. It goes without saying that the consular courts at this time were vastly different from the Japanese courts. Also, Japanese law did not have a discrete civil commercial code. Such non-legal tools of ensuring compliance as damaging reputation, gossip, and other forms of social censure were initially ineffective in the volatile and unstable treaty port community. Neither Japanese nor Western merchants had organized collective groups, such as guilds or formal registries, that regulated one another's behaviour. Hence, contracting, and thus credit, were difficult to establish in the Japanese treaty ports. Finally, to complicate matters even further, some of the merchants, Western and Japanese, were dishonest to begin with and had no intention of complying with their agreements.

What happens when two groups of people who are eager to trade find themselves operating in an environment of cultural and legal ambiguity? This study seeks to explore the problem by examining the experiences of Japanese and Western merchants in the period 1859-76, which is about two decades before the fictional story of *Madame Butterfly* took place. The main source of data are the English language transcripts and court summaries of civil disputes and complaints published in the local press such as *The Japan Weekly Mail* and *The Japan Times*. Also important were other primary sources such as letters, diaries, contemporary newspaper and magazine articles, and business papers. The treaty ports provide an opportunity to examine the impact and outcomes for two distinct communities who came together to trade without an established enforcement mechanism. When the ports opened in 1859, the two groups were relatively ignorant of one another. In order to trade, each merchant had to create solutions to overcome the problems and barriers he faced. Merchants, if they were to have long-term relationships with one another, had to create networks for credit and the exchange of information. How did these very different, and often very complex, communities form relationships? Did they trust one another from the outset? Did they choose to create complex agreements to avoid the risk? When did these transaction costs become obstacles in closing a deal? How did the merchants surmount the problems when expectations were not met? What were the mechanisms of trade on a day-to-day basis?

It is hoped, therefore, that this volume will fill a gap in the scholarship of treaty-port life in Japan by directly addressing the fundamental question: how did Western and Japanese merchants trade with one another? Although the treaty ports have been central in the body of Bakumatsu and Meiji Japanese history, the relevant studies, particularly those in English, have focused on either the nature of early trade, or on straightforward descriptions of treaty-port life. On a broader canvas, E. S. Crawcour, an authority of Japanese economic history of the Tokugawa and Meiji period, has also written about the treaty ports, but has emphasized internal Japanese trade and trade volume.

In Japanese, the treaty ports in the closing years of Japan's 'seclusion' have been the subject of both popular and scholarly interest. Novels, television mini-series, and comic books have been produced on the subject. A huge volume of scholarship on the treaty ports' ramifications for Japanese culture, economics, and society has also been written. Particularly notable is the high quality research and exhibitions from the Yokohama Archives of History, which has published monographs, books, and articles on all aspects of treaty-port life, ranging from maps, military personnel, to the sporting habits of Westerners, Chinese living in the treaty ports, and trade in the treaty ports. K. Ishii has published a number of works on banking and trade in the treaty ports, particularly *Kindai Nihon Igirisu Shihon: Jyarudin Maseson shyokai o chushin ni*, which centred on Japanese trade with the British.

On the treaty ports themselves, there have been only a handful of studies in English. J. E. Hoare's study, *Japan's Treaty Ports and Foreign Settlements*, is by far the most comprehensive work on treaty port life and the tensions that existed in these communities. Hoare's book focuses on the Westerners themselves and their lives, obsessions and beliefs in Japan in great detail. Other notable works are books by H. S. Williamson and P. Barr: however, both these authors wrote for a popular audience rather than a scholarly one. J. McMaster has written an unpublished Ph.D. thesis which also addresses the problems that British traders faced in the treaty ports and is well documented with research from Jardine Matheson and Co.'s papers. In addition, a number of biographies and memoirs have been published on the Westerners' lives in the treaty port era. However, unlike this study, all of these works have sought to describe and explain the *Western* residents' experiences in Japan, rather than focusing on the merchants' interactions with their Japanese peers.

Few have yet exploited the wealth of information contained in the treaty-port press as a source for trade practices. Thus far, no one writing in English or Japanese has sought to examine merchant interactions using the court documents. R. T. Chang has written a study of the court records of the Japanese treaty ports, but his work focused on the issue of justice and bias in Western consular courts. Dan Fenno Henderson has published a number of volumes on Japanese law and contract, but has focused on relations between Japanese, and not problems between Westerners and Japanese. J. H. Wigmore's detailed studies on Tokugawa Japanese business and law make for fascinating, if dated, reading. There has been one brief paper published in a Japanese law journal which translated a few mixed civil dispute documents of the Kobe British consular court into Japanese. In short, there has been little research on the subject at hand using the records of civil court disputes published in the treaty-port press.

The conceptual framework is based on the economic definition of contract. The word contract can be quite misleading as there are multiple definitions of contract depending on the legal, economic, or historical context. In this study, contract is an agreement for an exchange of goods and services that depends upon the principle of fully developed property rights. Given these rights, traders use contracts to exchange goods at an agreed price. Thus, contracts are mechanisms that can reduce transaction costs and stabilize expectations in an unstable market, as in the case of the newly-opened treaty ports. Transaction costs, in this thesis, are defined as those costs that are incurred in the trade of goods and services other than the price. For example, in the case of traders in the treaty ports, a specific transaction cost may be the costs for a translator needed in obtaining information and negotiating agreements. A particular contract cannot provide for every contingency because there exists potentially a wide variety of scenarios.

The economic perception of contract is intimately tied to the existence of transaction costs. Until Ronald Coase's seminal 1960 work, *The Problem of Social Cost*, the place of contract in an efficient market was ambiguous in terms of economics. Contract had been traditionally thought of mainly in legal terms. Coase's theorem stipulated that given zero transaction costs, production assets would end up in the hands of the most efficient users regardless of the initial distribution so long as property rights were well defined.

Coase's assumptions are admittedly heroic. In the world of Coase's theorem, three conditions were assumed: well-defined property rights, no transaction costs, and legal liability. In this study, we investigate the conditions of treaty-port Japan. Defined property rights, high transaction costs, lack of shared assumptions, and unpredictable legal remedy. Transaction costs are unavoidable in the real world. If we assume transaction costs exist, under Coase's theorem we can have two outcomes. Transaction costs are either not enough to prevent productive assets being allocated to the most efficient user, or the opposite, transaction costs prevent the assets from going to the most efficient user. In one study by R. Ellickson on Californian cattle ranches as an empirical example, it was found that Coase overestimated the influence of law and that actors reached their own mutually acceptable solutions through informal deals.

The idea of internalizing the obstacles to trade has been seductive and some economists have assumed that transaction costs are negligible when only two parties are in conflict. This assumption is false. Even among the tightly-knit community of Shasta County cattle ranchers, the transaction costs were enough to influence behaviour and their approach to problems. Among the heterogeneous group of treaty port merchants with few shared cultural assumptions, the effect of transaction costs was potentially even more disabling. We look here at the merchants' solution of what to do when one's business partner's behaviour is not predictable. Merchants made contracts with one another even though there was no legal structure to enforce contracts. Here, we go one step further than Ellickson's study by asking what happens to production assets when even law is unpredictable as a system of redress. Intuitively, one might think that a merchant would use all means available, even an unpredictable legal system, in order to clarify expectations in a contract. Coase's main point that conflicts could be resolved by the market alone is considered here in a different environment, arguably more realistic as transaction costs are taken into account. Another way of viewing the problem posed here is asking whether 'law' really does equal 'order'. What happens when law is uncertain? Does society descend to a Hobbesian state of nature? Given a market, do the actors create order?

Much has been made of the 'Japanese perception of contract' or lack thereof. A common preoccupation among legal scholars is the lack of a commercial code in the Western legal sense. Many scholars emphasize the fact that there was no formal legal concept or definition of contract during the Tokugawa period. The Japanese word for contract, *keiyaku*, had not existed in common parlance until the late nineteenth century and was invented by resurrecting the term from classical Chinese. Scholars have focused on the legal aspects of the formation of modern Japanese law, rather than actual contracting behaviour. In many of the studies of Japanese civil law, the tacit assumption exists that once a law was made, people would accept or reject it. In reality, the laws could play a more passive role: laws could exist in the background until a crisis forces actors to apply them. More subtle studies of how the law was used, if at all, have been lacking. The Japanese legal system in this time period was indeed different from the Western system, and this difference did have significance for Japan's legal development. Because the Western governments regarded the Japanese legal system as 'backward', the Western legal system was essentially forced onto the Japanese government as a precondition for the lifting of the unequal treaties. Modern Japanese law, such as the 1889 Meiji Constitution, was modelled on Western law.

Thus, we are principally concerned with what happened when law as a recognized and familiar system of redress was largely absent in this particular market. In the treaty ports, law was not strictly absent but was unfamiliar with high entry barriers to both parties: yet, both Japanese and Westerners managed to circumvent them. In addition, both Japanese and Western merchants had little legal consciousness. They made deals, and each had in his mind a notion of contract in which goods were to be exchanged. Their knowledge of proper contractual forms and rights was vague. Such ignorance of laws is not surprising as even in the present day, contracts in the arguably litigious United States are formed and dissolved with little reference to proper legal form. In the nineteenth century, it was unlikely that even the Western merchants were operating with precise legal notions of contract but rather with ill-defined ideas of fairness, justice, expediency and, at times, venality.

A merchant is defined here as any person, usually male, who bought and sold goods or services. In this admittedly wide definition, 'merchants' could include both merchant houses such as Mitsui or Jardine Matheson, and the proprietor of a bakery or a tea-stand. Cases in which one party is an institution of an official capacity, such as the Japanese or British government, will not be included as that changes the nature of the problem: the profit-seeking tendencies of a merchant house or single merchant are different from those of a public institution. Japanese merchants, when either a plaintiff or defendant to a Westerner's case, had their cases tried following Western procedure.

Western merchants, of course, were in an alien environment with a weak enforcement structure. The institutions of trade as

well as their business culture were transformed in Japan. Especially for non-British Western merchants, the court system was
weak and ambiguous because of a lack legal expertise. Among
Japanese merchants, social and official sanctions had long been
systematized. Japanese merchants, depending on whether they
were local to the treaty-port area, were sometimes subject to the
extra-legal pressures of other merchants and the Japanese community in order to ensure compliance. Whilst the question of
Japanese merchants' contractual procedure may be of historical
interest, we are concerned here only with the expectations of
Japanese merchants in order to form a basis of comparison.
Although a few papers have been written on general dispute resolution and adjudication in Japan, the treaty ports were a very
different trading environment from the rest of Japan. Unlike
shopkeepers in Japanese towns, the merchants were less accountable to their peers and their customers due to the particular
problems arising within the treaty ports. In fact, for some peri-
ods in the 1860s, it seemed to both Japanese and Western merchants that the treaty ports would be closed.

The seventeen-year period we are concerned with was defined with the parameters of this problem in mind. The starting
date of 1859 was chosen because it was the formal opening date
of the first treaty ports at Shimoda and Hakodate. Until that
date, Westerners were not allowed to trade freely with the Japanese, nor to reside in Japan. The treaty ports that opened in 1859
were different from the Dutch Dejima compound during the
Tokugawa period, in which the Dutch were limited to their small
island and access to trade was controlled by the Tokugawa authorities. Hence, an argument can be made that the majority of merchants were relatively ignorant of one another's business
practice. As we are concentrating upon the problems of cooperation and contractual compliance, the closing date of 1876
marked the end of this kind of relationship. In 1876, Japanese
merchants were able to make the first direct shipment of goods
to the West. With the advent of direct Japanese shipments, the
structure of the problem shifts; the Japanese merchants no longer had to cooperate with the Western merchants or accept their
terms. Compliance with the local Western merchants, therefore,
was no longer a necessity for trade with the West.

The use of court cases, of course, has a number of drawbacks. First, there is the issue of using dysfunction to describe function. Not much information remains on contracts that did 'work'. They may well have been quite different from those presented in court. At this point in time, all evidence of verbal contracts are purely circumstantial and second-hand. Moreover, court cases describe the situation when the disagreements could not be resolved. Thus, it could be argued that the deals that are described in court documents are not an accurate depiction of the deals that passed without disagreement. Karl Llewellyn characterized litigated cases as 'pathological' and as representative as 'homicidal mania or sleeping sickness [is] to our normal life'. However, we can assume that cultural norms are understood by both parties, and hence, the law is a solution of last resort. The legal arena was the place in which litigants argued their view of what correct contractual procedure should be, and thus provided an accurate picture of the merchants' expectations.

Another problem is credibility. Litigants may lie or be economical with the truth in order to further their case. Although the cases studied have used other corroborating sources of data to verify the statements, it was not always possible to check the background and validity of the testimony. However, even if the litigants did prevaricate, they told lies that they believed to be credible. Taken as a body of evidence, it is possible to draw conclusions on what was or was not considered acceptable behaviour. Because we are observing breakdowns of procedure, we can construct an idea of what normality was for these merchants.

Another potential problem is that the bulk of the evidence comes from the court records: the records were generated by a legal structure which was possibly marginal to the contractual negotiations. On the surface, it seems odd to use court documents when the court was seen as unpredictable. There are a number of ways of dealing with this issue. First, the court documents are not used to investigate the legality of the court decisions. The documents are used for their wealth of description. The legality, that is, the legal rights and duties of the merchants as stipulated by law, is not the central issue of this study, but is reviewed in relation to the problem of contractual compliance. For example, in the present-day United States, instigating court action is perceived as strategy of last resort because relations between parties usually become irreparable especially in small-scale cases. In the treaty ports, the merchants did not always have the resources to hire translators or research backgrounds and settle matters amongst themselves. Hence, the courts were used as mechanisms to settle disputes quickly, especially when a business relationship was not particularly involved or complicated.

Moreover, the fact that a legal system existed does not necessarily signify that the merchants had an understanding of legal rights or legal enforceability. In a case with a Western defendant and a Japanese plaintiff, the consular court system was based on the expertise and professionalism of the residing consul. For British defendants, the court procedures were well established because of the training that the consuls received in the British courts in China. The American consuls, on the other hand, were considered by some contemporaries to be corrupt and inept. For Western merchants in Japan, the boundaries of extraterrioriality were not always clear. On the Japanese side, the procedures in mixed cases with a Japanese defendant were equally uncertain. These cases were tried under the authority of the Japanese court but with the tutelage of a Westerner (usually the consular representative of the plaintiff) to ensure 'fairness'. For the Japanese merchant, this system of Western-influenced law was new, and for the Western merchant equally so, as substantial Japanese characteristics were retained. Finally, when these cases were settled under either court system, the results were not always enforceable. The fact that cases were tried did not necessarily mean that the treaty ports were under the rule of law. Both Western and Japanese merchants were able to evade their debts and obligations by leaving the treaty ports. The existence of a court system did not necessarily mean that the merchants knew how to exploit the legal system to their own ends. Indeed, the use of the court system involved a learning process.

Also, more importantly perhaps, successful Japanese-Western merchant relationships in the treaty ports seem to have stemmed not from expertise on a given commodity, but on a combination of reputation and opportunity. Expertise did not define the successful Western merchant; rather, the merchants' ability to manage expectations and information was the key to successful trade relationships. Indeed, the exchanges between the merchants may have been tied into a gift economy in order to lubricate the 'real' economy of goods and services.

Finally, it is worth remembering that merchants on both sides complained that the courts were biased, inefficient, and arbitrary, yet they still sought redress through them – perhaps because they were one of a few forms of norm-building.

THE TOKUGAWA LEGACY

My friends were envious. 'How is it that the tradesmen fall over themselves for you?' they asked. When I told them [I bought and sold swords], they said, 'That's no way to make money'. But make money I did – and plenty of it.

Musui's Story, the memoir Samurai Katsu Kokichi (1802-50)[1]

B E F O R E we fully investigate the problems of contractual relations in treaty-port Japan, it is necessary to outline the general historical context in which these merchants lived and worked in order to better understand merchant expectations.[2] Even before the arrival of Commodore Perry in 1853, Japan's economy and its governance were in a state of flux. While the creation of treaty ports and the sudden exposure to foreign trade did affect domestic trade patterns, the economy was already in a transition, which resulted in a series of economic crises. The treaty ports were not the only cause of the economic crises in Japan, but merely added to the disarray in Japan's markets, prices, and trade procedures. The trends towards urbanization and commercialization and the overall disorder in the Tokugawa economy, however, were rooted in the systemic breakdown of the governance structures of Tokugawa Japan.

THE EARLY TOKUGAWA BAKUFU: 1600-1750

The Japanese economy under the Tokugawa regime (1600-1868) was one that was based, at least officially, on the ideal of maintaining the political, economic, and social *status quo*. The 1500s had seen a period in which domains within Japan were in a state of almost constant war. Eventually, the disparate domains were unified, culminating with the creation of the Tokugawa regime under Tokugawa Ieyasu, the first of the Tokugawa shoguns. In this system, the Tokugawa shogunate (the largest of the domains and the *de facto* political authority) controlled a quarter of Japan's territory, and the other three quarters were controlled by roughly 270 daimyo (semi-independent domain lords). The Tokugawa government, or Bakufu, became the main administrative power in Japan, and the emperor and his court retained only a ritual significance. The domains were only nominally independent under the Tokugawa, and in the early Edo (Tokugawa) period, the Bakufu could essentially govern, either by persuasion or by command, the policies of the domains.

The seventeenth century was a period in which the Tokugawa systematically eliminated potential challenges to the Bakufu's suzerainty. To achieve it goals, the shogunate weakened the strength of the daimyo's domains by instituting a number of policies to maintain the political and military balance in its favour. For example, alliances between the daimyo were forbidden. Furthermore, the Bakufu limited fortifications and arms of the daimyo. In order to further occupy the resources of the domains, *corvèe* labour was also extracted for shogunate roads and other projects.

To prevent the daimyo from seeking foreign alliances, Japanese subjects were forbidden to leave Japan and most Westerners were expelled. The Bakufu perceived Christianity as a precursor to a Western invasion of Japan and took steps to eradicate the faith. Believers were made to renounce their faith or die. Trade with the West was limited to the Dutch on the island compound of Dejima in Nagasaki harbour. Similarly, the size and shape of sea vessels were regulated. All Tokugawa-period boats were small, without a keel, and flat bottomed. Such boats were only capable of coastal trips or travel by river. These regulations collectively formed the Tokugawa policy of 'national isolation', or *sakoku*.

One specific means of control over the domains was the system of alternate attendance, or *sankin kōtai*. In order to weaken the daimyos' local domain ties, the Bakufu mandated a system in which wives and heirs were left as 'hostages' in Edo (the political capital of Japan, later renamed Tokyo) and the daimyo themselves had to reside in Edo on alternate years. Under this system, heirs raised in Edo were cut off from their domains and were indoctrinated to accept Tokugawa authority. By living in the capital, the daimyos' opportunity to raise an army to challenge the Tokugawa was greatly diminished. This system had a two-fold advantage of preventing rebellions and financially weakening the daimyo. Maintaining a household in Edo was costly, and the Bakufu encouraged lavish expenditures on processions to and from Edo. These drains on resources diverted funds away from any potential insurrection. As time passed and the samurai became urbanized, they and their lords were transformed into bureaucrats and the threat of armed rebellion declined. Finally, the whole network was tied together with a system of road checkpoints, spies, and informants.

The Tokugawa economy was grounded on the principle of pacifying the warrior population which constituted between six and seven per cent of the population. It was in the Bakufu's best interest to maintain control over the samurai. The Bakufu's main strategy was to make them dependent on the shogunate for their social, political, and economic well-being. The shogunate gave all daimyo a fief of an estimated rice yield, and each samurai under the daimyo received a stipend in rice. This rice was sold and became cash. Disloyal behaviour resulted in revoking the fief or stipend. This system, called the *kokudaka*, replaced the *kandaka*, or cash-based system, in order to protect farmers and samurai from fluctuations in the rice market. In this way, all samurai received an income in exchange for loyalty.

The Bakufu created a social order by categorizing Tokugawa society into four groups deriving from Confucian ideals. In descending order of perceived value, samurai, farmers, artisans, and merchants. The groups were rigidly defined. Class proscriptions forbade samurai to earn a wage or farm, and farmers were forbidden to leave the land to trade or to soldier. With this measure, the Tokugawa guaranteed the loyalty of the domains and prevented farmers from joining armies. Merchants were, in theory, seen as unproductive actors who added nothing to the economy and were hence at the bottom of the social structure.

Economic growth was not a policy goal and was even eschewed because the Bakufu feared price rises which had the potential to unbalance the Tokugawa social order. In order to finance this system, rice was extracted in kind as a tax from farmers. The Bakufu forbade farmers to grow more profitable cash crops. In theory, farmers, who were taxed to subsistence levels, would not have disposable income for market activity, thus preventing economic growth and price rises. As coinage and its exchange was under the shogunate's monopoly, the exchange of rice to cash was to remain stable. In this way, the Tokugawa reasoned, the samurai would be satisfied and social stability would be maintained.

GROWTH AND CONSEQUENCES 1750-1800

Even with the best efforts of the shogunate, this arrangement did not remain tenable because the peace and stability established by national unification created an environment that fostered commercial activity. The resulting economic growth upset the balance of the Tokugawa policy of stability. Trade was no longer limited to local areas and coinage had replaced barter. The rise of urban centres was a major factor in the growth of commercial activity. *Sankin kotai* had transformed Edo into a city dominated by the daimyo and their attendants, and Osaka, which had already been a trade centre, consolidated its position as a entrepot city and a collection hub for tax rice.

The burst of commercialization and growth in the economy caused complications in the Tokugawa currency. The Bakufu had a monopoly on all metallic currency which consisted of gold, silver, copper, brass and iron. In the early seventeenth century, the official rate of exchange was one gold *ryo* (or *koban* coin) for 50 *me* of silver or 4,000 copper coins.[3] Silver was originally the standard, but by the 1770s gold was the main standard. The different metals were used concurrently. As the coins functioned independently of each other without restrictions, their relative values to each other were in constant flux. As the Tokugawa economy's need for currency grew, the Bakufu minted more coins. As the system was not rationalized, each issue had differing levels of purity so they too had differing relative values. However, the value of the coins was based on the assigned face value, rather than the metallic content. As consumption levels increased, the daimyos' consumption and therefore their need for cash increased. Because the Bakufu forbid the daimyo to mint coins, the daimyo resorted to issuing paper currency backed by rice. To further complicate matters, rice remained a form of currency throughout the Tokugawa period as taxes were expressed in bales of rice (*koku*) rather than in cash.[4] The shogunate and nearly all daimyo issued these notes in some 1,694 varieties.[5] The value of domain currency was not constant and varied from place to place. Besides these official issues, commercial paper became prevalent. The increased commercial activity resulted in merchant financiers providing banking needs by issuing drafts, loans, notes, and exchanging currency.

This initial burst of growth was not sustained beyond the early 1700s, but the social effects of the sudden growth disrupted the Tokugawa's original aims of social, financial and fiscal equilibrium.[6] Economic growth had resulted in the 'bottom' class of merchants becoming more prosperous, and the division between samurai and merchants was becoming less distinct. As the *Pax Tokugawa* wore on, the economic activity resulted in increased levels of consumption, and samurai sank into penury: the samurai class, whose income was tied to their fixed rice stipends, were now reduced in estate. Some samurai, though forbidden by class proscriptions, resorted to commercial activity.

Merchants, on the other hand, thrived under the Tokugawa peace and gained status and wealth. The market became more diversified. In Osaka and Edo, a rice futures market developed. Also in this period, the house of Mitsui, at present one of the world's oldest companies, developed from a small local saké and pawn-broking enterprise for pilgrims going to Ise shrine, to a dry goods retailer in the capital city of Edo. By 1691, Mitsui had branch stores in Osaka and Kyoto, and was established as the official bank of the shogunate. With this newly acquired wealth, merchant culture flowered; theatre, restaurants, literature, tea houses, and other amusements reached new levels of sophistication. Merchants, often flaunting austerity laws, began wearing fine silk stuffs, developed a quasi-samurai code of honour and formed academies to teach 'mercantile' ethics.[7]

Although the changes were slow and uneven, the agrarian

sector also experienced economic growth under the Tokugawa period. Improvements in farming technology and the commercialization of farming improved agriculture. Partial unification under the shogunate had brought peace; farmers were no longer called up for military service and were able to make long-term plans. Seeds, irrigation, tools, fertilizers improved in this period as well. Cash crops such as cotton, tobacco, and mulberry leaves (for silkworm feed) increased. With this shift towards cash crops came such cottage industries as cotton spinning, saké brewing, weaving, and dyeing.[8] With cash crops and regional specialization, wealth became concentrated in a few rural families and rural life became generally more commercialized than in the previous period of civil war which ended with the Tokugawa peace. The complex alliances of the large and tightly knit rural village farms were not as necessary for survival when peasants had other opportunities to make money. Village-wide farms were slowly divided into family units, thus loosening the land's hold on the populace.[9]

The economic growth and commercialization of agriculture was perceived as a threat to the stability of the Tokugawa regime. From the Bakufu's point of view, this shift from rice to cash crops and crafts diverted land and labour away from the rice tax base on which the samurai were entirely dependent for income. Less rice in an economy with growing consumption levels was seen as a twofold threat. Not only did the commercialization of farmers threaten the economic system of payments to the samurai, they jeopardized social stability as well. Namely, these changes in farming did not uniformly improve the life of the Edo-period farmer; cash crops and tenancy exposed peasants to price fluctuations and famine. Peasants became more vociferous and expressed their grievances in organized demonstrations, called *ikki*, which occasionally became violent. These disturbances, which had been rare in the previous 150 years, became widespread by the mid 1750s, and averaged six per year.[10] The Bakufu perceived the existence of rich peasants as a symptom of moral decay in the Confucian order of Tokugawa society.

In this period, the merchant class was garnering more power due to the samurai's increased dependence on them to finance their day-to-day expenses. In order to spend their stipends, samurai had to convert the rice to cash, and then spend the cash for goods and services. If the price of rice fell, their stipend would be worth less, and if the price of goods and services rose, again, the samurai would have less income. Thus, the Bakufu had to pursue the difficult economic policy of maintaining a high price for rice at the same time as keeping the price of other goods low.

Samurai had increasingly become dependent on merchants to convert their rice income into cash as well as for loans to cover the rising living costs of the urban samurai administrator. Although samurai were in theory to live a frugal life, they too surreptitiously partook of the pleasures and entertainment of the cities and often lived beyond their means. The two classes began to reach a sort of convergence: the samurai out of economic circumstance, the merchants by aping their betters. The 'top' was now in hock to the 'bottom', severely straining the social fabric.

To achieve its goals, the Bakufu attempted to retrench and discourage growth in a rapidly commercializing economy. Already there was an increased demand for currency to feed the new urban economies, and the shogunate resorted to debasing the currency, leading to inflation, which only worsened the situation. Another Bakufu method for controlling prices and consumption was the licensing of monopoly privileges within the major cities. In this complex system, wholesalers (*tonya*) were organized into guild-like associations called *kabu nakama*. The latter were given monopoly privileges as the shogunate's official agents. Agents from one city could only accept shipments from an approved list in another city. The Bakufu supervised the entire network in order to maintain price controls, and a similar system existed at the domain level in the domain castle towns.

Another control on the economy was the *Junin Ryogae*, the Ten Exchange Houses that served as a quasi central bank. This group of ten Osaka banks lent money to the domains and to smaller 'banks', issued bills of exchange for trade between other cities, controlled credit, and the market for gold cash and silver-denominated money. As the credit of wholesale retailers was in silver, and retail sales in other forms of cash, a shift in exchange rates between the different types of currency affected price levels. Also, the metals market reflected bank credit to cash supply.

Loans from the banks financed trade and industry through advances to wholesalers who in turn advanced funds for goods.[11]

The Tokugawa system of controlling trade and prices was largely viable up until the nineteenth century, and kept inflation in check. During the Edo period, the Japanese economy experienced a four-to-five-fold increase in trade volume and the amount of the currency entering the economy doubled. As time passed, Japan moved further away from the ideals set out by the original Tokugawa shoguns.

JAPAN ON THE EVE OF PERRY

By the turn of the nineteenth century, Japan had begun the process of shifting from a largely rural, agricultural economy to a more urban, commercialized one. In 1800, Japan was a pre-industrial country with a population that had stabilized at 30 to 33 million of which 80 to 85% was rural. While the majority was classed as rural farmers, a significant minority conducted trade and developed nascent industries. Often these farmers would work away from the farm on non-agricultural labour such as construction and transport during the slack months. In this way, a segment of the population was shifting back and forth from agricultural to informal commercial work.[12,13]

Urban centres in Japan had become significant and began to concentrate the population in cities and towns. The castle towns and large cities were centres of commercial activity. Nearly two million lived in the three urban sectors of Edo, Osaka, and Kyoto, one and a half million in castle towns, and a half a million in port and communication centres. Merchants, traders, and artisans composed half of the Edo population and met military and administrative needs. By the 1800s the non-samurai urban population of Edo had gained enough critical mass to sustain a demand for the merchants' services and products.

Even the cities themselves had become specialized. As mentioned above, Edo had become the seat of administrative power and entrepot trade. Osaka, which had been a trade centre from the 1500s, had fewer samurai living within its borders. Taxes in the form of rice were sent to the city to be exchanged for cash. Agricultural and manufactured goods flowed into Osaka and were distributed to other parts of Japan, often through Edo.

Kyoto, the oldest city in this triad, housed the imperial court and its attendants. Consequently, the city became known for its artisans and their luxury goods produced for the court and senior officials.[14]

By 1800, the system that had been established two hundred years earlier was no longer viable; the usual Bakufu methods for economic control such as austerity drives, price controls, and supervised monopolies could no longer stem the tide of commercial activity. The system of wholesalers could not control prices because of the increased overall consumption and commercial activities of rural and domain level markets. Intensifying the Bakufu's woes was the fact that its tax base of rice had shrunk and efforts to increase revenue were met with resistance by the domains as well as by farmers.[15]

Market competition had begun to create conflicts between the domains and the Bakufu. Domains, by avoiding the Osaka wholesalers, sold their goods directly to Edo and to other domains thus garnering higher profits. In villages, where trading and commerce were supposedly forbidden, merchants bought and sold goods. Whereas in the 1600s the Bakufu and the domains were in agreement about exacting a maximum amount of tax rice, the Bakufu and domains were now at odds. The domains recognized the potential of cash crops to fund their own activities and thus encouraged their growth.

Unfortunate 'acts of God' further destabilized the *ancien régime*. Extreme summer cold and unseasonable precipitation resulted in bad harvests in 1833 and 1836 and drove the up the price of produce by half. Shortages led to famine and civil unrest in both rural and urban areas. The price of rice fell in the following five years, but the price of other commodities remained high. By this point, price controls that had so assiduously protected the Bakufu had failed; rural and domain enterprise had reached such a volume that the price of commodities would not decrease. In addition, the amount of currency in the economy had increased significantly; from 1818-1838, the amount of currency in the economy had increased by 75%, and in the years following, new issues of silver coinage further debased the currency. Further increases in copper coinage only exacerbated the problem by fostering inflation.

The Bakufu, finding its authority undermined, sought to re-establish its hegemony and took drastic measures to return the country to orthodoxy with the Tempō Reforms. In 1841, the Bakufu announced a retrenchment and a return to the rural economy. Farmers were prohibited from trade and craft work and were forbidden from leaving their land in search of work. At the same time, the shogunate announced an austerity drive to improve the 'morality' of the agricultural class which had, in its eyes, drifted into decadence and was a cause of the rise in consumption. In an effort to force the fall of prices, the shogunate drastically reduced its own expenditure in the cities to reduce its consumption and debt and to weaken the urban merchants. The network of wholesalers and government monopolies was disbanded in the course of the reforms; it had become clear that controlling the Osaka-Edo trade was impossible. In 1842, the Bakufu ceased to prefer Osaka goods in favour of those from the Kanto area surrounding Edo.

That same year, the Bakufu demanded that domain monopolies be dismantled, perceiving the domain level monopolies to be a source of financial strength for the domains. Moreover, the domain monopolies' profits were not added to the shogunate coffers. The financial strengthening of the domains was seen as yet another threat to Bakufu authority in this environment of economic activity. This edict to dismantle the monopolies was met with varying levels of compliance. Trade and monopolies were the lifeblood of some domains, many of which were deeply in debt. Products were now to be traded freely in all domains, but many domains suspected that the Bakufu planned to exert national control over trade. Some domains, most notably Satsuma and Chōshū, strengthened their trade and nascent industries.

In 1843, the Bakufu mandated a 20% price cut in Edo and Osaka in order to reduce producers' profits and to constrict the supply of goods. The price cut, they reasoned, would impoverish the merchant class and make agriculture look less unattractive as an occupation. Rather simplistically, the Bakufu assumed that this plan would adequately control growth and act as a deterrent to commercial activities in rural and urban areas. However, this measure was a failure. Demand within Japan, especially outside the three main cities, was sufficient to absorb the supply of goods. Ironically, the major effect of the reforms was to further reduce rural crafts and worsen the living standards of the farmer. Merchants did not escape unscathed under the Tempō reforms, however. In order to lessen the samurai's debt and their rapidly decreasing standard of living, the Bakufu announced a variety of programmes that would relieve or refinance samurai liabilities. These programmes were funded by a number of forced 'loans' on the merchant community at low rates. In addition, the government announced a number of loan amnesties that forgave samurai loans owed to merchants. Although these measures were not without consequences, the Tempō reforms and other economic retrenchment policies of the Bakufu did not destroy the merchant class nor completely smother commercial activity.

JAPAN AND THE WEST

It was within this environment of economic transition and political friction that Western ships first made their appearance in Tokugawa Japan. Japan had been closed to the West for the best part of 250 years. Along with the breakdown of the governance structures, the turn of the century saw a softening in Japan's isolationist policies. By the turn of the century, Japan's isolation from the West was no longer total; Russia was pushing for fur trapping rights in Hokkaido, and a number of failed missions from the US and Britain nipped at Japan's national isolation. It had become apparent to some in the Bakufu that the policy of *sakoku* could not be maintained forever in the face of the West.

Internally, there was a subtle shift in policy and in the manner elites perceived the West. As the hard attitude towards the West somewhat abated in the eighteenth century, a significant scholarly minority in Nagasaki began to study *Rangaku*, or 'Dutch learning'.[16] These scholars, though largely outside of government circles, were significant in two respects. First, they could read Dutch, which would later prove useful in dealing with the West, and second, they were aware that Western technology was superseding Japan's. By the 1800s, returned castaways were no longer executed and were instead treated as sources of information. Some domains had clandestine contact with foreigners.

11

The treaty the Bakufu signed with US Commodore Matthew Perry after his return to Edo bay in 1854 was both a turning point in Japan's relations with the West as well as in the Bakufu's relations with the domains. Perry's expedition into Edo bay publicly brought to a head the deficiencies of Japan's military defences against the West. It also exposed the Bakufu's political vulnerability to the domains, of which some had been garnering power and resources during the Tokugawa peace. Perry had left Japan promising to return in the following year to complete the treaties, and in his wake, he left a debate over national isolation. In an effort to garner a consensus on the policy towards the West, Abe Masahiro, a senior councilor (*roju*) sent copies of Perry's letters and sought opinions from the domains on a course of action. Not only did the very act of consensus-building expose the Bakufu's increasing political frailty, but also the domains used it as an opportunity to polarize opinions on foreign policy. The majority of the ruling class initially asserted that maintaining the policy of national isolation was best, but at the same time sought to avoid hostilities with clearly superior military powers. The *roju* were aware of China's troubles with the British and wished to avoid repeating such conflicts in Japan. A minority faction, which included Lord Ii Naoskuke of Hikone, a future regent to the under-age shogun, advocated defending Japan by modernizing the Japanese military with Western technology. On the other hand, an equally vociferous faction, which included Tokugawa Nariaki, advocated rejecting the West's demands. Military action against the West would have been preferable, in his view, to the potential loss in morale that would result from ending national isolation. These prominent and vociferous factions fractured both the consensus as well as the Bakufu's power base.[17]

When Perry returned in 1854, the Bakufu negotiated a treaty that was more a maritime than a mercantile treaty. Nevertheless, this treaty paved the way for future discourse with the West; it guaranteed the opening of Shimoda and Hakodate as ports of call from which US ships could obtain coal and supplies, good treatment of shipwrecked sailors, the appointment of a US Consul in Shimoda, the most favoured nation clause, and finally, a vaguely defined right to purchase goods at the ports of call. It was not until US Envoy Townsend Harris arrived in Japan 1856 that a true commercial treaty was signed. Harris had been ordered to obtain a treaty that was similar to that of Britain's 'unequal treaty' with China. In theory, this stipulation meant trade under the principles of equality and *laissez-faire* capitalism.

The reality was far less palatable to the Japanese than pure free trade. The US treaty stipulated full access in specified ports, low tariffs, and extraterritoriality. All this, presumably, was negotiated with and backed by gunboat diplomacy. The commercial treaty that Harris negotiated in 1858 managed to accomplish all of these goals. Harris obtained promises to open Kanagawa and Nagasaki in July 1859, Niigata from January 1860, Hyogo (Kobe) in January 1863. In addition, Edo was to be opened for trade in January 1862, and Osaka in January 1863. Within these ports, Americans were to have complete access to free and unrestricted trade. Each port was to have a consul by whom Americans would be tried. Tariffs on Japanese exports ranged from 5-20%. Unlike the Chinese treaty-port system, however, opium was prohibited except in medicinal quantities in deference to the Bakufu's fears.

Although the treaty was a success for the Americans, on the Japanese side, it only furthered the divisions within the ruling class. The treaty remained unpopular although the majority of officials and the daimyo had accepted that Japan could not avoid trade with the West. In order to obtain legitimacy, the Bakufu needed the sanction from the symbolic head of state; the emperor. Lord Hotta Masayoshi of Sakura, who succeeded Abe, had miscalculated the emperor's pliability; in 1858 the Emperor Komei refused to sign the treaty. The imperial house's refusal to ratify the treaty was not so much an anti-foreign reaction; the house did not want to commit to a policy towards the West while the divisions existed between daimyo and the Bakufu. To further entangle matters, the imperial house was using the issue as leverage to choose the shogunate's successor. Ii replaced Hotta, and with him, the entire council of *roju* was replaced. Ii first tried to the secure the emperor's favour by attempting to resolve the Tokugawa succession dispute, but the signing of the treaty between Britain and China at Tientsin forced Ii to take matters into his own hands. Harris claimed that the British fleet would immediately set sail for Japan to demand a treaty. If a treaty with the US was signed, he pressed, it would put Japan under US protection. On July 29, 1858, Ii signed the treaty without imperial sanction. The British under Lord Elgin did eventually arrive, but with only one ship. Within a month, Britain, Holland, Russia and France all signed treaties based on the US model with most favoured nation clauses. Although Ii later obtained imperial recognition that he signed the treaty under duress, he did not fare well as he made powerful enemies and was seen as overstepping his authority. By signing a treaty with the US, Ii had committed political suicide and actual suicide. Pro-imperial forces assassinated him in 1860.

By 1858, the scene had long been set for a confrontation between the domains and the shogunate. After the treaties were signed, the players were the five Treaty Powers, the Bakufu and the daimyo. The struggle over control of foreign trade became the struggle for power between the Bakufu and the daimyo. The Bakufu was more concerned with the domestic political dimensions of the treaty ports, and economic concessions were freely given away to the Treaty Powers. In the process, the political and economic equilibrium between the Bakufu and the domains began to shift.

THE TREATY PORTS

Treaty ports came into being within this framework of domestic and international tensions, and the ensuing political instability had real effects on the merchants' environment. The members of the Bakufu and daimyo regarded the treaty ports with suspicion. The presence of the Westerners – whether diplomats, traders, soldiers, or sailors – was seen as a threat to the Bakufu's political and economic governance. For this reason, the Bakufu sought to contain the ports away from the rest of Japan. The Treaty Powers and the Bakufu had to resolve the conflict between the shogunal agenda of stable domestic politics and economic control, and the official Western policy of maximum market access.

In the case of Yokohama, by trade volume and population the most significant treaty port, the Bakufu's efforts to impose physical separation from the rest of Japan's population were particularly marked. From the opening of trade, the Bakufu attempted to contain the foreign merchants. Under the treaty signed with Perry, some ambiguity existed over the first treaty port, Kanagawa. The Treaty Powers understood the word to mean to the village of Kanagawa, whereas the Bakufu assumed that the word referred to the region. The Bakufu decided that the village was not a suitable locale for the foreign population. Although the city itself was a thriving port and post town, Kanagawa was on the Tokaido, the main road by which daimyo would travel en route to Edo. The Bakufu regarded this proximity as hazardous: a potential flashpoint between foreigners and anti-foreigner daimyo. Again, any major incident would lead to larger concessions to the West and erode the Bakufu's authority. As violence against Westerners escalated in the 1860s, this concern was not entirely without foundation. The Bakufu situated the treaty port away from the Tōkaidō (the main east-west highway connecting Edo with Kyoto) in the village of Yokohama across the bay from Kanagawa village. The diplomats of the Treaty Powers protested, claiming that the Bakufu was not only violating the treaty but also plotting to create a new Dejima and isolate the Westerners.

The Bakufu successfully enticed the Western merchants to Yokohama by building warehouses and houses. To further convince the merchants to come to Yokohama, the Bakufu ordered the creation of a pleasure/prostitution district called Miyosaki, but more commonly known as Gankiro. Although the origin of this area is often attributed to a nameless foreign consul who had asked the Japanese 'to establish such a place for the unruly sailors, soldiers, and beachcombers who were streaming into the port and making life miserable for the sober resident', the Bakufu had included it in their plans from the inception of the port.[20] As the Rev. Dr William Elliot Griffis, a resident of Yokohama in the late 1800s, remarked, 'the Yoshiwara [pleasure district] and the Customs House were the two institutions supposed to be indispensable to a foreign port'.[21]

Beside the diplomatic technicality of whether or not the Japanese violated the treaty over the site of the enclave, the Western officials were concerned whether 'free trade', similar to Chinese treaty port trade, could be carried out in Yokohama. Treaty Power officials were particularly concerned with the geography of Yokohama. The port area consisted of two towns of approximately equal size – the foreign enclave and the Japanese town, which together occupied approximately two square miles in area. Each boundary of the enclave was bordered by bodies of water. The enclave took the form of a rough rectangle that had three major streets running east-west with lesser thoroughfares. The area along the bay, facing roughly north, was known as the 'Bund'. There was a slight elevation known as the 'Bluffs', which had the 'Creek' flowing at its base. Connecting to the creek was the river, and west of this was the Japanese town.[22] In addition, there was a swamp behind the foreign enclave where the river flowed into an estuary. In short, the foreign enclave was an island surrounded by swamp, ocean, and river.

The main landing facilities were two stone piers close to the Custom House. The French wharf was to the east, in a less ideal position. The activity on the wharf was well captured by contemporary print-makers such as Sadahide.[23] The centre of both Yokohama towns was sometimes referred to as 'Blood Town' due to the predominance of drinking establishments and subsequent brawling. On the European side, consignment houses, trading firms, and godowns (warehouses) set up shop, as well as service-oriented businesses such as hotels, clothiers, and grog shops. On the Japanese side, traders came from all parts of Japan to ply their wares. Thus, the central area of both sides of Yokohama formed an enclosed trading zone.

Access to the enclave was restricted. Behind the Japanese town, where the river reached the estuary, a bridge connected Yokohama to the rest of Japan. A causeway connected Yokohama to the village of Tobe, the residence of the Governor of Kanagawa. This structure, Yoshida-bashi, had heavily guarded gates at both ends that were closed at sundown. On the eastern side, facing the Bluffs, were three small heavily-guarded bridges which spanned the Creek and led to the town of Honmura.[24] In order to get to Miyosaki, one had to walk a narrow causeway of about 1000 feet across the swamp, which, like the others, had a gate at the end. Thus, the enclave was not only isolated, but could also be tightly controlled. The geography invited comparisons to Dejima where the Dutch were confined during the Tokugawa period. Neither the American nor the British officials wanted trade to occur under what they saw as humiliating prison-like conditions. The Treaty Powers were also concerned that the confined geography was a constraint on business transactions and that trade could easily be suppressed.

Yokohama, by population, was by far the largest of the foreign enclaves. In 1861 there were 55 British residents out of 126 foreigners. By 1864, there were at least 200 British merchants, and half that number of merchants of other Treaty Powers and transients. Although the US was first to secure a commercial treaty with Japan, the incipient Civil War diverted its focus. Britain, with its business interests and fleet in China became the leader among the Treaty Powers. In addition, the garrison and the fleet ensured a presence of 6-7,000 troops. The Japanese population in the area also increased. In 1863, the Yokohama area had a Japanese population of 8,000 inhabitants. By 1865, the number increased to about 18,600. Nagasaki, the other major treaty port, had a Western population of 200 in 1862 in a city of 50,000 Japanese.[25] In addition to the Western population there was a sizeable Chinese population. Some came attached to the Western merchants as domestic staff, accountants, translators, and clerks (compradores), whilst others were traders in their own right.[26] The total foreign population in 1875 was about 5,000 strong, of which approximately half were Chinese.

TREATY PORTS AND THE BAKUFU

It should be noted that not all Bakufu officials thought that the treaty ports were a necessary evil. Some of them regarded the treaty ports as an asset for Japan. To some extent, the shogunate chose the Yokohama area for its potential effect on the surrounding regions. In the negotiations between Harris and Tadanari Iwase, a key Bakufu representative, the latter chose Yokohama as an open treaty port on economic grounds. In Iwase's view, the new international port should be built near Edo, because unlike other sites, Edo did not have any natural advantages. As a city built on 'human effort [*jinryoku*]', Yokohama would bolster Edo by increasing trade. Like others in the government, he assumed that the trade with foreigners would be controlled by key Edo wholesalers known to the Bakufu. In Iwase's view, choosing Yokohama as an international port was the first step in assuring Japan's well-being in an increasing global environment.[27]

The result was not as Iwase envisioned. Harris' commitment to 'free trade' – to the extent of securing as many economic rights for the Americans as possible – made any scheme that included officially sanctioned middlemen impossible. The disarray of the Bakufu's governance over politics and the economy created an environment in which a new type of Japanese merchant flourished in the treaty ports. With the breakdown of economic controls, merchants no longer had to buy into a guild or be part of the domain system. Japanese merchants in the treaty ports were increasingly free agents who traded for themselves rather than for a representative. Within the treaty ports, 'men from nowhere', that is, men from rural areas and few inherited official connections, came into prominence by means of their ability. Edo did grow into a distribution centre for foreign goods, and Yokohama merchants' demands for silk further stimulated the silk-growing area of North Kanto. Although Edo merchants set up branches in Yokohama, these purveyors of craft goods were outstripped by rural merchants of silk, tea and oil. In this way, the Bakufu lost its major mechanism of control over the nascent trade.

The most obvious effect of the opening of foreign trade was accentuating the original problem that the Tempō Reforms sought to address. Inflation and price rises. Japan, after some 250 years of isolation, now had to contend with the world market. Although the Bakufu's financial disarray was not entirely caused by the foreigner's presence, the issues over the currency were a visible result of the treaty negotiated with Harris. Under the Chinese treaty-port system, silver was exchanged based on its weight. Harris had insisted on this arrangement in Japan so that currency exchanges throughout Asia would maintain uniformity. However, the currency system in place in mid-nineteenth century Japan was one based on gold with less than three per cent silver in circulation.[28] Small silver coins in circulation in Japan reflected a nominal floating value. The Bakufu did have a largely unused official exchange rate for its coinage which was coincidentally close to the international exchange of fifteen to one. However, Harris pressed to have these silver token coins exchanged for gold based on their weight, reducing the Japanese silver-gold ratio to five to one. The Bakufu attempted to regrade the currency by minting larger coins to replace the silver tokens.

The Treaty Powers, rather unjustly, protested that prices for foreigners would rise. For a few weeks, gold drained out of Japan in what was called the 'Gold Rush' in which Westerners made massive profits. In theory, Western merchants would buy gold with Mexican silver dollars, the international currency at the time, at the weight-for-weight ratio of five to one. Then they would take the gold bought in Japan overseas to Hong Kong, or other such treaty ports, and exchange the gold for silver at fifteen to one. In this way, Western merchants could make nearly a 300% profit. In reality the profits were more along the lines of 50% because the cash could not actually be exchanged at that rate, and rumours of a 'Gold Rush' was more part of popular merchant lore, rather than actuality.[29] In 1860, the Bakufu reduced the size of the gold *ryo*, effectively degrading the currency and causing massive inflation, which benefited gold-holding Japanese merchants. The income of tenant farmers and of samurai, who were on a fixed stipend, was suddenly reduced. By 1866, the general price level was four times the pre-treaty level.[30]

The domestic market was further damaged by foreign demand for silk and tea: 50-80% of export value was raw silk.[31] A silk blight in France that had destroyed most of its domestic production led to an increase in the value and importance of Japanese silk. In order to keep the industry employed, Western merchants began to import Japanese raw silk. With all the raw silk diverted into Western hands, not surprisingly, the Japanese manufactured silk industry suffered. Shortages became widespread, and within the urban centres, especially Kyoto, an entire industry of weavers, silk painters, spinners, and tailors began to starve. In one emergency measure, the equivalent of soup kitchens fed Kyoto silk artisans. The Bakufu, whether in an attempt to control domain monopolies or reduce shortages, moved to institute control of national trade. Faced with disruption in the markets and potential riots in its urban centres, in 1860, the Bakufu declared that raw silk, oil, grain, textiles and wax would first have to be sold to Edo, only after which the quantities for export would be determined. This system had a two-fold benefit for the government; it increased its revenue, and raw silk could be diverted into domestic markets to prevent shortage. By 1864, the Bakufu had all but stopped exports of silk under this system.

Domains, whose sovereignty over trade was eroded, and treaty-port merchants, who no longer had access to silk, and Treaty Power diplomats, who claimed treaty violations, all protested this policy.

Not surprisingly, the treaties became deeply unpopular among the samurai and those earning a fixed wage. Divisions between Bakufu and daimyo deepened and samurai harboured resentment against the foreigners who were seen as the source of all these social ills. The Bakufu tried to use the escalating violence against foreigners to postpone the opening of Edo, Osaka, Hyogo and Niigata and sent a mission to Europe to plead its case. The European Powers especially France, which depended on Japanese silk, refused to close any ports. Instead, the Japanese secured the London Protocol, by which trade with Japan would be expanded by reduced tariffs in compensation for postponement. Treaty Powers assumed that the Protocol would force the Bakufu to enforce the treaty throughout Japan, but this was impossible, due to the Bakufu's weakened state and the structure of governance. The result was far from what the Treaty Powers hoped. Daimyo were not mollified, and the West sought further concessions.[32]

'THE BLOODY 60s'

It was only a matter of time before the anti-Western samurai would attack foreigners. In 1859, one month after the opening of Yokohama, Russian sailors were attacked and killed. Within the next year, a Japanese interpreter and two Dutch captains were also killed. The January 1861 killing of Harris' secretary, Henry Heusken, and the July attack on the British legation pushed the Treaty Powers on to the defensive. The attack on the legation was an organized political action aimed towards disrupting Japanese relations with the Treaty Powers. In this respect, the action was almost a success; all of the Treaty Powers except the US (Harris) withdrew from Edo to Yokohama in protest. However, as the Tokugawa were not versed in Western diplomatic discourse, they did not see the retreat as a protest. Sir Rutherford Alcock, head of the British legation, brought troops from China and from this point on, the treaty port was 'guarded' by British troops.

In September 1862, the 'Richardson Affair' (*Namamugi jiken*) brought the tensions between the daimyo, Bakufu and the Treaty Powers to a graphically violent and public crisis. C. L. Richardson, a British merchant and his companions were attacked by Satsuma domain retainers when the Westerners did not dismount from their horses while watching the Satsuma daimyo procession. Richardson was hacked to death in the attack and the others were wounded (one of whom was a woman which only heightened the drama in Western eyes). The Treaty Powers, lead by Britain, demanded that Satsuma surrender the men responsible for the attack. Satsuma refused, and the Bakufu, embarrassingly, did not have enough political leverage to compel the domain to give up the men. Britain demanded an indemnity of 100,000 pounds from the Bakufu as well as a separate indemnity from Satsuma of 25,000 pounds. Britain stipulated that the attackers should be punished. The Bakufu, caught between the daimyo and the Treaty Powers, tried again to negotiate for closure of the port. The British representative, St John Neale, Alcock's temporary replacement, took decisive action against Satsuma; he seized three Satsuma ships and came under fire. Both sides inflicted enough damage so that each claimed victory over the other. In the end, Satsuma promised to pay the indemnity with only vague promises to produce the men.

During this time, the Bakufu had had to contend with an increasingly strident and anti-foreign imperial court. Since Ii had signed Harris' treaty without his sanction, Emperor Komei was frustrated and angry over what he saw as disrespect towards the court. He and the imperial house pressed for the foreigners' expulsion and the closing of the treaty ports. The Bakufu agreed to an arbitrarily set expulsion date of 25 June 1863 hoping to negotiate its way out of the agreement while it dealt with daimyo and the Treaty Powers. The Chōshū domain on this date, took matters into its own hands and fired on an American ship in the straits of Shimonoseki in an act of 'imperial loyalty'. After further sinkings of treaty-power ships, the straits were closed, greatly disrupting shipping to and from the rest of Asia. The Treaty Powers demanded that Shimonoseki be opened as the attacks were disrupting the silk trade in Yokohama, but the Bakufu was not able to guarantee the safety of ships going through the straits. Realizing that the Bakufu was powerless over the domains, a joint treaty-power punitive expedition against Chōshū was launched in 1864. British, Dutch, French and American ships shelled the straits and extracted a treaty from Chōshū which re-opened Shimonoseki.

The actions of Satsuma and Chōshū marked a turning point for the Bakufu's relations with the Treaty Powers as it exposed to the Treaty Powers the Bakufu's lack of political clout and inability to force the domains into following policy. Its status as a 'national' government was, in the eyes of some Treaty Powers, greatly diminished. Accepting that the Bakufu was unstable, Britain adopted a policy that recognized the domain's demands. Unlike Britain and the rest of the Treaty Powers, France not only followed a policy of recognizing the Bakufu as the legitimate power, but also actively seeking to sustain the government. At this point, within Britain, the public and Parliament lost its taste for Chinese-style gunboat diplomacy in Japan and Alcock was replaced by Sir Harry Parkes in 1865. Parkes, ironically, had been a diplomat in China and was very much a proponent of armed diplomacy.[33]

When the Treaty Powers discovered that the Bakufu had acquiesced to the 25 June expulsion edict, the Bakufu's bargaining position with the West was further weakened. The treaty resulting from the Chōshū expedition was a financial blow: the Bakufu was to pay an indemnity of three million Mexican dollars as well as pay for the incursion. The Bakufu again pressed to close the ports, but the Treaty Powers refused. The Bakufu could not pay the indemnity due to its large size, thus trading rights were expanded in lieu of payment. The resulting tariffs convention of 1866 fully 'opened' trade within the treaty ports. The vast majority of imports and exports, including silk and tea, were set at a five per cent duty. Treaty Powers were allowed to trade with all Japanese without government interference or control. Finally, Japanese were to be allowed to trade with foreigners abroad. Economic rights were handed to the Treaty Powers in exchange for momentary political stability.[34]

THE MEIJI RESTORATION

The Bakufu's inability to balance the demands of the imperial court, the daimyo, and the Treaty Powers culminated in 1868 when it was overthrown by the 'pro-imperial' domains, led by Satsuma and Chōshū, who 'restored' the emperor as the head of state, removing the Tokugawa from Edo. In 1867, Komei was succeeded by Emperor Meiji, who was a mere teenager at the time. Armed conflict erupted in January 1868 when the daimyo converged on Kyoto and continued until 1869 when the Tokugawa fleet surrendered in Hokkaido. By spring of 1868, however, Edo had fallen, thus ending the political conflict between the daimyo and the Tokugawa Bakufu. The new government, it was claimed, returned authority to the hands of the emperor and took it away from the self-serving Bakufu who had, among other sins, handed the country to the Treaty Powers. The reality was far from their stated aims: the resulting centralized government was not emperor-led, nor did it overturn the agreements that had been formed under the Bakufu. The government, similarly, was led by a group of elders chosen from the 'imperial' forces, thus merely replacing one group of warriors with another. However, rather unlike like the *roju*, the new system, as delineated in the Charter Oath of 1868, laid the groundwork of a constitutional government in which all classes could participate. Ironically, the former xenophobes of the Tokugawa era also swore to seek 'knowledge' throughout the world in service to the new imperial Japan.

Although 1868 is used a sort of historical shorthand for the starting date of modern Japan, the next decade was a turbulent one in which the Meiji government shed, in a process of trial and error, the old samurai-centred rice political economy for a more Westernized market-based one. Although the old order had collapsed, the new government had not yet been founded.[35] Early Meiji governance remained similar to the old regime in that it was authoritarian and suppressed disaffected groups. The main difference was that the Meiji government succeeded in putting down peasant and samurai sedition with thorough efficiency. The problems that the Meiji government faced in forming economic policy were similar to those of the Bakufu; in short, effective governance of the urban and commercial economy while maintaining social stability. In the first year of its rule, it established a trade system that echoed the monopoly and licence system. This system was dismantled less than a year later. Like the *ancien régime*, the Meiji leaders sought to do away with the daimyo monopolies and centralize control of Japanese trade. In addition, the government needed steady tax revenue to fund itself. As much as 80% of the government activities were funded by a new land tax based on the land value, rather than the value of the harvest. Land became a tradeable commodity; peasants had the option of selling their land and leaving the countryside.

The main drain on Tokugawa resources had been the rice stipends for the samurai. The new government revoked their class privileges and reduced their stipends to nothing over the next ten years, using government bonds to avert insurrections by the armed class. In this respect, the government was not entirely successful. In 1877, Saigō Takamori, a former architect of the new government, rebelled and led a group of 40,000 samurai in revolt. Peasant conscript forces of the Meiji government defeated the elites, thus ending the chapter of samurai rule over Japan. In 1871, the government had dissolved the domains and thus dismantled the basic unit of economic governance and organization; domains were now prefectures. Edo, the former seat of Tokugawa power was now Tokyo, literally the 'eastern capital'. The emperor and his court were conveyed from Kyoto to the new capital Tokyo. A new system, based on a proto-national bank with a fully backed currency. The domains' debts and contracts, some of which were made with foreigners in the treaty ports, were absorbed by the new state. In this decade, the Japanese government shifted its primary focus from maintaining and supporting the samurai, to one struggling to maintain and fund its own activities. Unlike the policies of the Tokugawa, growth was now welcome.[36]

TREATY PORTS: BOUNDARIES AND BORDERS

When I first came to live in Yokohama
My duty was simple and plain:
To dazzle the nation with civilization
Implying more money than brain;
In a mansion as big as the Bluff
I had servants and horses enough
While the native possessions
Outside the concessions
Appeared to me very poor stuff.
I shall live on a different plan,
When I mix with authentic Japan.

A merchant in Yokohama, (Set to the
music of 'When I first put this
uniform on' by Arthur Sullivan)[1]

ON 11 NOVEMBER 1864, the English language local newspaper
The Japan Times reported that the French mail had arrived in Yokohama from Shanghai on the *Dupliex* at ten o'clock the previous
night. The custom had been to have the mail ready for pick-up at
11:30, an hour-and-a-half later. However, the postmaster had
been ill that night, and a large number of unpaid packages complicated the billing. A rumour spread that the delivery of mail
would be delayed until the following morning. The foreign re-

sidents reacted with, as paper termed in uncharacteristic under-statement, 'a few hours of excitement'.[2] A crowd had gathered at ten-thirty and began to pummel the French Consulate building with sticks to force an entry. They chanted for their mail so ob-streperously that they had to be beaten back at bayonet-point. In the next few issues of *The Japan Times*, the French Postal services published this notice:

> To avoid a repetition of the unpleasant exhibition presented by certain ill-regulated individuals at the Consulate General of France on the 11th. . .the French and other foreign communities are hereby notified that in the future, the gates of No 31 will be closed on the arrival of each French Mail, a notice posted outside will announce the hour when the gates will be opened for the delivery of mails, and no one will be admitted before the time named.[3]

The mêlée over the late mail was indicative of the fragility and isolation of treaty-port life; it was life on the periphery, far away from the metropolis. The Western residents of treaty-port Japan had such trappings of Western life as Worcestershire sauce, clubs, and cricket. However, mail by sea was the primary line of communication to the rest of the world, and through mail, enclave members traded, received news, sent reports, and com-municated by letter to loved ones at home. The lack of mail, or even its temporary delay, threatened the very way of life of the residents. Late mail, in the Western settlers' eyes, was a very ser-ious matter.

As illustrated by the panic and desperation over late mail, life in the treaty ports could be easily destabilized. The treaty-port environment, particularly in the 1860s, was not a predictable business environment either politically or economically. Busi-ness expectations, from the point of view of both Japanese and Western businessmen, were often frustrated by sometimes vio-lent political developments. The difficulties stemming from communication, instability, credit, and the lack of information in general drove up transaction costs between Japanese and Wes-tern merchants. Volatile markets throughout Asia only served to complicate relations. Furthermore, the continued existence of the treaty ports was not at all assured from the point of view of Japanese and Western merchants. And yet, on a day-to-day basis, the treaty ports were a source of opportunity for Japanese and Western merchants. The basic human propensity to 'truck and barter' occurred in the face of these considerable barriers.

The treaty ports were neither a case of Westerners recreating London or New York with 'Orientals' in their midst, nor was it a case of the Japanese business communities allowing Westerners to trade among them. Within the enclaves, both Western and Japanese traders were strangers in a strange land. The language, trade practices, business community, and authorities were as alien to the Japanese as they were to the Westerners. The treaty ports of Japan, although arguably similar to other treaty ports throughout Asia, offered a unique trading environment for both Japanese and Western merchants.

Neither the Western nor Japanese community was mono-lithic; rather, the treaty ports were a network of many small communities, Japanese and Western, which often overlapped. This complex mosaic of complementary and conflicting interests existed in a constantly shifting environment which threatened to destabilize a delicate balance of trust, suspicion and greed. Yet, in spite of many barriers, merchants managed to conduct trade.

BACKGROUND: JAPANESE TREATY PORTS AND THE CHINESE PARADIGM

In Western literature, Japan's treaty ports and, by extension, treaty-port trade practices, have been traditionally overlooked and treated as a footnote in the West's relations with China. Japanese treaty ports had been seen as the younger siblings of the British system of treaty ports in place in China.[4] This assumption is partially true as the treaties signed between the Western nations and Japan were systemically identical to those made between China and Britain. As in China, Western merchants in Japan were expected to live in enclaves protected by Western police and military. Non-diplomatic staff were prohibited from travelling beyond treaty-port limits. All other trips inland could only be for medical purposes and had to be authorized by the proper authorities. Westerners in China and Japan both had the privilege of extra-territoriality and were not subject to local law, and their consuls adjudicated their cases.

27

In addition, the Westerners themselves in the Japanese treaty ports perceived the two countries to be similar. For example, Western merchants made the same assumptions about the respective markets. In China, the British assumed that the market potential for trade expansion was large and untapped. Although the Mitchell Report of 1852 had shown that China had reached the limits of Western trade expansion, merchants were convinced that vast stores of untapped wealth existed in the interior. Somehow this wealth was denied to Western merchants due to what was perceived as market interference by the Chinese.[5] Likewise, Western merchants concluded that Japan also had a vast store of riches. When the ports first opened, the large profits of the metals trade and profitable transactions of Jardine Matheson & Co. (which was to grow ever larger) only further convinced the Westerners of the existence of a vast market for Western goods. Any evidence to the contrary, such as losses or sluggish trade, was blamed, as in China, on obstruction by the 'native' government. A conceit existed among Western merchants in both nations that if their diplomatic representatives concentrated their efforts on overcoming the 'native' resistance to trade, the market in Asia would expand.

However, the Japanese treaty ports had a number of characteristics that made them distinctly different from those in the Chinese system. In the case of China, the treaty-port system was a result of Britain's sometimes decidedly strained trade relations with China, which originated in the seventeenth century. Although the treaty ports in China were the direct result of the Anglo-Chinese War (1839-42), Western trade in China had been long established. When the East India Company withdrew from Canton in 1834, companies such as Jardine Matheson & Co., operating in Asia since 1828, as well as other merchant houses, filled the gap that was left in the expatriate business community.[6] Japan, on the other hand, had been 'closed' to the West for almost two-and-a-half centuries, with no trade with the West except a small amount with the Dutch located on Dejima island. The business networks and institutions for Western merchants did not exist as they had in China where a system of middlemen, who were either Indian or Chinese 'compradores', facilitated trade outside the treaty ports and through the rest of the country. Initially, no such middlemen network existed in Japan, so merchants either had to learn to trade with one another, or make do with the Western merchants' Chinese assistants.

Another difference between Japanese and Chinese treaty ports was the absence of the opium trade. The relationship between Britain and China could be described as one of shared addictions. Tea (grown in China and India), which produced a stimulating liquid with minimal nutritional value, had become a staple in British life. The far less benign substance of opium had become a staple in China's. Opium grown on the Indian subcontinent was used to pay for tea. A rough triangle trade had formed, and China's hunger for opium had outpaced its trade in tea by the nineteenth century. Companies such as Jardine Matheson & Co. traded thousands of the chests of opium at a substantial profit. Although the opium trade was no longer officially sanctioned after 1842, opium smuggling still existed in Asia. Until the Communists took power in the twentieth century under Mao Zedong, opium remained a social and economic drain on China. Those in the Japanese government were aware of China's example and the dangers of opium, and thus the Bakufu specifically negotiated that opium not be allowed into the country except in medicinal quantities. The first treaty with the West was negotiated with the Americans who had a smaller stake in the opium trade, and the US acquiesced to this stipulation. The lack of an opium trade meant that Western merchants in Japan did not have a ready-made trading staple.

Unlike Chinese treaty ports in which the British influence and interests predominated, Japanese treaty ports were in a state of institutional disarray. Within the Treaty Powers, there were significant differences of policy. The American interest, represented by Townsend Harris, was not insubstantial and did not always chime with the British view. To further complicate matters, foreign residents did not always agree with their diplomatic representatives.

Treaty ports were environments, which were neither part of the internal Japanese trading system nor totally under the control of the Western Treaty Powers. Not all Western consular courts were equal, although they appeared on the surface to be identical.[7] To further confuse matters, the mechanisms of authority in the shogunate were not only ill understood by Westerners, but were themselves unstable. The Treaty Powers were no more organized than the shogunate. Indeed, the Treaty Powers were a multinational group with no official leader, and diplomatic altercations between the Americans, British, and French were quite common. The group was not bound by a single cohesive policy or system of law. As a legal and economic 'no man's land', the treaty port was subject to the caprices of both Japanese and Western officials.

OVERVIEW OF TRADE IN THE TREATY PORTS

Fortunately for the early Western merchants, trade in Japan was initially profitable, especially in metals and foodstuffs exported from Japan to China. In the first year, (1859) trade totalled some 1.4 million Mexican dollars involving a little over twenty permanent Western merchant residents.[8] The Japanese market, especially at the beginning, was volatile: Jardine Matheson, a British firm, reported 200-300% per cent profit in the first months of trade, but this margin became a loss by the following year.[9] Exact figures on the amount of trade are not reliable as Japanese record-keeping on foreign trade was not dependable until well into the Meiji era. Another complicating factor regarding Japan's nascent international trade statistics was smuggling. Until the Meiji Restoration, the actual volume of trade with the West may have been up to double the official figures. Goods, such as silk and silkworm eggs, sometimes bypassed official accounting in order to avoid quotas and duties. By the 1870s, Asian trade began to experience a downturn, and Western merchants throughout the East suffered losses. The shift in the economy wiped out many of the smaller Western trading firms in Japan. Even the large firms such as Hearn & Co. and Walsh, Hall & Co. suffered. By the end of the decade, the economy had recovered, and those firms that survived once again began making profits. By 1876, total trade was about 57.7 million yen.[10]

Although the treaty ports went through cycles in which certain products were popular – for example, in the year of the rabbit by the Chinese Zodiac, there was a boom in rabbit sales from Australia – for the most part, silk and tea were the main goods exported from Japan. In the West, Japanese green tea, seen as poorer quality than the black tea from China, was drunk in the mid-west and other rural parts of the United States. Silk and silkworm eggs were exported to Europe to supply the silk lost in the silkworm blight. Besides the sale of arms and ships, Westerners sold fabrics such as woollens, as well as other finished goods. In addition, Westerners did a brisk trade in foodstuffs, such as seaweed, cuttlefish, fish oil, rags and other sundry goods which they exported and sold in China.

SYSTEMIC PROBLEMS

The Japanese treaty ports were a market in which merchants from two very different trade systems came together to pursue profit. Structurally, the treaty ports lacked the trade facilities and institutions required to adequately deal with the complexities of international trade. Goods from the West and China were sold to the Japanese, and Japanese goods were shipped to the West or China.

One major blockage to trade was the lack of cash. For the Japanese merchants, the problem stemmed from the merchants' relationship with the Bakufu. Because the merchants were periodically forced by the shogunate to give 'loans' or donations to pay for government programmes, they often tried to keep as little cash as possible in their hands. Thus, they suffered from a lack of liquidity. Western merchants, too, suffered from the same problem due to the opaque policies of the Bakufu. In particular, the Bakufu restricted the amount of Western money that could be exchanged for Japanese currency.

The chaos over currency and the supposed drain of gold out of Japan shortly following the opening of the treaty ports caused the shogunate to take actions to protect the Japanese economy. When the treaty ports were first opened, the customs house exchanged only a fraction of each request. Thus, especially in the early days of the treaty ports, the Western merchants were in the paradoxical position in which they came to the port with large amounts of Mexican silver but were unable to find merchants who would accept it.[11] Without Japanese cash, Western merchants were unable to buy goods or establish credit. The amount received for each application was not predictable, and Western merchants were thus unable to plan for future payments. Barter was used for small purchases and curios, but was not generally used for any large-scale transactions.

Trade between Westerners and Japanese was complicated by the lack of a common banking system. Western merchants used the branches of banks based in China and India such as the Chartered Mercantile Bank of India, London and China.[12] If a Japanese merchant wished to use the facilities of a Western bank, he had to find a Western merchant to borrow the money for him. Japanese banks were not a factor in the financing of foreign trade until 1885.[13] Bills of lading, remittances, or cheques could not be drawn in the other's currency. Because the Japanese merchants, and as well as many Western merchants, were unaccustomed to the mechanisms of international trade, the absence of common business practice further complicated early business relationships.

Finally, the sheer distance between markets, Japan and Western cities such as London, New York, and San Francisco, was another complicating factor. Although steamships were already in use, the physical distance between Japan and the West was significant. The majority of correspondence was by mail which was shipped by sea. Telegraph communication from China was seen as an expensive method of communication. Yokohama was four-and-a-half thousand nautical miles from San Francisco, or under the very best possible circumstances, a two-and-a-half-week journey on a ship travelling at a constant twelve knots. More often, ships stopped at Hawaii and Hong Kong and were not able to always maintain twelve knots; passages of two months were not uncommon. Goods to and from New York then travelled overland by rail. Goods to London took even longer. Hong Kong, a major British colonial port, was a three-day journey. Pirates and shipwrecks were not unheard of, so important official documents were sent in duplicate via different routes; for example, documents to London were sent via San Francisco to New York to London, and via Hong Kong to India to London around the Horn of Africa, and later the Suez Canal.[14] News and market intelligence was not only scarce, it was always at least a month out of date. Any decision made by the merchants and diplomats in the treaty ports was imbued with an element of risk. Both had to anticipate the wishes of the home government or firm due to the distance and incomplete information.

WESTERN MERCHANTS

Merchants in the treaty ports of Japan were a diverse group with differing expectations, practices, capitalization and skills. Among Westerners, merchants ranged from small one-man operations to Jardine Matheson with its networks throughout Asia and the rest of the world. Among the Japanese, traders included men from the countryside trying to make a fast fortune selling curios, to the large merchant houses with branches in all the major Japanese cities. The costs of setting up shop in Japan differed among Western merchants; the outlay for passage and kit for merchants in a major consignment house from Britain was about 300 pounds, not an insubstantial amount in the nineteenth century.[15] However, other merchants avoided these high costs by entering Japan as sailors and simply stayed on to open establishments that catered to the sea-going public. In the 1860s, W. H. Smith, one of the first managers of the Grand Hotel of Yokohama, came to Japan as an officer of the Royal Marines and simply stayed in port.[16] Information about the opening of firms, ending of partnerships and closing of firms was published in small, one, two or three line announcements in the local press.[17] Others still were merchants on a part-time basis. Sailors sometimes traded curios from port to port. Thus, the embeddedness of each merchant, and the extent to which each merchant was invested in the Yokohama community varied.

Some independent merchants came to port with the express purpose of starting a business in Japan. Joseph Heco, also known as Hamada Hikozo, a Japanese-American merchant, described men arriving in port with capital and a letter of introduction. Heco reported starting a business with a 'Mr K' with whom Heco been acquainted in San Francisco in 1859. Heco agreed to the partnership in which K would fund all the capital and Heco would do all the sales. All profits would be split, and a contract formalized the agreement.[18] The following year, K arranged for $10,000 worth of capital and the furniture and fittings for an office shipped from the US. Heco wrote that he had been also expecting goods, which he had planned to sell in Japan. With this influx of capital, Heco became a general commissions agent. In his early business ventures, he reported having difficulty converting the dollars to currency with which to buy local goods to send back on the barque which had come with the money and goods.[19] A year later, the sales had not gone well, so the partnership was dissolved without ill feeling on either side. Soon after, the market improved to such an extent that Heco was able to hire a Western clerk.[20]

Western women were by far the minority, those few that did come to the treaty ports were an essential part of 'society' and popular hostesses. Although most women came as wives or daughters of male diplomats, merchants, or missionaries, some women worked alongside their husbands as assistants. For example, British Consul C. P. Hodgson's wife and daughter accompanied him in his tour of duty in Nagasaki and Hokkaido.[21] Although few in number, some women opened their own businesses, usually haberdashery and sewing shops. Many women did not acclimatize to life in the treaty port and returned to the West to raise their families. Due to the scarcity of women, some men took Japanese mistresses, though not necessarily in the same way as Lt. Benjamin Pinkerton. By the 1880s, however, formal, mixed, marriages, including Western women to Japanese men, became more common, although still relatively rare.

Because merchants were such a diverse group, they were difficult to characterize, except that they were predominantly male and under thirty-five. British officials at home and in the treaty ports regarded the merchants as men of poor character and education. The British stereotype was that men went East only because they were failures in the metropolis. A significant minority were American and European Jews, who were integrated into the trading community.[22] In general, most treaty-port diplomats shared this bias against the merchants. Alcock crystallized this attitude with his comment that the merchants in the treaty ports were the 'scum' of Europe.[23] Since much of the research on the foreign presence in Japan has been based on consular dispatches, this jaundiced view of the merchants has permeated the literature of the treaty ports. Western merchants have been dismissed as a class of crass adventurers.[24] Some merchants, especially the transient sailor-merchants, were almost illiterate. However, not all were what the British Consul C. P. Hodgson termed 'greedy vultures' and 'unscrupulous specimens of all nations'.[25] For example, George Hall of Walsh, Hall and Co. was a graduate of Harvard Medical School. Francis Hall (no relation), who later joined the firm, was also well educated and the son of a schoolmaster. F. Hall had built a successful book business in his native New York and consorted with intellectuals and authors such as Samuel Clements (Mark Twain), Thomas K. Beecher (abolitionist and brother of Henry Ward Beecher), Ralph Waldo Emerson, and Oliver Wendell Holmes.[26] After leaving Japan, he devoted his retirement to philanthropy and public service.

Although some scholars posit that fortunes were not made in the Orient,[27] memoirs of the Beecher family state that John Walsh of Walsh, Hall and Co., left an estate worth 500,000 yen in 1897 – worth about US$10 million in 1992.[28] Francis Hall returned to the United States with a substantial fortune.[29] Of course, not all Western merchants made profits. One notable example was 'Professor' Risely, known in the Yokohama community for his spectacular business failures. Among other ventures, he had a dairy in which all his cows died, and an ice business of which the majority of the product melted while waiting for customs clearance, various circuses, and later a troupe of acrobats. The latter met a moderate measure of success. The Yokohama public enjoyed the spectacle,[30] and the troop later travelled with P. T. Barnum to the United States.[31] The residents were not without humour: the dairy and its odorous carcasses were lampooned in *Japan Punch*, the local satirical magazine.

SOCIETY IN THE TREATY PORTS – BOUNDARIES INSIDE AND OUTSIDE THE WESTERN COMMUNITY

The Western treaty-port residents created institutions and mechanisms to define the borders of their community. One way in which the borders of Western treaty-port society were defined was through creating a social network consisting of 'insiders' and 'outsiders'. Settlers in the treaty ports created a society in which etiquette and the manners of their home country were preserved. A wife of one American consul remarked, 'The etiquette and hours of society are those of England, and most of the American residents are more English in these matters than the English.'[32] Only members would know the appropriate etiquette, and those on the outside, such as sailors or new arrivals, would have to be invited in. In this way, membership in the network would be, in theory, restricted. Dinner parties were the measure of social success.[33] Social calls, especially the etiquette of calling on Yokohama's few 'ladies', the wives and daughters of the social elite, developed intricate procedures. Within the ports, particularly in Yokohama, a class system developed wherein '. . .with ludicrous exactitude drew a line between a man who bought and sold in an office and the man who kept a shop for the same purpose. . .'[34] Visiting theatrical productions, a popular amusement, would advertise 'select' nights in which only the elite, presumably diplomats, clergy, officers, and those merchants in established houses, were allowed to attend. All others attended the shows on 'ordinary nights'.[35] The class system was self-enforced, and members were expected to know their social place.

This intricate system of treaty-port society remained the norm throughout the 1890s. The creation of a classed society indicated to themselves and to those in the West that they were still members of the same social system. The merchants were creating a world in which reputation could be relied upon in a community in which many of its members could default in their agreements by leaving port. Clubs, for example, established a routine and a schedule. Those who were members were socially and economically invested in the treaty ports' institutions, and were therefore seen as more respectable. The 'snobbery' served an economic function, as it was used by Westerners as a sort of indicator of the trustworthiness of another Westerner. The received wisdom was that the more an individual knew the social mores of the treaty port, the more trustworthy the individual. The rigorously enforced social status may have been a reaction to the stereotype that the East was the land for opportunists, adventurers and social climbers.

At the same time, a prevalent image of Yokohama treaty port is one of a Japanese 'Wild West', which contradicts the description of obsession with social propriety. Western tourists, those in the West, and many Japanese and Western scholars have described the ports as an area of licentious lawlessness. In the first five years of the treaty ports this description was certainly not unwarranted. Most Westerners were armed, and violence, whether committed by Japanese or Westerners, was quite common. Adding to the picture of lawlessness, the sexual mores of this 'frontier' town were seen to be of a lower standard than that at home or in other parts of the Asia. In 1859, women could be hired for 33 Mexican dollars a month to provide sexual services on a live-in basis.[36] The large and opulent pleasure district contained the Gankiro 'tea house' which housed roughly 200 women and their attendants. The bishop of Hong Kong, George Smith, condemned Yokohama as the 'brothel of the Pacific' and announced that only the morally corrupt thrived in Japan. For a Western population of a few hundred, the numerous grog shops, prostitutes, and 'tea houses' seemed excessive to historians and contemporaries alike, and captured the imagination of writers; hence the origin of the 'Wild West' of the East.[37]

Yet, even in the early 'Wild West' period, Western merchants delineated boundaries and borders within their treaty-port communities; Yokohama settlers distinguished themselves from the sojourners that drifted into port. Western merchants were clearly stung by criticism of the diplomats and those at home: Alcock's and the Bishop Smith's comments annoyed the merchants, who responded to both with indignation. In another example of merchant sensitivity to external opinion, Western merchants, in reaction to Alcock's less than flattering comments in his book *The Capital of the Tycoon*, banned him, as well as other diplomats, from the Yokohama Club.[38] The residents defended the large pleasure area because it catered not just to the Western population but also to the Japanese. They also claimed that it mollified the sailors and soldiers who would otherwise wreak havoc. Although the treaty-port population was only a few hundred, troops and sailors were the steady market for the sex trade. Although some of the permanent merchants settlers did hire mistresses, the dominant market was not the settler population.[39] The sexual amenities were as much for transients as for the settlers. In addition, the treaty ports, whether Nagasaki, Kobe, or Yokohama did not remain 'frontier towns'.

After the violence of the early 60s, amenities of the British way of life had taken root in treaty-port Japan. Clubs, rowing, riding, concerts, and theatre became staples in port life. Within the compounds, the Westerners strove to create a pocket of Western society, divorcing themselves from the rest of Japan.[40] Food was imported from abroad; for example, butter was at times imported from as far away as Australia, often arriving rancid. Residents organized celebrations for the Queen's Birthday as enthusiastically as for the Fourth of July. Balls, although short of female dance partners, were another popular feature on the treaty-port social calendar. The physical appearance of the enclaves themselves reflected their roots in the West. Open parks, complete with band stands, were a feature of most treaty ports. In the Japanese treaty ports, businesses and residences copied the architecture of the Chinese enclaves. Inside the treaty port houses, residents filled the rooms with carpets and heavy wooden furniture that was impractical in fire and earthquake prone Japan.

The Western residents also started institutions such as the Municipal Council to deal with issues such as rubbish, lighting, amusement and security. Membership in this institution attempted to create boundaries between Western residents and transients and met with varying success in different treaty ports. Kobe's community was successful in collecting enough funds for their activities. The Yokohama Municipal Council, on the other hand, had a high number of transients in port, and combined with serious personality conflicts, failed to achieve any of its goals. The group had difficulty in collecting regular dues from residents to fund services as rubbish collection, lighting, and drainage. Members of the council failed to attend meetings, and those meetings with a full quorum were unproductive as they had little social or monetary capital to develop or beautify the enclave. The Chamber of Commerce in the respective treaty ports also served a similar purpose. Subscribers and those that attended meetings were defined as 'residents', thus creating an incentive, in the form of political franchise, to belong to the more permanent and supposedly reliable network of settlers.

The newspapers were another element that tied the ports and the Western community together. In the period 1859-76, roughly twenty Western newspapers and seven periodicals were published in Japan.[41] Although most closed within a few years, the existence of a Western press was important to the settlers. The press transmitted a wide range of information. News of the West, market intelligence, the history of Japan, and local gossip. As the publications were often sent back to the settlers' families and friends, they described treaty-port life as well. The world described in the press was presented as 'respectable' and largely ignored the Western transient population, except perhaps to note its more apparent indiscretions. Although the press was not always complimentary of Japan, the publications criticized Westerners as well, including the behaviour of their diplomatic representatives. Editorials and 'reports' occasionally railed against the drunken excesses of sailors on leave, and sometimes took up collections to compensate the Japanese families of those that incurred losses at the hands of 'ruffians' and 'brawlers.' Information in the newspapers was disseminated in an attempt to regulate the behaviour of those in the treaty ports: they informed the Western world outside the treaty ports about the boundaries of Western trader communities in Japan, and they advocated collective action to attempt to show the Japanese the distinction between settlers and transients.

Another important publication was the *Japan Directory* which published the name, business and address of most members of the treaty ports. In the early years of the treaty ports, the publication was a section in the *China Directory*. Later, a new directory was produced specifically for the Japanese treaty-port market and published in Japan. The directory, which was similar in format to the *China Directory*, can be read as a list of the self-selected *members* of treaty-port society. For example, not all businesses were included. Bars were not listed, nor were boarding houses, nor were all hotels. Nor were all people; sailors, soldiers and drifters were also not listed. All males listed in the directory nominally held a profession. It is unclear if these exclusions were editorial decisions or whether individuals simply adhered to their social 'place'.

As the population not listed in the *Japan Directory* was seen by the residents as a source of disruptive and sometimes criminal activity, the residents organized charities and organizations to curb this sort of behaviour. For example, Kobe and Yokohama set up a volunteer quasi-police force from among Westerners in order to maintain order. Residents also made voluntary donations to a fund to pay for the passage back home of indigent Westerners who had incurred debt. They donated funds for a hospital that mainly serviced the armed forces and treated venereal disease, among other afflictions. These charitable organizations not only made life more pleasant for the Westerners, but also worked to control what the self-appointed 'residents' considered as 'bad elements': namely, defaulters, disorderly behaviour and sexual excess.

'Natives', Japanese merchants and residents, were excluded from the community that the Western merchants sought to build. Although some Western merchants did have close friendships with their Japanese counterparts, the Japanese merchants did not regularly mix in any of the organized activities such as clubs or theatricals. This exclusion partially arose out of the racial prejudice prevalent among Victorians, but also because the community was trying to define its borders to create a stable, predictable environment for trade. The obvious physical and racial differences, from the point of view of the Victorians, signalled that the Japanese were different, and differences such as dress, language and customs introduced an element of uncertainty into the community. Treaty-port residents sought to reduce ambiguity. The one exception to this exclusion was horse racing. Both Japanese and Westerners went to the Yokohama races to compete and speculate. However, the Japanese were not invited out of pure goodwill or altruism; they were invited in order to defuse a rivalry and factionalism among the Western race clubs.[42]

This activity in creating borders, networks, and distinctions inside and outside of the treaty port was an attempt to form a predictable and stable trading environment. However, the networks and distinctions cultivated by residents were not always effective. The boundaries were permeable and fungible. Social distinctions that had been signals of class or wealth at home did not directly translate in the treaty ports. Consequently, it was difficult for the residents to tell if a new arrival was a bad risk until he ran up debts that he was unable to pay.

One such example was 'Drunken' Smith (no relation to W. H.

Smith) who was a former remittance man. As a businessman with an office, he would have been one of the business elite of Yokohama. After his marriage, he became an alcoholic, hence the nickname. In order to support his habit, he ran up debt in Yokohama. He then moved to Shanghai and took part in 'respectable' treaty-port life, going as far as becoming a member of the Race Club. Eventually, he defaulted again on his debts, and finished his life as a workhouse superviser.[43] Unless the Western merchant was from a Chinese treaty port, and even then, other Westerners in Japan could not easily judge the trustworthiness of a new arrival in port. Perhaps because the numbers of Westerners were so few or because information was scarce and expensive, the Westerners accepted most white individuals who came to port, provided they went through the motions of socially investing in the community. The 'exit barriers' were low: Westerners could leave easily. By the 1870s there were regular ferry services to China, and from there, one could gain passage to anywhere in the world.

JAPANESE MERCHANTS

Like the Western merchants, Japanese merchants who came to trade in the treaty ports varied in status, education and wealth. Because of the breakdown in Bakufu controls on prices and consumption, combined with the internal and political stresses, the mid-nineteenth-century Japanese economy as a whole was undergoing a shift. Within this framework, was a dynamic and unique trading environment in Japan. The treaty ports, due to the agreement between the Bakufu and the West, were areas of relatively unrestricted and unregulated trade, although not free from bureaucratic interference and trade institutions such as guilds. In addition, trade that had formerly been in the hands of urban Japanese merchants faced competition from new merchants from rural areas who had come directly from the countryside to the ports to sell their wares. Thus, the Japanese merchants in the ports were a mix of the trading establishment with its fixed customs and procedures and of outsiders from the countryside.

A digression is necessary to depict the changes that were occurring among Japanese merchants of the period. Those Japanese merchants who were part of the traditional trading community organized their enterprises around the family unit. These businesses were run by families from the merchant class as defined by Bakufu and Confucian law. Legally and socially, business was seen to be the property of the family entity, rather than the individual. Businesses were, in theory, to be passed on from generation to generation. The importance of the business as a family enterprise was reflected in the organization of the business, which was structured not only around the family, but also in the form of an extended family. That is, most merchant houses, such as Mitsui, were organized along the family network. The central house, *honke*, belonged to the direct descendant family of the original founder. When the head of the family died, the property was not divided but handed down to one son, usually the eldest. If there was no male heir, or if the sons were particularly inept at business, the master would adopt a relative's son or particularly skilled clerk from his organization who would then take the master's name. Often the adopted son would marry a daughter from the house. All other sons would not inherit. They would be sent to other branch houses to be apprenticed, or, if particularly skilled, they would be allowed to set up a branch shop (*bunke*) which would be part of the overall family business. Other sons would marry into other families, or work in other fields, or work for the family itself. Like the family unit, the dissolution of the business would only occur under unusual circumstances.

Even within each individual store or office, relations were paternal. The business was organized as a family with the head of family as head of the business and the employees as 'children'. Meals were prepared by the women of the family, and employers and employees were served around the communal table. Many employees were taken into a business at the age of about ten to work as apprentices. They lived on the premises and their masters paid for their food, clothing, and education. From about the age of fifteen, the child began his formal training as a clerk. If the clerk was especially talented, he became a *banto*, a term roughly meaning 'chief clerk'. In small houses, the term referred to the general manager, but in large houses, they were a separate class above clerks. *Shihai-nin* was the individual responsible for all management within the business house. A faithful and skilled manager could expect to be well rewarded and treated as quasi-family, or allowed to marry into the family itself.[44]

In the mid-Edo period, each merchant house belonged to a guild, called *kumiai* or *kabu nakama*, that grouped similar enterprises. For example, all rice dealers would be in one 'guild', all weavers in another, and all saké sellers in yet another. Merchant houses bought membership in the form of stock in these guilds, of which there were a limited number. Guild stock prices in the 1840s were in the tens to hundreds of *ryo* depending on the trade. One *ryo* was roughly the cost of one man's yearly consumption in rice. Usually the stock was inherited from father to son, or in other cases, the stock was bought and sold. Guilds defined who and what could be traded within a given business. In addition, they protected guild members from competition; not only were the numbers of competitors in a given trade curtailed, but also the guild defined rules of practice such as the prohibition on the hiring of any employee in a given trade without the former employer's consent. Guilds occasionally withheld goods from market in order to drive up the price.[45] Finally, the guilds worked collectively in their dealings with the government. Prior to the Tempō reforms, the guilds and middlemen wholesalers (*tonya*) reported to the Bakufu and collected 'thank-money' (*myoga-kin*) which amounted to a kind of tribute-tax for the government. Government requisitions for the non-commercial samurai class were filtered through guilds. Other forms of co-operation included guilds in the second hand goods business working with police authorities to prevent the fencing of stolen items.

The family entity was a system in which each member of the family business was individually responsible for the collective financial well-being of the firm. In their dealings, each individual and his or her behaviour was seen as representative of the entire family business. Any one clerk acting in ill-faith reflected badly on the family and the business. It was thus in the interest of those in authority to monitor the behaviour of their employees very carefully. The family business' membership in a guild also helped to ensure good behaviour in its business dealings. The stock that each member bought upon entry could be used as collateral for loans.

One of the most important functions of the guild system was the establishment of trade procedures, dispute resolution, and mechanisms for trust (reputation) and credit. The guild was a network that ensured the function of credit. At the turn of the century, credit was solid to the extent that bills and notes passed like currency without the intervention of banks.[46] In order for such a system to function smoothly, the guilds had to ensure accountability. The guild was the first port of call in case of dispute. The guild official recorder had a record of major sales, thus an impartial third party had an alternate record of the sale. Even without the recorder's books, however, a merchant's account books with his official seal were considered sufficient proof of the existence of a transaction. Contracts, if broken, resulted in the rest of the guild shunning the merchant; any serious complaint lodged against a defaulter resulted in the notification of all other members of the guild. The tarnishing of a reputation resulted in the loss of business, or possibly expulsion from the guild. If a merchant was expelled from a guild, it was impossible for him to work in the same field again, and moving to a new trade was difficult, if not impossible. Even rumours of a breach of an oral agreement resulted in informal sanctions by other members in the guild.

Among Japanese merchants, contractual defection was rare. Like the Western custom of the handshake, the clapping of hands signified to both parties that a deal had been reached. Sales were found through word of mouth or through guild auctions. Contracts, if written at all, were usually brief notes made by sellers and presented to buyers. Down payments, or 'bargain money' as it was called in the treaty ports, were not used. Sales by sample also were common. Another type of contract was *makase chūmon* ('entrusting order'), which was indicative of the level of mutual trust among merchants. Buyers would entrust sellers to bill them for goods appropriate for the buyer. For example, if the buyer ordered a quantity of cloth, the seller would send goods sight unseen that he thought were suitable for the buyer.[47] Although the merchants would check price and quantity with the other party, such orders were indicative of the traders' knowledge and trust of one another.

Finally, the guild specified procedures for payment and credit. For example, bills of lading were always packed with goods, so that goods had to be opened by the consignee.[48] Guild members were generally knowledgeable of the rules of their particular trade. Due to the importance of the guild and its emphasis on mutual trust, Japanese merchants rarely breached even their oral contracts.[49]

In 1843, however, this system of guilds was dissolved under the Tempō reforms. Edo's indebtedness to Osaka and the growing consumption levels of the urban population were some of the major factors behind this decision. By Bakufu decree, no group could call itself a guild, or could work exclusively as a wholesaler. All merchants had to be some form of retailer. Merchants were discouraged from working in collusion to raise prices. The reforms lowered the entrance barrier to trade. Merchants no longer had to pay the high guild fees to buy and sell goods. Bakufu officials assumed that the increased competition from new merchants would help lower prices. In order to compensate for the loss of the guilds, the merchants no longer had to pay thank-money to officials.

These reforms were designed to lower prices and at the same time, decrease levels of consumption of the urban population. The result, however, was not as the officials envisioned. Prices did not go down as the consumption had increased outside the urban areas; the sumptuary laws in Edo resulted in the merchants diverting their goods to other, newer markets. In addition, the loss of the guilds allowed any individual from the merchant class the right to trade without regulation from the guilds. New merchants or even those shifting into different types of trade were not familiar with appropriate business procedure. Soon after the edict was published, the price of some commodities was reduced, but at the sacrifice of quality. Short weighted goods became more common. Merchants in Osaka became unwilling to forward goods to Edo, and the government-mandated price cuts caused chaos in the Edo market. The dissolution of guilds and the mandatory cut in land and rents, resulted in a disruption of credit and contracting. Merchants were now unable to borrow money on their guild stock, as the guilds had been dissolved. Their liquidity, which had always been limited, became even more constrained without access to guild loans. Thus, they offered land or houses as collateral, but because of a lack of demand, creditors were unable to dispose of property into cash.[50] Finally, without a guild, contractual breach could no longer be punished by social sanction or exclusion. A defaulting merchant could easily change markets, change his trade, or simply find a new trading partner as there was no organized way in which information on unreliable traders could be disseminated. Disputes became difficult to resolve as the guild records and personnel no longer existed to resolve them.

In 1851, the system of middlemen and guilds was re-established by the Bakufu because the expected price declines had not occurred. However, new licenses for guilds were not issued by the government, contributing to the disarray in the re-organization of guilds. Furthermore, the lifting of some government controls over trade caused a flow of merchants from outside of Edo to trade in the capital city. Also, merchants outside of the main cities requested membership in these new organizations. As no set criteria existed for separating out old guild members from the 1840s and new applicants in the 1850s, all merchants were accepted into the organizations. Even by the late 1850s, the number of guilds within a given trade was in dispute and their organization was still in a state of disarray. The new guilds were no longer cartels, and hence did not have the control over the trades enjoyed by the old guilds. The guilds never regained stewardship over trade, and the system of credit and reputation never recovered. The relationship between the merchants and the Bakufu became opaque as the guilds could no longer collectively bargain with the officials, and the government's additional demands on the merchants became still more onerous.

It was in this interval of ten or so years when the guild system was suspended that the merchant population came to include those outside the traditional system. Trade in rural areas had begun to grow in Japan. By the mid-nineteenth century, the rural economy had become more commercialized; for example, cash crops such as silk and tobacco became common. Farmers realized that they could gain more profits if they circumvented wholesalers and middlemen and began selling directly to the urban market. While some of these rural merchants were representatives of an extended family enterprise in the country, still others were individuals trading on their own. By the 1830s, silk trade wholesalers filed lawsuits against the outsiders, and at the same time, outsiders pressed for the merchant groups to open up trade. The Daimyo, who were at odds with the Bakufu, encouraged their farmers to commercialize and seek alternate markets in order to increase domain revenue.[51] When the system of middlemen and guilds was dissolved in the 1840s, the 'rural merchant's' hold on the market was deepened. By 1859 and the opening of the treaty ports, a new breed of aggressive rural merchant independent from the old business network of Edo and Osaka was ready to trade with anyone, including Westerners.

JAPANESE AND WESTERN MERCHANTS

The treaties with the West had placed emphasis on the importance of free and unencumbered trade. All Japanese merchants were, in theory, to be allowed to trade with Westerners. The breakdown of institutions that once regulated merchants and their trade practices only served to encourage trade with the Westerners. For example, the house of Mitsui was a traditional type enterprise and had about one thousand employees in 1840. Using its old connections with the Bakufu it had developed over the previous century, it was able to secure the right to open a government-sanctioned branch-shop in Yokohama. From the Bakufu's point of view, Mitsui was a trusted business as it had fulfilled and depended on government contracts since the late seventeenth century. The Bakufu assumed that they could maintain some control over foreign trade through Mitsui.[52] Although there was some dispute within Mitsui itself on the prudence of such an enterprise, the shop changed money and sold cloth goods with some success.[53] Mitsui worked with an American company, Walsh, Hall and Co. and established a joint venture, a paper mill in Kobe. A former clerk of Walsh, Hall and Co., Robert Irwin, worked closely with one of Mitsui's *banto* and future head of Mitsui Bussan, Baron Masuda Takashi, on the Meiji government's re-financing of *han* loans to the Bakufu.[54]

Still others came from rural areas and set up business in the treaty ports: some were meant to be nascent family businesses, others were set up to briefly trade with the Westerners, make a windfall profit, and then return to their home villages in the interior. Hoshino Chotarō circumvented the traditional middlemen and came directly to Yokohama from what is now Gunma Prefecture to represent his family's silk-producing business.[55] Iwasaki Yatarō, who founded Mitsubishi in the 1870s, also worked with Walsh, Hall and Co. to secure camphor rights in Tosa. Iwasaki Yanosuke, his younger brother and future head of Mitsubishi, travelled to New York to stay with the Walsh family and to attend a boys' school that was headed by Francis Hall's brother. In this way, it can be seen that neither the Japanese nor Western merchants fell into the easy categories that they had been pressed into in past histories of the treaty ports.

THE PROBLEM WITH FOREIGNERS

The prospect of a predictable trading environment was far from being a reality in treaty-port Japan; the world outside as well as inside the enclaves destabilized the treaty ports. For example, both the Japanese and Western traders who worked in these areas were often subject to anti-foreign behaviour that further lessened the stability of the enclaves. Furthermore, both Japanese and Western merchants were captive to their own prejudice. One cause of disruption came from fear of the unknown. Some of the Japanese public viewed the largely white, hairy, big-nosed, meat-eating Westerners as demon-like.[56] Superstition played some part in feeding the irrational fears and anti-foreignism. Both a cholera epidemic and severe inflation was blamed on the Western presence by high and low alike. Other rumours depicted the Westerners as flesh-eaters, an understandable conclusion to make for a largely fish-eating community upon seeing sides of salted beef. The treaty port was thus feared by some as a source of physical or moral contamination.

Stereotyping was not solely the domain of the Japanese. Westerners saw the Japanese, not so much as who they were, but in the way the Westerners wished them to be. Westerners, particularly the British, had their biases and assumptions; after the fraught experiences of Britain in China, the Westerners had pre-determined that Japan was nothing like China.[57] Britons, as well as other Westerners, wanted to see Japan as a fresh start to their presence in Asia. Contemporaries and travellers commented that physically the Japanese did not resemble the Chinese, and suggested they were Semitic in origin.[58] The Japanese, in the perception of early Western settlers and tourists, were cleaner, the women prettier[59] and their children cried less.[60] Later, when the relationship soured, so, too, did this rosy view of the Japanese.

Victorians in both China and Japan were convinced of their cultural, intellectual and physical superiority. Westerners saw Japan in almost an Orientalist manner:[61] Japan was part of the East with its unchanging, child-like, immodest, otherness. Even in the 1920s, business commentators wrote of Japan's 'oriental characteristics' such as 'shrewdness'.[62] Such observations were seen as fundamental and part of the unchanging nature of the Japanese 'race'. As Westerners, some merchants saw themselves as ambassadors of 'civilization'. Most merchants believed that open and free trade was always a positive development; by opening Japan to the West, they were convinced that they provided a service and a boon to the Japanese people. Ironically, this 'pre-eminence' seemed to be the justification of some Western merchants in beating their 'native' staff.[63] In wider policy, local organized resistance to the West was met with gunboat-style diplomacy.

Stereotypes, in combination with domestic and international tensions, resulted in violence against foreigners by the armed samurai class. These attacks affected official Japanese-Western relations and disrupted trade. In general, the samurai, perhaps because they thought themselves to have the most to lose financially and politically from the foreign presence, were responsible for the attacks. Japanese merchants, artisans, and farmers were not part of organized efforts against the settlers. Occasional name-calling and mild harassment by townspeople did occur, but by and large, merchants from both sides worked without violent clashes. The so-called 'Bloody 60s', a period in which there was a string of attacks on Western officials and residents, was the height of overt actions against the Western presence. The disturbances by domain and masterless samurai (ronin) alike, were motivated equally by xenophobia and a desire to derail the sho-

49

gunate's relations with the West.

By attacking Westerners and intimidating those Japanese who had any social or economic association with treaty-port residents, these disturbances managed to undermine Western diplomatic intercourse with the shogunate. Each killing and the shogunate's subsequent inability to satisfy Western demands for 'justice', introduced another element of instability. From the point of view of the merchants, two scenarios seemed evident from this escalation of tensions: either the ports would be closed, or the Treaty Powers would resort to force. In either case, the circumstances were not conducive to long-term planning in business or diplomacy.

Domain samurai and *ronin* used fear and violence to compel Japanese merchants to cease trading with the Westerners. Such methods included death threats and displays of decapitated heads on spikes.[64] Francis Hall, a merchant working in the early 1860s in Yokohama, reported that harassment and rumours of assassinations drove Japanese merchants to close shop.[65] Dankitchi 'Dan Ketch',[66] was also a target for his association with the Westerners. Ketch, along with Joseph Heco, was a Japanese who had been shipwrecked off the California Coast. After learning English, he worked for the British Consulate as an interpreter. Perceived by *ronin* as rising above his station, he was repeatedly threatened by samurai for his Western dress and manners. Ultimately he was killed; possibly by the brother of a tea girl whom he had somehow compromised. As Ketch was a registered British subject, Hall asserted that the threats of arson and assassination were 'political as well as personal'.[67] His colleague, Joseph Heco, wrote in his memoirs that he was convinced that his killer was an assassin.[68]

As a result, until after the restoration, trade in the treaty ports was highly volatile due to violence. During the British reparation crisis of 1863, Japanese merchants liquidated their stock and prepared to leave the area for fear of a military incursion. Hall described the general confusion in which Japanese merchants' wares were sold at any price, and debts, sometimes not even due, were collected from the Westerners. Servants robbed their employers in the stampede to leave Yokohama.[69] This panic was not an isolated episode: events repeated themselves in 1864 during the Chōshū operation when the Treaty Powers reopened the Shimonoseki Straits. In 1868, during the internal fighting prior to the Meiji Restoration, the capital, Edo, was all but deserted and trade ground to a halt. After 1868, attacks on Westerners subsided, as the new government adopted a policy of absorbing Western technology and thought.

Not all disruptions in trade were the result of *ronin* violence. Other disruptions occurred owing to political manoeuvrings of the Bakufu. In 1863, the shogunate tried to divert all silk into Edo in order to regain control over foreign trade and the domains. The policy was intended to ease the raw silk shortage for domestic consumption by diverting silk away from Western merchants back into the domestic market. The Bakufu hired *ronin* to intimidate Japanese merchants into complying with these orders. All silk export deals, which had been a major commodity traded by Japan, ground to a stop.

REACHING AGREEMENT: THE MECHANICS OF PROMISE AND PAYMENT

> . . . Irwin's dealings were so honest and prompt and I was extremely impressed, we decided instead of trading directly with the West, we would let Irwin handle our affairs.
>
> Masuda Takashi, *circa* 1874[1]

THE ENVIRONMENT in which the merchants traded was not a predictable one; contracts were easily disrupted and information was scarce. The mechanisms of self-regulation which had allowed for cooperation, as the Japanese merchant guilds, were in a state of disarray. Western merchants were not a cohesive group, and the law, which was to formally govern the actions of the commercial community, was fragmentary and inconsistent. No single set of laws regulated the actions of the Japanese, Chinese, and Western merchants. Japanese merchants were under Japanese jurisdiction, and Western merchants, due to extraterritoriality, under their respective flags. Finally, the continued existence of the treaty ports, especially in the 1860s under the Tokugawa regime, was not at all guaranteed. Armed conflicts, attacks, and murders all contributed to the political and commercial instability of the treaty ports. Yet, trade transpired nevertheless. What were the mechanisms that allowed for trade between Japanese and Western merchants under these circumstances? Given adverse trading conditions and merchants who were as diverse as they were unpredictable, how did merchants enter into contracts with one another?

Merchants trading with one another in the treaty ports used a variety of arrangements to limit their risk. When Westerners first arrived in the Treaty Ports, they depended primarily on a system of auctions to buy and sell goods. Although the use of auctions as a method to disburse goods continued throughout the period, merchants began to use other trade methods; they started to use contracts with one another in order to obtain specific goods and deals. Contractual compliance in the market for wholesale goods was notoriously unreliable. Contracts between Japanese and Western merchants did not always honour their agreements. This lack of credible agreements for wholesale trade resulted in merchants investing in the social capital of networks and information. For example, rather than choosing trading partners who were experts in a given commodity, merchants chose to work with individuals and firms with whom they were assured stable working relationships.

MARKET OF MIDDLEMEN[2]

Trade in treaty-port Japan was a market of intermediaries trading with one another. At the treaty ports, Japanese merchants were selling agricultural and handicraft goods, which were grown or made in the interior. The sellers of silk, tea, and curios were not, in general, the actual farmers or artisans who produced the goods. Intermediaries, whether family representatives of producers or traditional wholesalers, sold the goods at the ports as their primary occupation. Similarly, Western merchants were also intermediaries as they traded on consignment or shipped goods to and from a market in the West. In general, the Westerners were not consumers or producers of the goods they traded. In this respect the Japanese and Western merchants were similar: both the Japanese and Western middlemen were neither the consumers nor the producers of the goods they traded.

Within the treaty port, there were few primary producers selling their goods. The major exceptions were labour and entertainment. Coolies, porters, carpenters, prostitutes, domestic help, restaurants and sellers of such of everyday food and goods as vegetables, fish, and charcoal. These items were mainly consumed in port by resident merchants. Domestic help, and to some extent clerical help, was sometimes imported from China. Such individuals were delegated the task of buying everyday goods and services. Some Western firms with offices in China brought over Chinese clerks, often called compradors, to Japan to assist in business in Asia. As Japanese raw materials, especially foodstuffs, were often intended for the Chinese market, Chinese staff was especially useful.[3] Also, at the opening of treaty ports, all goods were sent to China; there the goods were placed on ships bound for Europe and the United States.

This market of middlemen faced a number of problems with contracting and credit because it depended on the attainment of reliable information. Because intelligence on markets in the West and those outside the treaty port was scarce, the trade was often speculative in nature. Profits were made and lost on a rumour or a panic. For example, one popular speculation was in the silver currency market of the early 1860s. In this case, success depended on merchants keeping information to themselves. Since the Bakufu's money policy was opaque and the exchange rate fluctuated widely, the Japanese government sought to remove some of the silver from the market in order to stabilize the currency. Rumours circulated that the Japanese might remove a certain type of silver coin, and then re-issue it at a different weight. If a merchant had information on which coin was to be removed from circulation, he could corner the market by hoarding this coin. By taking advantage of the floating value system, the merchants could then drive up the price by being the owner of a scarce commodity. If other merchants started buying the coin, the first merchant's coins would be of less value because he would no longer be in the position to dictate his price. This particular type of speculation was a zero sum game in which winner took all. Although not all deals were of this type, there were similar situations with other goods. For example, in the mid-1860s, silk was in short supply due to the Bakufu diverting supply away from the treaty ports.

Another rumour, and only a rumour, was over the purported liberalization of the rice trade. Western and Japanese merchants hoarded rice in the late 60s based on rumours that export restrictions would be lifted. They reasoned that once the restrictions were lifted, the demand and price for rice would be high. Unfortunately for the Japanese and Western merchants involved with the speculation, this did not come to pass and some incurred heavy losses.

Information was not only expensive in the treaty ports, it was not always reliable. Access to reliable information was constricted symmetrically. Both Japanese and Western merchants faced similar barriers such as language, lack of market intelligence and Western and Japanese government prohibitions on travel. Initially, they did not have the facility to read or write Japanese reports, messages or contracts. In order to facilitate business exchange, a pidgin language, which was a blend of Japanese and English, developed.[4] Before the creation of a workable form of pidgin, even a simple oral transaction was communicated with gestures and body language.[5]

Western merchants, for example, did not know the actual demand or costs of production of a given good because they were forbidden by the treaties to go into the interior. Thus, at Yokohama non-diplomatic staff could not go beyond a 10-*li*, or about a 25-mile, radius of the city. Such restrictions precluded trips to plantations, farms, workshops, or other markets outside this area. Some Westerners, however, took advantage of a loophole in the treaties which allowed for trips into the interior for 'health' purposes; this exception was probably allowed by the Japanese government to allow for visits to curative hot springs. Without special dispensation, overnight trips outside the enclave were prohibited by the treaties. Western tourists and merchants took full advantage of this allowance, but because such exceptions were regulated by the Bakufu and the Western consuls, they could not be relied upon as a regular method for access to the interior.

At the same time, the Japanese merchants did not know the effective market for goods in the West as they were forbidden by law to travel outside Japan. Some Japanese merchants, like some of their Western counterparts in their efforts to learn Japanese, made an effort to learn English in order to alleviate the language barrier.[6] Written Chinese was used as a kind of makeshift *lingua franca* because of the common use of Chinese characters. Many Westerners, especially those who had offices in China such as Jardine Matheson and Co., had Chinese servants and compradors who acted as clerks. Although some Westerners learned to speak passable Japanese, many did not. Some 'Old China Hands' assumed that their Chinese language ability would be sufficient in Japan as both languages used Chinese ideographs. In reality, spoken Chinese and Japanese were quite disparate. In order to obtain intelligence on Western markets, Japanese picked though the garbage of Westerners to obtain copies of reports published in metropole newspapers. By chance, silk merchant Hayami Kenso discovered in a copy of *The Times* of London that higher prices for Japanese silk were being quoted in the European markets than by the Western merchants.[7] Woodblock print artists disseminated information on the dress and habits of Westerners found in these newspapers from the garbage. Inexpensive wood block prints, called *ukiyoe*, based on observations on Western treaty port life and drawings in such publications as the *Illustrated London News* and *Frank Leslie's Illustrated Newspaper* sold to a wide Japanese audience. These pictures, called Yokohama prints, became popular with everyday Japanese in the areas around the cities.[8]

Because trade and therefore profit hinged on attaining information and successful enforcement of the contracts, trade relationships were affected by these constraints. Because many Western and Japanese merchants were involved in enterprises in which there was some element of risk, some Western and Japanese merchants abandoned specializing in one particular commodity. Rather than specializing in silk, tea, metals, or weapons, they instead traded in a range of goods – for example, merchants would trade in rice in one deal, coal in the next, and raw silk after that. For some Japanese merchants, such practices were a departure from the old guild systems in which merchants were experts on one particular commodity. For some Westerners, for example those who worked only as tea, silk, or opium experts in China, such methods were also a deviation from the norm.

As a result, some merchants specialized in developing human capital: in short, they became specialists in trading with the 'Other'. At times, Japanese merchants traded with one particular

Western merchant or house. In Western merchant houses, single commodity experts on items such as tea or silk were hired for particular deals. Very large firms were the exception and had the experts on staff, but the house itself took on all types of goods.[9] Those Western merchants in small specialized houses quickly diversified or found work freelance. Successful Japanese-Western merchant relationships in the treaty port seem to have stemmed not from expertise on a given commodity, but on a combination of reputation and opportunity.

Western merchants themselves diversified their businesses. In general, merchants also held multiple occupations as insurance against the caprices of the volatile Japanese market. A merchant could be a newspaper editor, auctioneer, and insurance agent at the same time. For example, M. J. Noord Hegt advertised himself in *The Japan Herald* as both a storekeeper and a commissions merchant.[10] Charles Rickerby, the editor of *The Japan Times*, also worked at the firm of Rickerby, Westwood, and Scare, bill and ship brokers, and commission agents.[11] His counterparts, A. W. Hansard and J. R. Black of *The Japan Herald*, were both auctioneers.[12] Francis Hall of Walsh Hall and Co. worked for his general commission house which also sold insurance, Japanese curios and antiques. He was also an occasional reporter.[13]

Ultimately, in this ambiguous and occasionally inhospitable environment, successful relationships and investment in social capital played a significant role in determining success. As success in the treaty ports depended on attaining information, a good relationship was a source of information and intelligence. In addition, once a relationship was established, costs of contractual planning could be lowered or even circumvented – due to the cost of translation, many merchants avoided formal contracts. A good relationship with a foreign merchant, furthermore, potentially engendered future repeat business; such an example of repeat business dealings was the relationship of Robert Irwin of Walsh Hall and Co. and Itō Hachibei. Although their relationship collapsed and eventually resulted in legal proceedings, they shared information, capital, socialized with one another, and worked together in a number of deals in different commodities.[14]

AUCTION

One solution that circumvented the problems of obtaining information, creating, and enforcing contracts was using auctions. Auctions were useful in dealing with unfamiliar traders because they minimized the risk. With an auction, merchandise was simply brought into the treaty port and sold immediately for cash. The merchants present at these auctions were predominantly Western, although Japanese merchants later participated in these quayside proceedings.[15] The local newspapers and the *Japan Directory* both list a number of auctioneers – auction crying was a common supplemental occupation. Goods shipped from the West would be unloaded on to the docks in Yokohama. Duty was paid at the Customs House, and then the consignor would take the goods away to store in a godown, pidgin for warehouse. In order to save storage costs, some auctions were immediately held at port. Goods were hauled to shore and potential buyers had a short period in which they could examine the goods for sale. Auctions were sometimes held by the docks in the open air. The highest bidder secured the sale, and after the auction, buyers took away their lots, or arranged for delivery and storage. Payment was usually handed in cash to the auctioneer at the end of the sale.

Two kinds of auction lots were sold in the treaty ports. In one type, the lots were large and of a single commodity such as tea or silk or lumber. In general, these items were to be exported. Some auctions in the Japanese treaty ports were similar to the Chinese treaty port opium auctions in which opium was sold in bulk lots. Buyers would then divide the lot and sell the smaller amounts to the 'retail' market of individual users. In Japanese ports, opium was a prohibited substance but some goods followed this pattern. Besides these bulk type auctions, small lots of goods were sold by auction in lieu of selling on the retail markets. Goods such as hats, trousers, and stationery were sometimes sold by auction in small amounts for individual use. Other lots, usually items imported to the treaty ports, were mixed; one auction might have had many small lots of one good, ranging from men's clothes to Western food stuffs to hats. In an advertisement published on June 4, 1863 for an auction on June 7th, auctioneer A. W. Hansard announces a diverse list of goods including furniture of all types, stoves, boxes, books, a fully fitted boat, paper for correspondence, and 80 boxes of gin.[16]

Auctions as a method of sale had advantages; namely, the speed in which goods were converted into cash. Goods would be sold at a given price, and there was no risk of default by buyers. Overhead was low, and information on the goods could be obtained by physically looking and touching. As sea captains were sometimes the importers, the auction was a convenient and fast method. As ships were in port for only a limited amount of time, auctions efficiently raised the cash for goods which could then be used to buy goods to sell at the next port. Auctions had the added advantage of being a familiar form of trade. Both Western merchants in Chinese treaty ports and Japanese merchants in inter-guild transactions used auctions to buy and sell goods. Francis Hall, a Western merchant, observed a Japanese auction in Osaka among Japanese merchants and commented: 'Samples are shown and the bidding and sale is conducted as near as I could ascertain, much as with us. The auctioneer cries the price exactly as with us.'[17]

Auctions, however, had limitations; in brief, planning was not possible. With auctions, specific goods, such as machine parts or even a special style of hat, could not be relied upon to appear in port – such items had to be ordered. For example, women's clothing, which required stays and corsets, had to be specially ordered from Europe. Due to size specificity and the intimate nature of the apparel, one could not rely on auctions to fulfill the specific needs of the enclave community members. A further disadvantage was that auctions functioned on the cash-and-carry principle. Treaty-port merchants were often cash poor due to the restrictions on the amounts of cash that could be exchanged; as transactions were completed with cash, not credit, after the crying of the lots, auctions were not always a preferred means of trade for the cash-poor merchants. Also, auctions could not be used for certain kinds of speculation or any other complex transactions.

THE CHIT SYSTEM

Interestingly, one type of credit system that arose immediately and functioned within the treaty port was the chit system. Chits were effectively IOUs signed by the foreign resident for transactions within the treaty port. Residents carried a pencil on their person instead of petty cash. The system was based upon a similar system used in the Chinese treaty ports. A resident paid for drinks or a meal, for example, by leaving a paper with his name and address and the amount owed. Chits were mainly used for retail goods or services, and were generally accepted in the treaty port area. It was said that only beggars and railways (once established) refused chits, and even churches accepted chits in the collection plate, although the practice was generally frowned upon.[18]

Depending on the status of the Westerner's credit, the seller would go (or send a servant) to the residence of the foreign resident to obtain payment at a later date. If the buyer had a man-servant, one of his duties was settling such debts. Following the Japanese tradition, all chits (and therefore debts) were ideally cleared by the last day of the year. In most cases, chits were paid within a month. In extreme cases, chits were carried over for three years. If residents were found by their government to have no means of support, the residents were unceremoniously sent back home to the West at the expense of their government.

The 'mini-contracts' of chits operated with little friction. Legal cases for small retail amounts such as refreshments and the cost of napkins were pursued in the consular court, but they were rare. Such an example was the case of Nakagawa vs. Fitzgerald in which Nakagawa sued for $17.25[19] over a refreshment bill and some supplies that had been delivered. The defendant claimed that he owed between $7 and $10, but not $17.25. In this case, there was no receipt, so the court examined the translated account books of the plaintiff. As the amounts matched the claim, the verdict awarded for the plaintiff.[20] Cases over small amounts of money were usually either tied to a criminal act, such as an assault, or another larger deal which had been breached. In another case, the same plaintiff, Nakagawa, sued another Westerner, A. Jaffrey over a rented pony carriage, and tacked on a bill of $6.25 for refreshments to the plaint.[21] Among Westerners, one case explicitly mentioned the word 'chit' in the suit.[22] By and large, however, the cases over small debts were few compared to the majority of cases in which disputes were over thousands of dollars or yen.

In contrast to the chit system for retail goods and services, coin was exchanged for export goods. Due to the currency chaos of the early 1860s, Japanese merchants would reject certain types of coin in circulation and would insist on specific types of coin for payment.[23] Merchants buying such goods as tea and silk required contracts, with what was termed 'bargain money', or a down payment. Any long-term or large transaction also required an oral or written contract, and could not be secured with a chit. Among Japanese merchants trading with one another, the system of chits was not used. Instead, the buying and selling of commercial paper, not chits, of Japanese merchant houses was common among Japanese traders. A reputable house such as Mitsui could have bills in circulation for years. Chits were only used by Japanese inside and outside the enclave for day to day household expenses. The Japanese chit system operated independently from the enclave chits and had existed before the Western chit system.[24]

There were a number of reasons for the smoothness with which the chit system operated compared to the import-export system of contracts, described below. First, chits were only used for small purchases or goods and services for personal use – transport, refreshments, or drinks. If a chit writer defaulted, not only was the total amount owed small, it was spread out over a number of people. Chits, however were not used for bulk purchases such as those that would be used in importing and exporting goods from the treaty ports.

Moreover, the chit system appears to have not been bilateral; Western residents only wrote chits to other Westerners and to Japanese merchants and workers. Westerners who were in the retail business served mainly a Western clientele. Retail goods and services were provided by Westerners in occupations such as butchers (most Japanese did not eat meat at this time), tailors, and bakers, all of whom belonged to a lower class within the treaty ports. The services or goods paid in chits had already been rendered or received. Unlike a non-spot contract, the price, quality, or quantity was not up for dispute. The chit system may have been asymmetric as there is no evidence of Japanese consumers writing chits to the Westerners. Japanese were probably by and large the recipient of chits; otherwise, they sent bills, or contracts were exchanged with Westerners. The chit system was unlike the larger import and export market in that it was not a market of intermediaries. Consumers, with a few exceptions, dealt directly with the producers of labour or goods. Chits were a market in which small transactions were iterated. Although most likely a stereotype, it was said that the Victorian male in the treaty port was said to be a creature of habit, preferring the same brand of cheroots, whiskey, and patronizing the same rickshaw stand.[25] Each of these transactions would be 'paid' for using chits. In the business of consignment, however, the trader did not have the luxury of assuming repeat business at such frequency.

CONTACT AND CONTRACT

Contracts, when compared to auctions, were advantageous to the merchant due to planning and specificity. A merchant could order particular goods at a given time for a particular customer. Spot contracts, or instantaneous exchanges, are weak when dealing with asset specific commodities. The more one tailored goods and services to specific needs and the less it can be substituted, the more parties prefer long term/relational types of contract.[26] For example, at Christmas time, among Westerners, the demand for turkey or ham increased. In another case, a Japanese merchant may have wished to order cloth of a particular colour or weight in a particular season's fashion. Even under the somewhat challenging circumstances of the treaty ports, contracts met the needs of both Japanese and Western merchants. Merchants could plan, establish credit, and order specific goods. Although auctions were a popular means of trade in the 1860s and were used throughout the period, contracts were used in transactions between Japanese and Westerners almost immediately. As early as September 1859, British Consul George Morrison wrote to British Consul General Rutherford Alcock, three months after the official opening of the ports, of contractual disputes between the Japanese and Westerners.[27]

In this particular case, the problems arose from the confusion that resulted from the Japanese using contractionary monetary policy to strengthen the currency. In brief, Bakufu treasury officials had taken almost a third of the silver out of the economy and minted less valuable coins. Such actions resulted in a dramatic rise in export prices. Western officials and merchants reacted with complaints and claims of treaty violations. The Japanese government was pressured by the West into devaluing the currency, thus lowering export prices. In this melee, contracts had been formed, but the shifting currency had shifted the terms of the contract in favour of the Western merchant. In Morrison's letter, he reported that Japanese merchants were unable or unwilling to fulfill contracts with Westerners. Moreover, Morrison reported that when Western merchants sought redress from Japanese authorities, the Bakufu officials were unhelpful as, in Morrison's opinion, 'they support the defaulter on such grounds as his stated inability to procure the goods, or change of price since the contract was made'.[28]

In order to contract with one another, a seller with a given good at a given price had to find a buyer, and *vice versa*. There was no systematic arrangement for Japanese and Western merchants to find each other. Contracts were made through word of mouth, or chance. Up through the early 1860s, the process was more of trial and error, and any information, even gossip, however unreliable, was mined for 'facts'. Deals were made in the street, by the wharf, or in firm offices. In the case of the treaty ports, there was no central market area like the Athenian agora to use as a clearing house for Western and Japanese merchants. The purveyors of licensed goods, such as silkworm eggs, on the other hand, were registered in the Customs House.

In some transactions, chance was the main catalyst driving trade. Most of the treaty ports had open air markets in which curios, groceries, and staples were sold, but such markets were for retail and sales involved cash and carry type transactions. However, cash and carry type transactions were also often used to buy curios for the overseas export to the West. Francis Hall, of the consignment house Walsh, Hall and Co., recorded in his diary numerous occasions in which he went to markets and wandered into stores to look at curios and antiques or simply to look at the price of everyday goods. He, like many others, bought curios and antiques to sell back West. Some Western merchants

were approached by Japanese merchants with business propo-
sals. Hall also described an occasion in which Japanese antique
dealers brought goods to Hall for his inspection.[29]

For larger transactions or for long term contracts, the merchants had to rely on word of mouth. Merchants gathered in
the Customs House area in the ports as this place was the first
port of call for cash, complaints, and questions. Another efficient method of obtaining information was using the pre-exist-
ing Japanese network by hiring Japanese staff as *bantō*. The word
'bantō' in the Japanese treaty ports came to mean Japanese compradores. Essentially, Japanese clerks were employed as secre-
taries and book-keepers by Western firms. The Japanese staff
would speak to one another and obtain information on deals.

Larger firms, such as Jardine Matheson, had separate rooms
in which *bantō* interviewed prospective clients.[30] For example, in
the case of Itō Hachibei vs. Walsh Hall and Co., the two parties
initially met though the introduction of Walsh Hall and Co.'s
bantō, Kumagai Iske.[31] After this initial meeting, the two parties
traded hundreds of thousands of dollars over the course of three
years. After working for Western firms for a while, some *bantō*
resigned and started their own businesses or worked for Japanese firms. Such men, with an understanding of and connection
to the Western firms, often facilitated relationships among Japanese and Western merchants.

Despite the obvious cultural and language differences, Western and Japanese merchants formed social networks in order
to facilitate transactions and to collect information. Some Western treaty-port merchants maintained distance between themselves and Japanese merchants, while other merchants
socialized regularly with Japanese counterparts. In the case of
Hall's dealings, the lines between social and business life
blurred. Hall, for example, reports in his diary numerous visits
to Japanese merchants, sometimes buying goods, sometimes
not. More often than not, he went and shared a cup of tea or
saké with the Japanese merchants; a business visit sometimes
became a social visit and *vice versa*. He received special gifts
from Japanese merchants, such as young tea rolled by the hands
of virgins, and spent evenings with the merchants' families.[32]
The information and opinions of his Japanese colleagues in-

formed his business dealings and newspaper articles that he wrote for a US audience.

On the surface, the environment of the treaty port was hardly conducive to trade, let alone long term contracts. In order to have credit, contracts, and therefore trust, must first exist. Without credit, trade was limited to auctions and cash sales. Although Western merchants could obtain credit from Western banks, and Japanese merchants from Japanese lenders, the Westerners could not borrow from Japanese lenders, and *vice versa*. Contracts were one method in which orders for specific market niches could be fulfilled.

With contracts came the need for building information networks. Networks had a dual function of enforcing contracts and allowing for information flows. When the Western and Japanese merchants commenced trading with one another, networks for information were non-existent. With the increased volume of trade and the compounding factors, Western and Japanese merchants began to create networks in order to find further trading partners and to attempt to form an enforcement mechanism. Merchants needed to verify the credit of their potential trading partners. In a letter to *The Japan Times*, a merchant complaining of the lack of contractual compliance among Japanese merchants wrote:

> Most of us doubtless regard some half-a-dozen native dealers with whom we have done regular business through the long term with a kind of wavering confidence, with a kind of hope that we might trust them around the corner, but the large majority of them keep or break their contracts as suits them best. . .[33]

The 'trustworthy' type or merchant – that is merchants with predictable business methods – was of importance to the Western merchants.

The first step in building networks was to amass information. Merchants obtained information by physically going to the Custom House, not only to exchange funds, but as a place to congregate and collect information. Western merchants have been maligned as aloof and prone to sending Chinese compradors to transact business.[34] At the start of the treaty ports period, many firms were small operations which were unable to hire staff, and therefore, the Western merchants went themselves to transact business with their Japanese counterparts. Merchants also explored the other's environment. Merchants visited one another on a social basis as well as simply exploring the markets and stores around them. Although Japanese merchants were forbidden by law to leave Japan, they acquired information by observing the Western enclave and scrutinizing Western publications. Japanese and Western merchants formed networks in order to collect information on new deals, market intelligence, and to assess the risk on their dealings.

THE ANATOMY OF A DEAL

An open-ended contract, in brief, is a contract in which the exchange is not completed until a later date; in such an arrangement a transaction is completed sometime after the agreement is made. A 'spot' or immediate contract is one in which the contract is completed simultaneously; the purchase of newspaper at the news agents is such an example. In another modern example, one such instance of an open-ended contract is a consumer buying an item from a catalogue. In this example, the buyer writes down his order, encloses his payment, and sends his request via post or e-mail. The seller receives the order, processes it by packing the item for the post, and mails it off. If all goes well, the item reaches the buyer, which he may or may not accept as the item he ordered. Until the item is shipped and accepted by the buyer, the contract is uncompleted. In the case of nineteenth-century Japan, a treaty-port merchant might obtain goods on consignment from the US or Britain, and the contract would remain unfulfilled until the goods were sold in Japan. Similarly, a Western merchant may have ordered goods, such as silk or tea, from the interior.

In the treaty ports, such open-ended contracts for goods followed a rough pattern. In general, open-ended contracts using bargain money involved goods that were tailored for the buyer – for example, the good or the specific quantities of the good could not be had on the 'open' or auction market. The buyer and seller first established which goods and at what prices they wished to exchange. In cases when the goods had to be imported into the treaty port, a contract fixed the price and specified the date of the goods' arrival. Usually, the agreement allowed for a range of dates in order to allow for mishaps such as late ships, problems clearing customs, and bad weather. For example, if a Japanese merchant ordered wool cloth from a Western merchant, the buyer would most likely specify the colour, weight, quality, quantity, and the dates by which he wanted the cloth. Good weather, in this example, would be necessary when landing the goods – rain could damage cloth when it was brought on to the piers where they customarily sat until collection by the buyer. In the monsoon season, this requirement could cause serious delays.

If the seller, in this example the Western merchant, agreed to the conditions set by the buyer, and *vice versa*, they would have an agreement. Both parties, in theory, understood that they would transact business by exchanging goods at an agreed price. In some exchanges a contract was drawn up, but written contract was not always used – the details of the transaction were sometimes exchanged orally. However, in order for an open-ended contract for goods to be valid, the merchants almost always paid a deposit, or 'bargain money'. In some cases, the balance was handed to the seller when the goods reached the buyer. It was customary to give a receipt for the bargain money. In the absence of a contract, the receipt for the bargain money functioned as proof of the agreement. Bargain money was customarily 10% of the total value of the deal. For example, if the buyer ordered $500 worth of wool cloth, he would pay the seller $50 when they sealed the contract. At this point, both sides generally understood that a contract existed between the two parties, and default on either side constituted a breach.

When the items arrived in port, the buyer inspected the goods, and if it matched the sample or the description in the contract, the buyer paid the remaining balance of the money. If the goods did not meet the buyer's expectations, the trade was not completed. In some cases, due to damage in shipping or because the goods did not match the sample, the price was sometimes re-negotiated. It was acceptable for the seller to offer a lower price for his goods. It was considered unacceptable for sellers to demand a higher price for goods because the market had changed; however, many Japanese and Western merchants breached their contracts in favour of buyers willing to pay better prices.

Bargain money sealed the agreement. In almost every incomplete transaction in the treaty ports, some sort of bargain money was exchanged. Bargain money was used both in Western-Japanese transactions and between Western merchants. Bargain money functioned on a number of levels: first, it helped secure the contract compliance from the buyer, second, the contract was legally binding, and third, it gave the merchants funds to secure goods from outside the treaty ports. Because the treaty port market was volatile and was an environment where a supply of cash could not be easily or predictably obtained, so bargain money was a source of ready capital to finance trade. Bargain money was distinguished from 'purchase money', which was given to an agent to procure goods on the buyers' behalf. For example, a Westerner would give a Japanese agent funds as purchase money in order to buy silk on his behalf in the interior. Any remaining funds would be returned to the Westerner. The buyer might remunerate the agent by paying him a salary or giving him a commission. In cases in which bargain money was exchanged, the buyer was not an agent; any transaction with a third party was a separate agreement.

Bargain money helped bind the relationship between buyers and sellers by giving them the incentive to fulfill their promises. The advantages of using bargain money changed throughout the transaction. Initially, the seller had the advantage; he held the goods and 10% of the of the total payment. Early Western traders may have envisioned trade in which the goods were sold *to* the Japanese. In such a scenario, the Western seller would have had the advantage. At the same time, however, the reality was such that there was Western demand for Japanese goods, namely silk and tea products, and the bargain money system made the Western merchants vulnerable to Japanese defaulters. However, there was nothing preventing the seller from defaulting on the agreement and absconding with the buyer's money. Indeed, letters, articles, and complaints made to Japanese and Western officials accused Japanese and Western sellers alike of defaulting on their obligations. Bargain money not only gave the buyer incentive to go through with his agreements, it also protected the seller. If the buyer failed to buy, the seller held 10% of the contract which would presumably buffer his losses. In some cases, instead of pursuing a court claim, sellers simply took the bargain money as the penalty for non-compliance. The buyer could also default on his obligations, but at the expense of losing 10% of his payment. Once the goods were handed to the buyer, and the seller was awaiting payment, the advantage shifted; the buyer had the goods and the remaining 90% of the payment owed to the seller. The seller now had no leverage over the buyer. The bargain money system was one that initially favoured both Japanese and Western sellers. A Japanese merchant, however, had an added advantage: if he could not sell his goods in the treaty port, he could unload his goods in the indigenous market, whereas a Westerner could not. The only other markets available to Western merchants were markets in China and the West, both of which were at some distance from Japan and therefore additional costs would be incurred.

Bargain money in the form that it took in the western treaty ports was a Western legal conceit. One significant function of bargain money was that it made an open ended agreement a legal contract under Western legal codes. In order for a contract to exist, at least in Western (British) law, some form of consideration must be exchanged.[35] Consideration is defined as some form of compensation for something promised or done in order for contract to be a legal entity. In short, something must be exchanged for the contract to be legally binding; mere mutual promises for a future exchange, at least under British law, were not legally binding. Bargain money can also be viewed as an expression of declaring the intent to enter into legal relations. Although the courts were not always effective settling contractual disputes, Westerners, because of this unstable environment, may have structured their contracts with the express intent to enter legal relations in order to protect their agreements in case of default. Bargain money, however, was not used in agreements between Japanese merchants outside the treaty ports. Under Japanese law and business practices of the period, the mutual promises were sufficient in securing a binding agreement. The concept of consideration was initially an alien one to Japanese merchants.

4

DESCRIPTION OF CASES

'A merchant shall hardly keep himself from doing wrong; and a huckster shall not be freed from sin;' and again: – 'As a nail sticketh fast between the joinings of the stones: so doth sin stick close between buying and selling.' It may be so: Commerce seems to tend to corrupt the morals of a people. . . and we know no place in the East where the text may be expounded with greater edification than Yokohama.

Editorial on Kingdon vs. Wilkin and Robison in *The Japan Times' Overland Mail*, February 12, 1869

COURT CASES, whether civil or criminal, are a reflection of society. However, the picture they present is sometimes like that of a fun house mirror; warped and distorted beyond recognition. Certainly, some contracts were made under duress and these trade relationships became twisted as relations soured. However, some elements of the cases remain true, and certain patterns arise from the discord. These court cases are only one tool of many in which we can ascertain how merchants traded in the treaty ports. The cases often illuminate the problems and expectations of the treaty port merchant. The purpose of this chapter is to focus on the cases themselves as evidence. Here, we seek to describe the cases collected, the limitations of the cases in describing the treaty-port merchants, and some generalizations that are evident from the cases.

From the body of evidence from 1859 to 1876, it cannot to be said that Japanese merchants had particularly unique or different attitudes towards their trade commitments when compared to their Western counterparts. Although the legal conception of contract was a purely Western conceit, the manner in which 'contract' as an agreement for trade was understood – or in some cases, not understood – among both Japanese and Western merchants, was similar. By and large, the disputes in mixed, or Japanese-Western, cases were similar to disputes among Westerners. In addition, one might assume that because they had similar legal traditions and assumptions, Westerners would have few disputes with one another, and more with Japanese merchants. From the court records and merchant writings, it is evident that Western merchants had wide-ranging disputes and had no clear consensus on business norms or procedure. Westerners readily sued one another. In this trading environment there was no single authority to which the traders were held accountable, and Western and Japanese merchants both pursued their own interests.

THE BODY OF CASES

The body of cases was a catholic one. They ranged in issues and costs, and contained examples of cooperation, generosity, and venality. The cases ranged from the mundane – such as the accidental death of a pet – to international treaty violations. This portion of the study focuses mainly upon 77 mixed civil disputes heard in British, American, Italian, Swiss, German, and Japanese courts; these cases were examined in addition to hundreds of criminal and civil cases between Westerners in the period from 1859-76. More than one hundred mixed cases (Japanese and Western litigants) post 1876 were examined in addition to the main body of cases. Most of these cases came from newspaper and news magazine sources which contained fairly detailed summaries of court activity and procedure. Some articles of larger cases contained detailed information of witnesses' answers to the attorneys' questions, but at the minimum, all the newspaper law reports stated the plaintiff, defendant, court, charge, the defendant's response to the accusation, and the verdict. In longer trials, the newspapers would report a given day's activity in court, and each subsequent day was described serially in subsequent issues. In a weekly newspaper such as *The Japan Weekly*

News, the paper would summarize each day's activity in varying levels of detail. From 1861 onward, there was at least one newspaper in publication in at least one of the ports to report on court activity: the drawback in this method was the occasional lost newspaper issues which may have contained other cases.

In reality, there were probably more mixed cases than those covered here. However, two problems existed in collecting information. In the case of the British courts, Foreign Office documents, such as those in Series FO 262 and 46, tended to cover details of cases that deserved special mention; usually they were of a criminal nature or concerned treaty issues. The correspondence of the officials recorded the problems and complaints of the merchants, rather than their day to day routines and procedures. These files were mined for cases but few civil cases were covered in detail in the diplomatic dockets. These files were more useful for background and information on the general issues of the Western population in Japan. Unfortunately, the list of the court returns of the consular cases were lost because they were sent as enclosures, which were separated from the official reports; most of the early enclosures were lost. In US diplomatic dockets, the enclosures were separated from the reports, and were forwarded to the appropriate federal agencies. To this day, it is unclear whether the list of court returns are still extant.[1]

The actual number of court cases still remains to be ascertained. R. Chang's study of the justice of the consular court found 140 civil mixed cases in US and British courts for the period from 1859 to 1899, an average of 3.5 mixed civil cases a year. For the period of seventeen years covered in this study, this would result in about 60 cases. In this study, a total of 47 US and British mixed cases were found in the newspaper files. Considering that the number of mixed cases greatly increased in the late 1870s, these numbers seem reasonable for the period. Chang and other scholars of the treaty ports have relied heavily on Foreign Office papers for consular records of trade activity – of which one twentieth century British consul commented that the reports pertaining to trade were at least fifty per cent inaccurate.[2]

At the same time, the numbers seem suspect. Chang's findings seem low; for example, in 1877, the year after the period specified in this study, there were 17 US and British mixed cases out of 41 mixed civil cases – well above his average of 3.5 cases a year. Through 1878-80, the number of mixed cases remained high. Chang himself suggests that many more mixed civil and criminal cases existed than those mentioned in the consular reports. They were likely to have been listed in the lost court return enclosures; he estimates almost a total of 2800 cases from 1859-99, an extrapolation from the 668 mixed civil and criminal disputes. Because the number of the mixed civil trials recounted in the newspapers is closer to Chang's observed figure, the actual number of civil cases is probably closer to the observed figure than his estimate. At the same time, using this method, no mixed cases were recorded from newspapers in 1861. There is the tantalizing reference in one of official reports that $30,000 worth claims had been lodged by British merchants against Japanese merchants.[3] Thus, the newspaper-method figure seems rather low. The early 1860s were a period in which newspaper publication schedules were at times irregular. This also raises another issue. Was there a distinction between a 'complaint' and a court proceeding? Evidence suggests that there was; in the silk worm egg dispute described in Chapter VII, the Western merchant first reported to the consul to register his complaint; however, there is no record of a formal court appearance. This suggests that a registering with the consul was distinctly different from initiating court action.

Whatever the numbers may be, at the very least, a broad cross-section of civil disputes were collected. Because the majority of the cases extracted for this study were from the treaty-port press, they covered a range of cases and not just the cases that were deemed noteworthy from the diplomatic perspective. The press endeavoured to print a complete record of the court activity of all cases, ranging from one dollar fines for public drunkenness, to murder trials, to $10,000 silk deals gone wrong.

The body of civil disputes varied in their legal sophistication: some plaintiffs explicitly specified a 'breach' in the contract, whereas other parties mixed criminal and civil complaints. For example, there are a number of cases in which workers complained of unpaid wages – a breach of an employment contract

— and beatings by their employer. For example in 1869, a Japanese woman Nami, a keeper of a tobacco and 'saki' [saké] shop, pressed charges for assault and for unpaid sales of alcohol.[4] In R. vs. D. Welsh, Welsh was tried for assault, and at the same time an unnamed Japanese man sued him for a debt of $6.92. Both issues were addressed in a single trial.[5] Other civil complaints, although not strictly contractual complaints, pursued damages; for example, in one 1876 case, a *jinrickshaw* coolie' pursued 9 yen 75 sen of damages sustained in lost wages by an attack by a British resident's bulldog.[6] In another case, a Japanese pursued a claim of damages sustained when a British resident accidentally killed the plaintiff's mother.[7] Other cases were purely commercial and plaintiffs specified that they sought to compel defendants to take delivery or requested a return of bargain money. The body of evidence also includes a 1876 case which was an appeal of an earlier case in the British consular court.[8]

Of these mixed civil cases, the majority of the cases pressed for payment due to the plaintiff. In most part, these cases were treated as breaches of contract because at one point, some type of contract had been made in which a buyer agreed to pay money to a seller for goods or services. The disputes arose because buyers refused to purchase the specified goods, or sellers refused to deliver the specified goods. In cases where payment was withheld, the majority of cases were due to the buyer's belief that the contract was not fulfilled to his satisfaction. In a few cases, the buyer simply did not have the funds. More often than not, the merchant refused to comply with the contract because the goods were not satisfactory because they did not meet his expectations or because the goods had somehow been adulterated. At times the contract was breached out of simple convenience or greed; in such cases the market for a given item may have collapsed, or a better deal may have been found elsewhere. Both Japanese and Western merchants breached inconvenient contracts. In the opposite case where the seller refused to sell, the buyer asked the court to force the seller to keep his part of the agreement. Both types of complaints presented a breach of contract issue.

The majority of mixed cases occurred after 1872, with almost a third of the cases in 1876 alone. The sudden explosion of cases was partially a result of the establishment of the Kanagawa Sai-bansho, the Japanese court in Kanagawa, in which Western plaintiffs could more easily pursue claims against Japanese de-fendants. The majority of mixed cases found during the course of this study with Japanese plaintiffs were heard in British courts, with American courts a far second. After 1875, in addi-tion to the increase of the cases filed by Japanese against Western-ers, there was dramatic increase in the number of mixed cases filed by Westerners against Japanese: a trend that continued through 1880. Until 1874, there was only one case in which a Westerner pursued a claim in court against a Japanese. In 1875 and 1876 alone, there were 21 cases. Civil cases up until 1875-6 were cases in which Westerners pursued claims against each other, or Japanese plaintiffs sued Western defendants.

The cases and the issues in the mixed civil trials changed over time. Only 6 mixed civil cases were pursued in the 1860s, although Western merchants sued one another over a range of disputes. These early cases were over larger sums of money: Ja-panese merchants pursued claims ranging from $835 to $3488. One claim did not have a specified dollar value, and Japanese plaintiff instead requested the court to compel the Western mer-chant to take delivery of the contracted goods.[9] 1869 and 1870 were years in which there were few civil cases between Japanese and Westerners; probably due to the unrest resulting from the Meiji Restoration.

Nevertheless, during this time period there was much civil and criminal court activity between Westerners. The increase in cases was partially the result of an elevated criminal load; be-cause of the increased military presence, the sentencing of drunk sailors and soldiers increased. By 1873, the claims of both Western and Japanese plaintiffs became more sophisticated: in-stead of vaguely stipulating contract enforcement, both Japa-nese and Western merchants assigned a specific dollar amount to the breach. That same year, contractual disputes stemming from the debts of the old domains owed to the Western mer-chants were heard in Western consular courts. Although the old domains were clearly a Japanese defendant, the case was heard at the Japanese Foreign Ministry with the British Judge Hannen assisting the Japanese Commissioner. The legal sophistication of the Western courts increased as well. Once into the 1870s, fewer cases treated civil and criminal complaints in one case. 1875 saw the reappearance of Japanese defendants in the Kanagawa Saibansho (Court of Kanagawa) in which Westerners sued Japanese defendants under the adjudication of Vice-president Asaina Kansui. That year, six of the sixteen cases were pursued against Japanese. By 1876, 15 out of the 27 mixed cases were pursued against Japanese defendants.

In general, among the diplomatic personnel, contractual disputes between merchants were deemed as not urgent and a low priority. Consuls and their staff often complained of the overwhelming loads of paperwork resulting from civil disputes and were often behind on their case load. The courts were short of staff, which resulted in cases being backlogged when a time consuming case was brought into court. For example, the case of Itō Hachibei vs. Walsh Hall & Co. dominated the fall and winter of the British consular court of 1875. Certain cases appear to have taken precedence over others. For example, an inquest into a death – a suicide or other such sudden death – required immediate attention. Similarly, salvage cases and seamen jailed for drunkenness and fighting also had precedence over civil disputes. These types of cases were a priority because of the pressing time frame; bodies could decompose, sunk junks could float away, and ships had schedules to meet. In the 1860s, diplomatic tensions were particularly high and staff were occasionally called away to their core duties rather than resolving disputes among merchants.

By the 1870s, some residents became regular users of the treaty port courts system. A British resident, Jaffray,[10] who was connected to a stable in some form, was the defendant of a number of disputes. Jaffray also sued a man named (most likely Thomas) Glover for $50 worth of horse-related items a few months later in September of 1872.[11] In April 1872, Suyamano, a Japanese horse-feed dealer, sued Jaffray for some alleged debts. Another Japanese, Nakagawa Mankichi also sued Jaffray for $13 3/8 in 1876.[12] Nakagawa was also no stranger to the courts: in 1876, he pursued another claim against Westerners. Cocking & Co. filed three separate cases in April 1876 against Japanese merchants for breaches of contract ranging from $84.73 to $3000.

THE JAPANESE PLAINTIFFS

The majority of mixed civil cases were filed by Japanese plaintiffs against Western defendants. Within a mixed case, usually a Japanese individual or group of Japanese merchants sued a single Westerner or group of Westerners or Western business. In the period up to 1876, there were no cases in which Japanese and Westerners cooperated together as either co-plaintiffs or co-defendants. In 1877, one such case appeared in the proceedings of Ishiya Kuibei and Emmanuel Schraub vs. Israel Isaacs.[13] These cases were extremely rare. In most mixed cases, a Japanese person who had a civil complaint against a Westerner filed his grievance at the consular court of the Westerner's nation, in accordance with the unequal treaties. Every Westerner had the right to have a civil or criminal trial under the laws of his home country. 53 of the 77 cases were Japanese claims made by Japanese against Westerners.[14] The uneven ratio of claims against Westerners was probably the result of an inefficient system of processing Western complaints against Japanese merchants. Of these civil disputes, five cases sought civil damages for accidents (versus those damages sought from non-fulfillment of contracts): they ranged from an injury stemming from a bulldog bite (9 yen 75 sen)[15] to the destruction of a boat ($6,616).[16] Other cases pursued the payment for services rendered: these included services for labour, entertainment, and refreshments.

Two groups pursued claims: merchants offering services and goods, and to a much lesser extent, branches of the Japanese government. Of the handful of the latter cases, the Japanese government also pursued its claims in the consular courts.[17] For example, there were a few in which the Kanagawa authorities pursued claims of land rent against Western defaulters. In general these cases were for no more than a few hundred dollars. Two major cases were pursued by branches of the Japanese government. The Ōkurashō (The Finance Ministry) of Japan, through their agent Yoshida D'Jiro vs. PMSS (Pacific Mail Steam Ship) Company in 1874 sought $10,250 for breach of contract. The 1875 case of Kaitakushi (Hokkaido Colonization Office) vs. Martin Cohen & Co., heard in the US court, was a breach of contract over 1600 rifles and ammunition. In addition to the $40,000 claim for the money paid to the American merchants, they also claimed $200,000 worth of damages for non-performance of the deal. Although these cases were significant, they are not the focus of this study which centres on contractual behaviour between merchants.

The bulk of cases focused on Japanese merchants pursuing Westerners for breaches of contract. In most cases, they pursued payments owed to them or attempted to compel the defendant to complete a contract. The issues were far from clean cut. Overt exploitation by Western merchants occurred in few cases, such as that of Alpiger vs. Shibia covered in the following chapters. There were accusations by Western merchants and diplomats that Japanese traders sued Westerners as a form of speculation, they are difficult to prove. Most cases seemed to result from unclear and conflicting expectations, careless bookkeeping, neglect, and unforeseen circumstances. In addition, a modicum of greed appeared to be one of the causes behind the cases. The case of Itō Hachibei vs. Walsh, Hall, & Co. encompassed all these problems, and is covered in more detail in a further chapter.

Another common dispute in the courts, also discussed in a following chapter, is the issue of 'bargain money'. Problems occurred when the seller defaulted or when the goods were not what the buyer expected. In such cases, a buyer could possibly lose not only his down payment, but also risked the entire amount of the deal. A suit over bargain money was a clear instance of a breach of contract because certain promises and consideration were exchanged, yet the transaction was not completed. Japanese merchants sued Western merchants for the return of the bargain money in contracts for Western goods. The reverse also occurred: Japanese merchants also sued Westerners to force Western buyers to take delivery of their goods and to fulfil their contractual agreements. In both cases, Western merchants found it convenient to avoid their obligations in the volatile treaty-port market. Some Japanese merchants pursing contractual completion and bargain money sued for monetary damages which had arisen from the contractual breach. But actual losses stemming from the non-compliance of a contract were difficult to prove, and those requests were generally dismissed.

One of the most striking aspects of the body of treaty-port civil cases is the range of complaints raised by Japanese and Westerners. Japanese plaintiffs suing for breach of contract ranged from the wealthy, such as Itō Hachibei, to carpenters and labourers who were arguably poorly educated and paid. In cases similar to Itō Hachibei vs. Walsh Hall & Co. in which the parties sued over thousands and both parties were relatively affluent, the plaintiff had the means to pursue his case. A wealthy man such as Itō could afford the risks and costs to sue.

At the other end of the spectrum were small cases pursued by menial workers. Some of this group were most likely illiterate such as women in menial labour and uneducated labourers – a group with few resources – who sued for lost wages, expenses, and breach of contract. Although the mixed cases were rather similar to the Western cases, the Japanese plaintiff faced considerable barriers in pursuing a case.[18] In addition, the Western adversarial court was unfamiliar to most Japanese. They were essentially navigating though a system that operated by different laws, norms, and languages. For example, in 1877, a female servant, sued her female employer, Angel Ramon, for $50, the arrears of her wages ($35) and for an alleged beating.[19] In another case that same year, Uchida Waka, an 'amah', sued her Danish employer for travel expenses.

A notable group in these service-oriented cases were those pursued by carpenters and builders, where the conflicts centred upon issues over the definition of the 'completion' of a building project. The carpenters' complaints resulted partially from the problems of inflexible contracts. Carpenters and builders sometimes initially had a written contract with their Western employers. However, as many who have undertaken a home improvement plans may have experienced, the project's goals sometimes change. These additions – such as an extra window or a new wall – or unforeseen problems – such as rot or damage – were not part of the original contract. As work was already in progress, a new contract incorporating the extra materials and costs was sometimes not drawn up. When the work was completed some time later, the final costs were in dispute. The language barrier made it even more unclear; instructions were misunderstood, and the responsibility over who should bear the extra costs and materials was not transparent. Another problem stemming from lack of information was that Japanese carpenters often did not report problems that occurred in the projects and improvised their own solutions rather than tell their employers. Such initiative sometimes did not meet with approval.[20] Some merchants, who often faced their own cash flow problems, attempted to escape their obligations by finding obscure faults in the workmanship.

In order to pursue their case, plaintiffs had to lodge a complaint to the proper authorities. They had to appear in court on the appointed day, thus losing a working day, to present their claim, and to argue their case following Western consular court procedure. Most of these small claims, if not all, were self represented, and did not use the services of an attorney. If they used one, they had to find a way to communicate with him, as the lawyers were usually Westerners. For small cases, the lack of a lawyer was probably due to a lack of funds, and the small amounts contested.

The courts did offer some facilities and procedures that may explain the existence of some Japanese cases in Western courts. Translators and interpreters were available and they helped ease the communication barrier. Also, in the British courts, the individual who lost the case generally bore the costs of the case. If the plaintiff lost, he would have to pay court costs, and *vice versa*. The custom of the treaty port courts was that Japanese plaintiffs did not have to demonstrate that they had the means to pay for court costs or to leave a deposit to pursue their claims. In some exceptional cases, when a mixed case became extended, the Japanese merchant plaintiff was required to deposit funds with the court.[21]

Thus, the barriers to pursuing a court case in British court were lower for a Japanese litigant than a British one. If a plaintiff was confident that he was going to win his case, pursuing a legal case was a rational course of action. If the Japanese party believed he would win, and was willing to take the risk, he could pursue the case at almost no cost. The usage of the courts for small, petty disputes suggests that entry barriers to the legal system were low, and that in an environment in which information flows were difficult, it was easier and cheaper to resolve disputes though the court. The court appears to have been an efficient means of dispute resolution in the treaty ports for these small claims.

THE WESTERN DEFENDANTS

The Western defendants of cases pursued by the Japanese were by and large merchants or their firms. The majority of the plaintiffs sued individuals into the 1870s rather than firms, after which the Japanese began to hold Western companies responsible for their debts. An 1866 claim against Glover by Aburaza Ihei, for example, was made against the person, rather than firm he represented. The shift in focus from the individual to the firm was probably a result of Western firms expanding from one-man operations to companies with several members. In this period, the man was very often the firm. Merchant houses in the 1860s were often literally a single room in which the merchant ate, slept, and conducted his business. This shift also suggests an increased sophistication on the part of the Japanese plaintiff in recovering his claims. Whether the individual or the firm was responsible for the debts was not a problem in most cases. An exception was if a Japanese merchant sued a Westerner who had a partner of another nationality, the consular courts had no jurisdiction over the partner, and could not adjudicate the case. By suing the firm, the plaintiff was able to sue all members of the firm regardless of nationality.

Western defendants shared one attribute with their Japanese counterparts; both groups ranged from small-time dealers to large merchant houses. Japanese plaintiffs sued the large merchant houses such as Walsh, Hall, & Co. Smaller merchants, such as G. Blass who owned a general store, were involved in civil disputes. Finally, at the lower end were individuals, such as W. H. Smith and A. J. Wilken, who had defaulted on their rent. These individuals had irregular employment and uncertain means of support.

WESTERNERS PURSUING CLAIMS AGAINST JAPANESE DEFENDANTS

Under the consular court system, only complaints from Japanese plaintiffs could be adjudicated. The consular court did not have jurisdiction over Japanese defendants, except on the rare occasion in which a case involving Japanese plaintiffs was appealed by the Western defendant. In cases in which a Westerner had complaints against a Japanese merchant, the case had to be heard under Japanese law. Although Japanese courts which processed Western complaints technically existed throughout the period, until 1875, they did not function as an effective means to resolve civil disputes. The courts existed in name, but until that date, Western plaintiffs did not have a functioning court in which to lodge their claims.

In the 1860s, disputes under Japanese adjudication were heard in the British consulate parlour with British 'assistance'; an uncomfortable state of affairs for the Japanese who, in theory, had jurisdiction over cases with Japanese defendants. The Japanese court was preoccupied mainly with criminal issues. In an 1860 circular written by George S. Morrison, British Consul, the emphasis on criminal issues is evident. The first portion describes how to deal with theft by the Japanese. Civil issues are addressed in the shorter second part, 'With Reference to Disputes arising out of Trading Affairs'. In cases of criminal and civil disputes, a British officer's presence was required to resolve the dispute. The Japanese defendant, if found liable, was responsible for his actions under Japanese law.[22]

Western merchants found these arrangements far from satisfactory. For example, these impromptu courts had no permanent locale. In addition, the Western merchants had grave reservations about the justice handed out in these Japanese courts. They did not mince their words: 'justice' at the hands of Japanese authorities was 'an evil. . .'.[23] This was 'natural circumstance' resulting from 'the Japanese (authorities who) wish to render as little desirable as possible (sic)'.[24]

The first official mixed *civil* case on record in which a Westerner sued a Japanese was in January of 1864, in which A. Edelman sued Shibiya Segerō for $665.80. At the same time, Shibiya Segerō sued his counterpart for $4908 over a silk dispute in a British court. Both cases were the result of an agreement between the two merchants in which Edelman had contracted to buy 19 bales of silk. When the silk arrived, Edelman inspected the silk without Shibiya's presence, and immediately exported it out of Japan. He then claimed that the silk was not of the same quality as the sample and refused to pay the price previously agreed upon in the agreement. In the case of A. Edelman vs. Shibiya Segerō, the defendant was Japanese, so the case was heard in a 'Japanese' court held on the premise of the British Consulate sitting room with Marcus Flowers, the consul, 'assisting' in the case. This case resulted in a statement in which the unnamed Japanese court official deemed that Edelman had acted irregularly in inspecting the silk in the Japanese merchant's absence, and passed responsibility on adjudicating the matter to the British Court: 'A number of English resident merchants bore unanimous witness at the court to the honesty of Shibiya. I therefore beg you to settle the matter as it ought to be.' The case of Shibiya Segerō vs. A. Edelman was then heard under the British Court with Consul Flowers adjudicating the case. He found Edelman's action 'irregular and censurable in the highest degree',[25] and awarded the plaintiff the full amount claimed.

In the 1870s, after the Meiji administration had gained some footing, cases against Japanese defendants were regularly heard in Japanese courts, albeit with continued Western 'guidance.' In 1873, four suits were brought forth against the indebtedness of the old domains under the Tokugawa by Western merchants. They ranged from a few thousand dollars to $15,000. Because the defendants were Japanese − albeit of a non-existent government − the case was heard by Japanese authorities. Interestingly, the civil complaint was heard in the Gaimushō, the Foreign Ministry, in the presence of Western authorities. In 1874, with the establishment of a dedicated courtroom for the Kanagawa Saibansho (Court), cases brought by Western plaintiffs against Japanese defendants began in earnest. That year, almost half of the mixed cases were those pursued by Westerners against Japanese; few cases were heard in the British court because that fall and winter, the prolonged case of Itō Hachibei against the Walsh brothers' company dominated the British court's schedule. The next year, over half of the cases were heard in the Kanagawa Saibansho. In February of 1877, the British Secretary of State for Foreign Affairs sent Harry Parkes, the British representative in Japan, a revised set of rules of procedure for the Japanese courts, which was later translated and published in June of 1877.[26] Later that month, the British Legation released a circular that specifically addressed the rules and procedures for British subjects pursuing a claim or an appeal against Japanese defendants in the Japanese court.[27] The trend of Westerners suing Japanese continued through to 1880. In these Japanese cases, the majority of Western plaintiffs pursuing a civil claim were merchants pursuing a breach of contract dispute, including cases in which they asked the court to compel the defendant to take delivery of goods. The defendants all tended to be merchants who had at one point made some sort of agreement to trade with the Western merchants; some were individual merchants, other were firms such as Mitsu Bishi Steam Ship Co. (*sic*).[28] Most of the civil cases were contract disputes over goods, but also included cases over services and employment contracts. The claims ranged from just over one hundred dollars to $13,000.

The most remarkable aspect about these cases pursued by Westerners was the fact that they were not remarkable at all. In short, the cases pursued against the Japanese were similar to the cases that Japanese pursued against Westerners. Although the cases against Japanese of 1875 and 1876 tended to involve higher amounts, the types of disputes were similar. Westerners sued for the return of bargain money, to compel the completion of the contract, to settle debts, and for wages owed for services rendered. For example, in the case of H. Arhens & Co. vs. Omia Shobiya, the Western plaintiff sued the Japanese merchant to force him to take delivery of a specific type of cloth. The Japanese merchants refused to take delivery on the basis that the cloth did not match the sample that had been initially shown. Ten years earlier, Aburaza Ihei and Isuruya Kanezo sued Glover & Co. to compel the Western firm to take delivery in much the same way. Cases pursued by Westerners against Japanese all had analogous examples in the body of cases between Westerners and mixed disputes.

INSTITUTIONAL MEMORY

Within the treaty ports, there was interest in establishing some sort of 'institutional memory' among the business community. Although it is difficult to make an assessment of how representative the cases were of trade in the treaty ports, judging from the body of evidence, it would be safe to say that trade relations did not go as smoothly as all parties would have wished. The Western press, aside from calling for the creation of trade norms, also published the letters from merchants seeking a standard form of accountability and establishment of norms of business practice in the treaty ports. The law, and by extension, the courts, were seen by merchants as one of the main means of establishing sound trade practices. The courts also worked to clarify the unspoken business norms and procedures so as to bring order to business transactions, but these efforts met with little success.

The commercial disputes were a source of tension with the members of the treaty ports. If we were to believe the letters sent by Western merchants to British officials, the contractual problems were due to the Japanese merchants' and officials' lack of moral rectitude and inherent rapacity. Japanese merchants made the same argument concerning their Western counterparts. But, as early as November 1859, Alcock, Parkes' predecessor, was skeptical of the Western merchants' complaints. In a report to Lord Russell, he censured the behaviour of the foreign residents, calling it 'indiscreet conduct, to use the mildest term. . . both to the nature of trade they enter into and the mode in which they conduct it – often in many instances to grave objection'.[29] The lack of business norms, procedures, or 'morality' and the ensuing problems were clearly not limited to transactions between Japanese and Westerners. Yet, 'morality', with its multitude of definitions was not the issue here. The understanding and the willingness to comply with the terms and duties of a contract is of issue. Westerners did not have clear procedures for trade in the ports, and the lack of understanding and shared norms caused many contractual disputes.

Among Western merchants, the case of Kingdon vs. Wilkin and Robison generated much commentary by observers in the treaty ports;[30] it became a *cause celebre* among the treaty port residents as being an exemplar of the lack of commercial morality. Wilkin and Robison sold a consignment of N. P. Kingdon's rice without his permission. There was some confusion as to whether or not this deal was a partnership:[31] In any case, a lack of transparent business procedure resulted in losses for both parties. The problem then became an issue of who should bear the loss: the court ruled that Wilkin and Robison bore three fourths, and Kingdon a fourth. 'ONE OF THE PUBLIC', a reader, wrote in a letter to the editor of *The Japan Times' Overland Mail* that he had followed the case, and condemned the affair as an indication of 'commercial morality generally' of the treaty ports.[32]

In much the same way, the British court ruled on a number contract disputes between Westerners by evoking the 'custom' of the treaty ports. In the case of Ross vs. Burke in 1865, the plaintiff stated that he brought the civil case to court as a test: he wished to force the court to rule in order to set a precedent in trade procedure.[33] The court and merchant community were thus caught in circular logic: in order for the business custom to become customary, it had to be recognized by the court. For the court to recognize a business custom, it had to be accepted by the merchant community, thus obviating the immediate need for the court's ruling. One judicial official wrote of the confusion that arose:

> Another matter on which I should wish to touch has reference to what is called the 'Custom of the Port' or the 'Custom of the Trade'. More than once, in the course of the cases that I have been called on to decide, my attention has been called to these so-styled customs. I have never been able exactly to understand what is really meant by these terms, but witnesses have been called and I have been favoured with their views on the subject. I hardly have to say that they have generally been contradictory.[34]

In short, throughout the period there was no real consensus, even between the Western merchants, on how to conduct business in Japan.

As early as 1861, an article in *The Nagasaki Shipping List and Advertiser* warned that Western merchants should not rely on their diplomatic representatives as an 'agent for the recovery of bad debts' and argued that it was better to forgive some debts and contracts for the sake of 'sound trade'. Although the article complained that Japanese officials never punished the 'fraud' of Japanese merchants, they also warned that the Western merchant must be prepared for, and accept, these losses as a consequence of trade in Japan. Contracts, they argued, were not sufficient forms of protection. The solution suggested by the editors of the paper was that 'some evidence of stability' be given by Japanese merchants. Western merchants would then keep a list of trustworthy partners, and information on dishonest traders would be disseminated by a 'system of "posting" to expose the names of the dishonest as a caution to all'.[35]

In reality, the courts were used as means of collecting bad debts from both Japanese and Western defaulters. A system of sharing information on bad risks as envisioned by the editors of *The Nagasaki Shipping List and Advertiser*, never came to light. The high turn-over rate of both Japanese and Western merchants in the treaty ports, especially during the late 1860s and early 1870s during the economic downturn, did not make such a list feasible. Furthermore, because only a limited number of Japanese merchants were willing to trade with Westerners and because of the short supply of such desirable goods as silkworm eggs, Western merchants were willing to take the risk of trading with a possibly unreliable trade partner. For example, Itō Hachibei, discussed in Chapter VII, made one of his many fortunes by selling oil doctored with water. Yet, even with his decidedly suspect record for honesty, an establishment such as Walsh, Hall, & Co., a large American consignment house, traded with him on the order of hundreds of thousands of dollars. The consular courts and the Japanese court indeed became a forum in which to recover debt. However, as a source of institutional memory, it was not effective. For the most part, contracts were concluded and broken, and then forgotten.

This is not to say that treaty-port members were not conscious of the idea of norm building. In many of the articles in the merchant press, the idea of courts 'teaching' Western and Japanese merchants the 'correct' trade behaviour was reiterated. Western merchants were also aware of the effects of reputation. In the case of Cook vs. Frey, H. J. Frey bought space in *The Japan Herald* to advertise his grievances over the court proceedings in the British consular court. He claimed that he had been treated unfairly. 'Letters to the Editor' were a popular forum for Western complaints. Letters poured into the merchant press expressing opinions ranging from the lack of drainage to observations on Japanese plant life. The minutiae of these small communities were faithfully recorded – no club, party, or game could take place without it being recorded in the press. In the end however, the merchants did not form a unified community which could enforce contractual compliance. The municipal council in most ports was without teeth, and the Chamber of Commerce was mainly a social club. The municipal council of Yokohama was in name a government organization; the residents banded together to improve the welfare of the treaty port. But they functioned mainly as a civic club of sorts, as they were not accountable to any one legal system. At the same time, they were accountable to all because the members were of different nationalities. The councils dealt with such issues as drains, lighting, and fire protection, and collected money for civic improvements. The group consisted mostly of merchants. In Yokohama, the group continually suffered from poor funding. In the end, the merchants and their civic organizations turned to the Japanese to bail them out of their civic duties and to the consular courts to establish their business norms.

In 1866, there was one attempt by the Yokohama Municipal Council to establish its authority in the ports; it used the courts as a means of enforcing norms of behaviour. The Municipal Council pursued civil cases in the American and British courts in an effort to collect liquor licence fees. It was not unusual for branches of the Japanese and Western governments to sue over civil issues in the consular courts for breach of contract; usually the non-payment of ground rent. In the 1866 cases, the Municipal Council sued a group of American and British residents who owned public houses and did not pay licence fees to the Municipal Council. By 1865, judging from the newspaper and magazine articles and the number of cases concerning drunkenness of sailors, the consumption of alcohol had strained the social fabric of the settler community. The Municipal Council sued the public houses as a way to control behaviour that was detrimental to the treaty port residents, as well as collecting needed funds. The courts were used to disseminate information and damage the reputation of the owners of the public houses. In the case filed with the British court, one of the public house owners went to the trouble of hiring two Western lawyers to defend himself against the $100 contested in the trial. In both the American and British cases, the lawyers were not a good investment; both groups lost against the Municipal Council.[36] In the end, it was the court, not the council which admonished the public house keepers to 'keep respectable houses'.[37]

THE UNIVERSAL DISPUTE

In the case of small petty disputes for minor amounts, Japanese cases against Westerners were similar to cases Westerners pursued against their Western peers. Looking only at the complaints lodged by Japanese against Westerners and vice versa, it would be tempting to assume that the litigiousness of the merchants was a result of the misunderstanding that occurred when dealing with the foreign merchants. However, if we examine the cases that Westerners pursued against other Westerners, it is evident that they sued one another over much the same issues. For example, both groups had plaintiffs pursuing claims for unpaid labour, debts arising from unpaid refreshments, and payments due for the for shipments of goods. Both Japanese and Western merchants sued over debts that arose out of unclear business procedures. Occasionally, the cases pursued by Westerners against other Westerners and mixed cases were remarkably similar. For example, both groups had disputes over claims of as little as a few dollars. In addition, both groups had disputes about the accepted use of promissory notes and other treaty port financial instruments. The 1862 case of Cook vs. Frey,[38] which centred on the dissolution of the business partnership, was similar to the problems addressed in the case of Itō Hachibei vs. Walsh, Hall, & Co.[39] Another 1862 case, S. J. Gower vs. R. Schoyer,[40] had a resemblance to the mixed 1866 case of Aburaza Ihei and Isuruya Kanezo vs. Glover & Co. Although the Western 1862 case was nominally a trespass case, both dealt with the problems of trade procedure and payment. In Gower vs. Schoyer, the issue was over who had rights over a cargo boat. Property rights were at issue. In the case against Glover, the problems stemmed from unclear trade procedure and property rights. Hansard vs. Da Souza,[41] in a parallel vein, was dispute over employment. A number of mixed cases, such as Kimoto Simpei vs. R. F. Livingstone[42] were over employment issues and wages.

Some issues pursued among Westerners did not immediately have analogous cases in the body of mixed trials. The shipping industry is such an example. Until 1870, disputes surrounding the shipping trade were exclusively against Western defendants, because the Japanese did not have shipping companies that could compete with Western shipping. Some cases, such as E. M. Van Reed vs. Masters and Owners of the British Schooner *Bezaleel* and Knight & Co. vs. W. M. Robinet,[43] were brought forth by Western plaintiffs. In other cases such as Yennomoto Rokubei vs. Pacific Mail Steam Ship Co.[44] and Suzuke vs. Pacific Mail Steam Ship Co.,[45] Japanese plaintiffs sued a Western defendant for damages. The fact that shipping cases of the 1860s were dominated by Western defendants was not surprising because shipping, especially in areas outside Japan, was dominated by Western ships and Western shipping companies. However, as the historical reality changed, so too did the body of cases. By the mid 1870s, the Japanese shipping companies had gained a foothold in the shipping market. 1875 and 1876 saw a number of cases against Japanese shipping companies such as National Mail Steam Ship Company[46] of Japan and Mitsu Bishi (*sic*) Steam Ship Company.[47]

THE AVENUES OF LEGAL REDRESS

WANTED – A BARRISTER
If any young member of the English Bar, educated at Oxford or
Cambridge – any where [sic], indeed, but at the London University
– a gentleman, of pleasant manners, agreeable address and a very
moderate knowledge of Law, is pining in briefless indolence in
England, we venture to recommend him to give up his chambers,
renounce his hopes of the Great Seal and the custody of his Mon-
arch's conscience and take a passage ticket for Yokohama.

Japan Weekly Mail, December 10, 1870

THE CONSULAR COURTS of treaty-port Japan were based
upon the extraterritoriality stipulated in the 'unequal treaties'
signed between Japan and the West in the late 1850s. Western
powers, led by Britain and the US, patterned these agreements
after the treaties between China and Britain after the Opium and
Arrow Wars. True to the phrase 'unequal treaties', the agreements
signed between the Treaty Powers and Japan were designed so
that the citizens and subjects of Western nations received privileges that the Japanese could not have enjoyed in Britain, or for
that matter, when pursuing complaints against Westerners.

Under extraterritorialty, Treaty Power subjects were not accountable to Japanese law even outside of the enclave; any criminal or civil infraction was tried under the laws of the
individual's home country. Extraterritoriality in Japan extended
to non-diplomatic personnel; that is, a merchant, or any other

such private citizen, was not bound by the laws of Japan. For example, when a Japanese rickshaw driver accused a German, H. Hohnholzt, of assault in 1874, the case was heard in German consular court.[1] In the case of a breach of contract, one significant form of redress was the law. In the case of such a civil dispute, a merchant would lodge a complaint with the consul of the individual with whom he had a complaint. In the contract dispute between the Japanese merchants Yamatia (Yamashiya), Sagamia (Sagamiya), Yuroshia (Yuroshiya)[2] vs. E. Alpiger, the consul of the Swiss Confederation heard the case because the defendant was Swiss.[3]

Perhaps because the Treaty Powers had negotiated similar treaties of extraterritoriality, the distinctions between the actual mechanisms of the various consular courts has been overlooked. The most favoured nation clause, common to most agreements with the Treaty Powers, gave the agreements the veneer of uniformity: those countries with most favoured nation status had the same rights and privileges extended to any other country. At best, the legal system of the ports has been regarded as part of a coherent treaty port system, or at worst, as a weapon of Western imperialism. The treaty-port consular courts were similar in that they all derived from some form of Western law. In all the major Treaty-Power legal systems, the concept of contract law, as a part of civil law, was recognized. They resembled one another especially in comparison with the legal system of the late Tokugawa period.

If the consular court systems of the Treaty Powers were all founded on the right to extraterritoriality, they were not similar in practice. The Treaty Powers each had differing levels of commitment in Asia. For example, Britain had far more resources in the form in money and manpower in the region than any other Treaty Power. Subjects and their businesses in the region were part of the Empire, and in need of defence – whether through the force of arms or through the force of law. Externally, the Crimean War impelled Britain to maintain a foothold of power in Japan against Russia, which held territories in Sakhalin directly north of Hokkaido. On the other hand, the presence of the Kingdom of Sweden and Norway was nominal at best; at times, it had no diplomatic representatives in Japan.

The civil court cases of the consular courts often reflected this disparity in commitment, resources, and knowledge. Although contract law had reached its zenith in sophistication and influence in the nineteenth century,[4] Western law in treaty port Japan did not attain the same level of sophistication; the professionalism of court officials and lawyers was inconsistent from one country to another. For example, the legal training of a British consul differed greatly from that of an American merchant consul. In early mixed cases adjudicated by Japanese courts, Western legal theory and jurisprudence were gradually introduced. The combined ignorance of Westerners of Japanese law and vice versa, further complicated matters. Because of the multiplicity of consular courts all with slightly differing rules, the legal systems of the treaty ports, and the expected outcomes, were not always transparent to the merchants.

Alternate extra-legal avenues of redress existed; these will be covered in further chapters. At the very least, judging from the ink used up and the passions expressed in the treaty-port press, the legal system was an important form of redress to the Western merchants. This chapter seeks to investigate and describe the legal mechanisms for contractual redress available to Western and Japanese merchants in treaty-port Japan. It also seeks to establish that the legal systems in place under the treaty-port system were inconsistent and ambiguous as a result of the low level of professionalism and resources.

WESTERN MERCHANTS AND THEIR RELATIONSHIP TO WESTERN LAW

Merchants in the treaty ports were decidedly litigious; in the period 1859-99, the British courts alone heard nearly three thousand cases.[5] This figure included both criminal and civil cases, and Western merchants suing one another far out numbered 'mixed cases'; mixed civil and criminal cases constituted about 13% of the total cases.[6]

Most Western merchants adhered to the notion that some sort of official court system was needed to adjudicate commercial disputes: as a writer for *The Japan Weekly Mail* commented: 'Men should look to the law as a friendly protector, not as an ogre, who, under the pretence of defending them, devours them instead.'[7] No records exist of merchants questioning the need for an official judiciary. In fact, Western merchants not only regarded law a necessity in conducting business, it was also seen as an appropriate venue for resolving conflicts between all merchants, Western or Japanese. The perceived lack of civil law in Japan was seen by Westerners as a deficiency and the sign of a backward society.[8]

Attitudes towards extraterritorialty, which formed the basis for the Western court system, were mixed. Some scholars have argued that the merchants clung on to the privileges which defined the treaty port system even at the expense of commercial gain.[9] While this attitude might have been true in practice, some Western residents believed, at least in theory, that extraterritoriality was a necessary evil in Japan's development: 'We cannot too often repeat that the Western World looks with no favour upon extra-territorial (*sic*) rights, regarding them only as conditions of and pupillage incidental to such admission the removal of which, as early as circumstances permit, is not only agreeable to, but demanded by, justice.'[10]

Western merchants, in general, took seriously the duties attached to the rule of Western law. In Western legal practice, the knowledge of the law was, and remains, the responsibility of the individual. The treaty port press, for example, was preoccupied with legal issues. Almost every major publication, except for *The Japan Punch*, printed a regular law and police column. The press reported arrests for assaults and theft, official announcements, consular court activities, and any Japanese legal case in which a Westerner was a plaintiff. Although the amount varied from publication to publication, the notes on the court proceedings were detailed – even for a straightforward drunken assault. Depending of the number of cases, the law report consisted of up to a third of the publication. In addition, many of the papers contained articles, which ranged from the sublime to the ridiculous, on the legal systems and their failings.

The Western merchant press also disseminated information on the legalities of contract in this uncertain trading and legal environment. The Western merchant's anxieties about trading in an environment with unpredictable legal redress manifested itself from the very inception of the ports. The treaty-port press, such as *The Japan Weekly Mail* and *The Japan Times*, published articles, clippings, and letters addressing the specific problem of contractual disputes that arose from trading with the Japanese. For example, a sample fill-in-the-blank-type invoice used in Hawaii was reprinted in *The Japan Herald*.[11] In 1866, the British consul published in the same newspaper a circular suggesting ways to avoid contractual disputes when hiring builders.[12] A few years later, *The Japan Weekly Mail* published a fill-in-the-blank contract written by the Japanese government. In order to alleviate the increasing problems of breach and misunderstanding, this contract was written specifically for the Japanese treaty port market, and published in English, transliterated Japanese, and Japanese in the subsequent issues of the weekly newspaper.[13] Ironically, the majority of the contractual disputes were between Westerners. Such didactic literature was designed to avoid misunderstandings with the Japanese, and thus to avoid the loss of time and money of going to court.

Western merchants had a 'love-hate' relationship with their court systems. Whilst they actively utilized the court to settle disputes, they were not always satisfied with the results. Western merchants had conceptions of their legal 'rights', which were sometimes neither accurate nor based upon actual law. Matters were not helped when the courts were stretched thin while processing the constant flow of petty criminal cases, usually committed by drunk Western sailors on shore leave.[14]

For example, in the 1875 criminal case of R. vs. Archibald King, the tensions between the treaty port residents and consular courts came to head. In this case, King was accused of raping a thirteen year old girl in a drinking establishment. The British Court found King guilty of rape, and sentenced him to six months in prison. The verdict was contrary to the Western residents' expectations, and they protested that justice had not been served. The assessors of the case, who acted in a capacity loosely similar to jurors, had dissented from the official verdict, stating that they were not satisfied that the evidence had shown that King had committed the crime.[15]

In the aftermath of this case, residents protested the lack of proper legal procedure and protection of their rights. Some merely expressed their confidence in King's innocence due to lack of evidence. Other objections centred on the perception that the court had erred by having assessors, rather than jurors, examine the proceedings. Assessors did not affect the verdict of a trial, although their dissent opened the possibility for an appeal. Had the trial been heard in Britain, the case would have had jurors, but since the case was tried in Japan, assessors were used as per the Order in Council of China and Japan which established the English legal system in the East. The residents complained vociferously in print and in letters to authorities.[16] In their assertions, the problem of this criminal trial stemmed partly from King's purported innocence and partly from the larger issue of a legal right to a jury trial.

Treaty-port residents assumed they knew their rights and duties under the law, whereas they often did not. The fiercely-held belief that trial by jury was the right of a Westerner was, in fact, not the case in the treaty ports. This degree of ignorance may have been the rule rather than the exception. In Robert Ellickson's research on conflict resolution and the perceptions of law, he found that the legal expertise of the layman was at best superficial, and at worst, wrong. In a study of the cattle ranching in Shasta county, he found that 'not even the most savvy members of the Shasta County Cattlemen's Association' knew about the applicable boundary fence laws in ranching.[17] Ellickson found a similar type of legal ignorance among university professors. Most did not know the particulars of copyright laws pertaining to the photocopying of class materials.[18] One other point is well illustrated by the reaction to the King case: Western residents displayed a keen interest on law and its proceedings. They also expressed a sense that the rule of law belonged to each and every treaty port 'citizen'.

JAPANESE MERCHANTS AND THEIR RELATIONSHIP TO JAPANESE LAW

Japanese law, and the subsequent attitudes towards civil law, differed from that of the Western consular courts. Much could be written on the subject. Under the Tokugawa legal system, an individual was not responsible for knowledge of the law.[19] Broadly speaking, justice was 'handed down' by an official to an individual, rather than being any person's 'right'. Unlike the Western feudal tradition arising from the English Magna Carta of 1215, an 'inferior' had no 'rights' in front of his 'superior'.[20] Civil law, or the lack thereof, in Tokugawa Japan differed from the Western common and constitutional law tradition. At the risk of over-stating the case, the Tokugawa Bakufu regarded criminal and ci-vil law as one seamless legal entity. The Japanese government did not attempt to expand its authority to popular transactions or private disputes. A justicible contract is a Western legalism de-pendent on a system of private law. Because the Bakufu was more concerned with law upholding the strength of the state, it perceived criminal acts and other such social ills as having the potential to destabilize the regime; thus the preoccupation with the criminality of its subjects. Civil law, in the Western legal sense, did not exist in Japan; a Japanese court hearing a civil dis-pute centred on the criminal implications of the dispute, rather than the civil ones.[21] Minor criminal offences, for example, were arbitrated in the same manner as civil disputes.[22] Although the Tokugawa system of law has been characterized as a mainly crim-inal legal system,[23] perhaps this legal system would be more ap-propriately classified as a system of 'public law'.

The legal system of the late Tokugawa period fostered concil-iation in civil disputes. For a case to reach a shogunal court, both parties were first required to submit to the arbitration of the village headman. In the case of merchants, most contractual disputes were handled among themselves, or by guild officials. Only when the headman acknowledged that these negotiations had failed was the issue allowed to proceed to a higher court.[24] At the higher court levels, conciliation and arbitration contin-ued to be both encouraged and mandated by court officials.[25]

JAPANESE AND THEIR RELATIONSHIP WITH WESTERN LAW COURTS

In the treaty ports, Western legal concepts of adversarial civil law were superimposed on this construct of conciliation. Japanese officials and the founders of the Meiji government abhorred the treaty courts as unfair and an instrument of Western imperial-ism. The courts, they argued, were biased against the Japanese.[26] As Baba Tatsui, a Meiji pamphleteer charged, the Western courts existed 'to protect their countrymen rather than prosecute or convict them'.[27] Similarly, Fukuzawa Yukichi, a Meiji statesman and educator, stated in *An Outline of a Theory of Civilization*:

Even when there are grounds for litigation over some business dealing, to press charges one must go to the five ports, where one's case will be decided by their judges. Since under these circumstances it is impossible to obtain justice, people say to one another that, rather than press charges, it is better to swallow one's anger and be submissive. They act like a young bride before her old mother-in-law. [28]

Fukuzawa practically exhorts Japanese to use the courts as a weapon against the West; to 'beat them at their own game', as it were. In the eyes of these Japanese, not only were the Western courts fundamentally alien to Japan's legal system, extraterritoriality and the courts were also used to weaken the Japanese spirit.

Yet, is this assessment of the consular courts fair? Chang's research on the justice of mixed court verdicts demonstrated that the majority of cases adjudicated by Western officials were fair within the parameters of Western law.[29] Of course, justice within 'the parameters' of Western law was sometimes different from justice perceived by the Japanese. The other problem with the idea of the courts as an instrument of the Treaty Power is that it assumed that all the courts of the Treaty Powers were similar and uniform. It needs to be remembered that these impressions of law were those of Meiji officials and statesmen, not merchants. Japanese merchant impressions of the consular courts, especially as users, may have differed significantly from the point of view of officials.

Few Japanese merchant impressions of the court system remain. But if we assume that the consular system was biased and unjust, why did Japanese merchants use the court systems at all? Japanese merchants certainly sued Westerners and such litigation was against the legal traditions of conciliation that had been fostered by the Tokugawa state. What did they have to gain from the system? As Chang's research showed, Japanese merchants sometimes won their cases and found redress in the system.

THE BRITISH CONSULAR COURT SYSTEM

The British Consular Court was by far the most complex and formalized as it was part of the British treaty port system which had been extended from China. Under the British system, consular staff were part of the diplomatic system which was under the authority of the Foreign Office. Consuls were professionals who were prohibited from trading. In a Foreign Office letter of appointment to a consul, the latter is explicitly admonished, 'You will further understand that you are strictly prohibited from trading either on your own account or as a request for any other party. . .'[30] Most candidates were vetted by the Foreign Office or their representatives, and were required to have some knowledge of British and international law. Most positions were filled in Britain; candidates sometimes wrote lengthy letters directly to Lord Malmesbury, the Foreign Secretary.[31] They were encouraged to pass the bar examination, and diplomatic staff in Japan were sent to the British courts in China to undergo further legal training. Occasionally able men already in the East, such as businessmen, were selected to fill posts. Such appointments had to be approved by the Foreign Office.

Most consuls were well educated and paid. Ernest Satow's salary as a student interpreter, one of the more junior positions in the British Legation, was £400 per annum.[32] Consuls in Japan were in the range of £750-£1,200. Alcock as Consul General, later Minister, made between £1800-2000 per annum.[33] By 1879, Harry Parkes, in the same position, had a salary of £4000.[34] The salary allowed for the individual to enjoy a comfortable standard of living without having to seek supplementary occupations. Of course, the diplomat's work for the consular court was one of many duties.

In the early period of the treaty ports, British cases were adjudicated by the consuls and appeals were heard by the British Minister who was also the Consul General. The British, like most Westerners, found Japanese law to be severe and inappropriate for international trade.[35] Under the original Treaty of 1858, signed between Britain and Japan, extraterritoriality was intended to cover criminal, not civil disputes. Civil disputes between Japanese and the British were to be arranged by 'competent officials of the two countries'. No specific provision was made for cases between Britons and members of other Western nations nor for disputes between British subjects. Maritime or admiralty cases, such as salvage rights, were not under the adjudication of the consular court; an inconvenience in a port enclave. The issue became particularly ambiguous when seamen committed offences on land. In addition, the British Minister in Japan was empowered to make additional regulations to govern British citizens in Japan.

In practice, the court did not strictly follow the treaty guidelines. Consular court cases between Westerners were a kind of a diplomatic and judicial afterthought: in fact, the majority of the courts' resources were expended on disputes among Westerners. In the first five years of the treaty ports, assaults and offences committed by British subjects on Japanese were tried in the consular courts. In these cases, the state, the Crown acted as the plaintiff to prosecute these crimes. Japanese plaintiffs were rare in such criminal offences. Japanese subjects pursued civil disputes throughout the treaty port period. Also, the same consular court officials conducted admiralty hearings on salvage and on the conduct of sailors and men.

The Order in Council of 1865 formed the basis of the consular courts and established their basic structure. After 1865, disputes were resolved in a circuit court, ostensibly adjudicated by the same consular officials. Appeals were heard under the Supreme Court of Shanghai, bypassing the British Minister in Japan. Further appeals were heard by the Privy Council in London.[36]

Although the court procedures were organized and transparent, the British consular court system did have its deficiencies. By 1869, the load on the courts had doubled from 1864 in Yokohama alone. In 1869, the court processed 106 civil and 277 criminal cases, with no increase in staff.[37] Consuls were strained for time, money, and resources, and relayed that information in their dispatches home. Money for the support of the courts and improvement of the jail was not readily granted by the Foreign Office. In addition, the system was framed such that the responsibility of adjudicating consular courts would fall to the inexperienced young diplomatic staff in the absence of the experienced consul. In 1870, E. Satow, a young British official at the time, wrote:

> Fancy me an acting Vice Consul. Such is the truth. It is quite absurd. I did not know how to register a birth till the constable showed me. Now I live in daily terror lest a case should be brought in my court and I am compelled to sit in judgement.

Not having the faintest idea of how to preside. To say nothing of complete ignorance of the law.[38]

Because many of the British officials in Japan were under thirty, this situation occurred often.

By 1870, activity in the courts reached such levels that the situation demanded a full time judge, and not just the attention of the consuls. N. J. Hannen, the Assistant Judge at Shanghai, was appointed to preside in Japan. However, due to ambiguity in his orders, it was unclear whether his court was a branch of the court of Shanghai, or whether his appointment initiated a new court of Japan. If the Japan court was a branch of Shanghai's, any appeal of a verdict in Japan had to be heard in London by the Privy Council. Such an appeal would take the great time and expense of travelling to London and engaging a London litigator. Although Hannen had been correct to assume that his court was a branch of the Shanghai system, Sir Edmund Hornby, the Chief Judge at Shanghai, resolved the situation by creating a separate court of Japan. Consuls became assistant judges to Hannen, the appointed judicial officer. Appeals were heard in Shanghai, then finally in London. This *ad hoc* resolution was formalized eight years later, under the Order in Council of 1878.[39]

In the British consular court, the barriers to bringing a suit to trial were different for Japanese. Under the British system, a Western plaintiff deposited money and paid fees for initiating a case. If the plaintiff lost the case, the court retained the deposit and billed him any further costs. The local custom in the consular courts of Japan was to forgo the filing fees for Japanese plaintiffs, and waive the deposit.[40] Judge Hannen, when he arrived in Japan, did not recognize the custom, and insisted the Japanese pay fees. The Japanese government protested and retaliated by threatening to force Westerners to pay fees in Japanese courts. Since the British community did pursue cases in the Japanese courts, the fees for Japanese courts would have been a financial drain on the Western merchants. The problem was resolved when the Foreign Office ordered that the fees be waived.[41]

British consular court judges in Japan had a fair degree of latitude in their decisions. They were allowed to adjudicate on civil cases worth less that $1,500 dollars in value, and in criminal cases, they were allowed to pass verdicts on cases involving less than two months imprisonment, and a fine of less than $200. The court had the authority to judge all other cases provided that two to four assessors assisted in the case, and to inflict a sentence of no more than one year and a fine of up to $1000. Assessors were men of 'good repute' who attended proceedings, but unlike a jury, had no effect on its outcome. The assessor could concur with or reject the verdict, but the judge's verdict stood in either case. However, the dissent of an assessor paved the way for an appeal hearing. Unanimous juries of up to five men, instead of the usual twelve in Britain, were also required for all juried appeal cases. Any cases beyond these given parameters were heard at the court in Shanghai.[42]

Official fees in British courts were not exorbitant but were not inconsequential. In 1874, fees for civil complaints ranged from half a dollar to 50 Mexican dollars. Fees for filing a civil suit ranged from 1 dollar to one per cent of the amount contested. However, the fees quickly accumulated. For example, an official translation of a document started at 10 dollars.[43] Every summons, motion, application, or demand, taken out, made, or filed, cost one dollar.[44] Any time a communication was made with Japanese officials, the cost ranged from five to fifty dollars, depending on the circumstances.[45]

THE AMERICAN CONSULAR COURT SYSTEM

The American justice system in the treaty port was less formally structured when compared with the British model. Furthermore, the American consular corps were ill supported and poorly paid. Joseph Heco, a bilingual Japanese American, initially worked for the United States consulate out of possibly patriotic and personal motivation. However, even Heco eventually left the consular service in order to start his own firm. He wrote in his memoirs that he left the service because of the low salary and the lack of job security.[46] Compared to the British system, the duties of consuls and the diplomats were ill defined, and unclear. In general, consuls heard cases, but in 1859, when the treaty ports first opened, appeals were heard in California and the American Minister, the consul general, was bypassed. By 1860, the consul and Minister heard cases with the Minister having appellate jurisdiction, and the federal circuit court of California was the appellate court above the minister. The US Minister had some authority to make additional regulations for the American residents in Japan. Unlike the powers of the British Minister, any actions taken by the US envoy were to be reported to Congress.[47]

By the 1860s, law in the US was largely in the hands of the US Minister rather than a professional judge. US Consuls adjudicated cases in which fines did not exceed $100 or 60 days imprisonment. If the fine exceeded $100 or if the punishment was more than 60 days, the defendant could appeal his case with the US Minister. If the Consul saw fit, he could have one to four members of the public assess the case. The law required assessors for any civil case exceeding $500. Unlike British assessors, if one US assessor dissented from the Consul's judgment, the matter was automatically referred to the US minister. Both Ministers and Consuls tried felonious and capital cases, as well as major civil disputes. However, if a Consul adjudicated any of the above cases, the Minister and assessors all had to concur with the verdict for the result to be legal.[48]

One peculiar characteristic of the US system was the existence of the merchant-consul. Although the US had some paid consuls, merchant consuls were hired for posts mainly outside of Yokohama in Japan. Unlike the British, American Consuls were not professionals selected by the State Department. Instead, local American merchants were appointed by the minister to carry out consular duties. This arrangement posed a host of problems: most merchants had little training in international law, the salary was low, the merchant-consuls' interests were divided between business and the court, and the merchant could conceivably be part of the case he was adjudicating.

An article of *The Japan Weekly Mail* alluded to a specific incident of merchant-consul misconduct, but unfortunately for the historical record, 'tenderly withheld names or dates'.[49] The authors may have been alluding to the autumn 1865 case in which an American, probably Gustave Glackmeyer, was suspected by his British employer, Alexander McKechnie, of pilfering, and was arrested and placed illegally in a British jail. Although it is unclear, the American was probably placed in the British jail because it had superior accommodations. The

American brought a suit of false imprisonment against his employer in a British court.[50] The only lawyer available in port was the American Consul. The American engaged the Consul and the case went to court. Tempers frayed and resulted in the American inflicting a 'severe cow-hiding' on a British news editor, probably Charles Rickerby, who had published some remarks unfavourable to the American. The British editor brought an assault and battery case in the American court. The judge of the assault case was formally the lawyer of the defendant in the false imprisonment case in the British court. Due to the perceived conflict of interest, the British community refused to cooperate with the American court. Further exacerbating relations between the British and the Americans, the US court awarded 6 1/4 cents damages to editor for his pains.[51]

The lack of funds for the upkeep of the US court caused problems beyond conflicts of interest. Yokohama, the highest court in Japan, had no law library. For US diplomats with little or no law training to begin with, the lack of a law library further exacerbated the situation. For example, in the 1860s, the final appellate power in Japan was Minister Townsend Harris who came from a mercantile, not a legal, background. The enforcement of criminal sentences posed problem as the US did not have a jail, and had borrowed the facilities of the British. In the early years of the port, the American jail was seen fit only for drunk seamen. Women, gentlemen, and officers were usually accommodated in the British jail.

The poor pay of the consuls did not increase the professionalism of the corps, and led directly to corruption. In the first few years of the treaty port, diplomatic staff were allowed to exchange as much money as they desired at the Customs House while their merchant colleagues were allowed to exchange only limited quantities of dollars. Merchant-consuls, especially poorly paid American ones, used their position to exchange currency for their business purposes. In the US case, the pay was so low that such activity was necessary. Merchant consuls were paid at best about $1000 per annum, but the cost of 'respectable living' was about three to four thousand dollars a year.[52] Some officials, especially in the early 1860s, took advantage of the difference in Japan's gold-silver exchange with the rest of the world. They bought gold in Japan where it was cheap and then shipped their treasure to China where they sold it for silver. The silver was shipped it back to Japan to buy more gold, making profits in the range of 100-300%.

The exchange ceiling for non-officials was $3000 to $5000 monthly ($36,000 to $60,000 a year), but exchange requests often took more than a month to process. And since the Japanese would not process more than one request at a time, the actual ceiling was far lower. Consequently, the amount of money that a merchant could exchange realistically in a year was a sum far below given Bakufu limits. In the merchants' view, many times that amount was necessary for their overseas ventures to be profitable. In order to increase their currency holdings, the merchants resorted to subterfuge such as requesting huge sums of money, hoping to get some fraction, or by making up names. They requested outrageous amounts, once as high as $1,200,666,777,888,999,222,321. Yokohama gained new citizens under names such as 'Mr. Smell-bad', 'Mr. No-nose', and 'Mr. Doodledoo'.[53] The diplomats rebuked the merchants and the practice stopped.

One merchant, Francis Hall of Walsh Hall and Co., took up his pen and began to publish articles against what he perceived as official abuses by the Western diplomatic corps. Hall and another resident, Dr. Duane B. Simmons, charged that diplomats and other officials were using their position for profit in the US treaty port press. Prussian Consul Von Brandt's compilation of Custom House documents noted the full currency returns for various Western governments and individuals. Hall's conclusion: 'The documents are all authentic from the Custom House and show an amount of official rapacity that is lamentable to behold.'[54] Diplomats were profiting, not merchants, Hall and Simmons maintained. By their calculations, the English fleet received exchange of $180,000 per month, the American Minister Gen. Pruyn, $70,000 per year, French Minister de Bellecourt exchanged $5000 on the eve of his departure. The total amount exchanged by officials, the fleet, and the military in one year amounted to $4,000,000.[55] The American Minister seemed to Hall to have the 'sharpest dodge':[56] instead of allowing the Japanese to take a 4% discount on his monthly sum of $3,000, he exchanged the full amount, and he then paid $120 in Mexican silver. He thus secured himself an additional $120 worth of *Japanese* currency. In 1863, the Minister arranged for a one-time special exchange of $20,000.[57] 'Sharp work for a high official,' Hall noted. Hall estimated that by taking advantage of exchange privileges, the US Minister made $25,000 in one year and the US Consul in Kanagawa made $8,000 to $10,000.[58]

Hall argued that official exchange privileges were no better than bribes paid by the Japanese to foreign diplomats.[59] He wrote:

> As I have before had occasion to say, this exchange and mono-poly is a favour allowed foreign officials by the Japanese, by which their salaries and places are doubled, trebled or quad-rupled in value – a corrupt state of affairs which if understood in all its influences for evil by the Western Powers would be once and forever forbidden by officials they send hither.[60]

Hall and others maintained that official position should not be used for profit, especially since merchants were sustaining losses in the same area. Another merchant, the Japanese-American Jo-seph Heco wrote that he would have had to wait two months to exchange $10,000 that he needed immediately in 1860; he ob-tained only $5,000, causing him to lose his profit.[61] Hall lamen-ted, 'What a picture [the scandal] presents of our boasted civilization and honour.'[62]

The diplomatic corps, on the other hand, did not think these exchanges were 'bribery', but viewed them simply as opportu-nities. Heco described an incident in which Minister Harris en-couraged Heco, as an official US interpreter, to ask the Japanese for special official exchange privileges. Heco was clearly uncom-fortable about the arrangement: only with the additional en-couragement of the Minister and the Yokohama Consul, did Heco accept a one-time exchange of $500. Heco stated that he did not use any further privileges during his term of office.[63]

The British officials in the treaty ports also had exchange pri-vileges. Harry Parkes, the second British Minister, received let-ters of complaint from merchants alleging that other British merchants were taking positions as merchant-consuls for other European nations in order to use diplomatic privileges for personal gain and privilege.[64] Shortly after Hall's articles, privileged exchanges by diplomats and military officials stopped.[65]

As in China, merchants in Japan had conflicts with diplomatic personnel. The problem was one of expectations; merchants expected diplomats to protect their trade interests, and the diplomats expected merchants to follow official policy. The division was not as clear among Americans as among the British whose diplomats were forbidden to trade. Given the class prejudices of the diplomats towards merchants, serious conflicts arose between the two groups. The most intense personality conflicts ensued between American merchants and diplomatic staff. Hall and Heco both negatively described the US Consul E. M. Dorr. Heco reported that Dorr threatened to beat him over a perceived slight, and Hall called him 'a man devoid of honour, honesty, or gratitude, save as they may serve some selfish end he desired to promote'.[66] Hall too had harsh words for Harris, of whom he wrote that Harris had acted with cowardice when H. Heusken was murdered by *ronin*.[67] This situation was somewhat ironic as most American diplomats and consuls came from mercantile backgrounds; John Greer Walsh, one of the founders of the Walsh Hall and Co., was the consul in Nagasaki. These pronouncements were not made simply out of jealousy over special privilege; both Hall and Heco worked in some official capacity for the US diplomatic services.

Although the enclosed area of the treaty ports probably only served to exacerbate tensions and personality conflicts between the American officials and American merchants, this friction was not without consequences. These very officials who were reviled and accused of cowardice, corruption, greed, and rapacity were those who maintained their legal system. Although not all American diplomats and merchant consuls were corrupt, the structure of the American system in Japan allowed for conflicts of interest. The combination of the two led to a legal system in which it is unlikely that the merchants had much confidence.

OTHER TREATY POWERS

Other Treaty Powers[68] in Japan had even less legal infrastructure than the US and had few or no consular staff. Those countries that did not have consular staff relied upon the British or US court system or employed merchant-consuls. If an individual's country had no diplomatic representation in port, he or she could apply to be under British or American protection. Under these circumstances, all trials pertaining to this individual as a defendant would be tried under the laws of his chosen country. For example, if a Portuguese citizen elected to be protected by British authority, he would then be tried under British law in the event of a legal proceeding.

One particular quirk of researching court documents in Japan is the inconsistency in the name of the courts' venues. The three major courts were in the treaty enclaves of Yokohama (Kanagawa), Kobe (Hyogo), and Tokyo (Edo). All three cities underwent changes in name; for example Edo changed to Tokyo after the Meiji Restoration. However, in British documents well into the 1880s, officials referred to 'Yedo'. In the case of Kobe, the confusion arose from the fact that the port town of Hyogo was opened to function as a port for Osaka. Major Treaty Powers such as the US and Britain recognized Hyogo and Osaka together as one consular district. Other Treaty Powers, especially those which had merchant-consuls in Osaka, did not have diplomatic coverage. Hence, in consular documents, it is occasionally unclear whether the writer was referring to Osaka, Hyogo, Kobe, or some combination thereof.

The Kanagawa/Yokohama name debate occurred out of a Treaty Power desire to maintain pretences. Under the treaty signed with Perry, some ambiguity existed over the first treaty port, Kanagawa. The Treaty Powers understood the word to mean the village of Kanagawa, whereas the Bakufu assumed that the word referred to the Kanagawa region. The Bakufu decided that the village was not a suitable locale for the foreign population. Although the town of Kanagawa itself was a thriving port and post town, Kanagawa was on the Tōkaidō, the main road by which daimyo would travel en route to Edo. The Bakufu anticipated conflicts between the Westerners and the daimyo and established the foreign enclave in Yokohama.

In order to entice merchants and traders to settle in Yokohama, the Bakufu took advantage of the fault lines within the foreign community; namely, the tensions between the merchants and the diplomats. The Bakufu constructed a town which served the merchants' needs. For example, the shogunate built housing and commercial buildings in Yokohama. In addition, Yokohama had a deep harbour in which ships could unload their cargo directly onto the piers. Kanagawa, on the other hand, had a shallower harbour that required portage by small boats, increasing cost and, at the same time, decreasing convenience. What Yokohama lacked in formal facilities, the Bakufu provided. In a very short time they built structures that could serve as bungalows, warehouses, and shops, as well as a Customs House in a convenient location.[69]

The Bakufu had correctly assumed that if the majority of foreign traders preferred Yokohama, the treaty port would be centred there. Dr George R. Hall, a doctor and merchant, was the first member of the foreign community to defy the consuls' wishes; he moved across the bay to Yokohama on his own initiative and purchased the lot 'No. 2 Bund' which later became the site of Walsh, Hall, & Co. Soon the representative of the firm Jardine, Matheson and Company, one of the largest trading houses in China, followed, choosing No. 1 Bund, and Dent and Company acquired Nos. 4 and 5.[70] These defections by key leaders of the foreign business community paved the way for other firms to establish residences in this area. Although the Treaty Power diplomats eventually moved out of Kanagawa into Yokohama to be closer to the population they represented, they still dated official correspondence from Kanagawa 'rather than admit that they had acquiesced to any departure from the terms of the treaty'.[71] Thus, in Treaty Power documents of the 1860s, court proceedings were reported to have taken place in Kanagawa, rather than in Yokohama where they actually took place. This fiction has caused much confusion on the exact court and location of Treaty Power legal proceedings of this period.

WESTERNERS IN JAPANESE COURT

In order to end the unequal treaties, a prerequisite mandated by the Treaty Powers was that Japan had to establish a Western style legal system. The process of adopting Western law codes into the Japanese judicial system was a slow one, and the Western merchants had to make do with Japanese law when pursuing Japanese defendants. In this period, those Western merchants who wished to bring suit against Japanese merchants faced the lack of Western style civil law codes.

Bankruptcy was ill defined under Japanese law and civil disputes were resolved in a different manner than in the West. In order to assure that their citizens' rights were protected, the Treaty Powers insisted that all cases involving Westerners in Japanese court were heard following Western jurisprudence. Complaints against Japanese merchants were processed through the Japanese Customs House. If a merchant had a complaint, he first went to the Customs House where he would ask for the police. The police would then examine both the (Western) accuser and the (Japanese) accused. If the accuser was British, a consul would either be called, or the police officer, the accused, and the accuser would all go to the British Consulate to conduct the interview. However, these procedures assumed a criminal intent of fraud or theft.[72] No provisions were initially made for the problem of civil disputes between merchants, such as breach of contract or restitution.

Initially, until the early 1860s, criminal offences by Westerners against Japanese were treated as crimes against the Crown or the State. After the establishment of Japanese courts, only particularly egregious cases were tried against the State. However, civil complaints were not addressed under this system. In 1865, British Consul Marcus Flowers convinced Japanese magistrates to try Japanese court cases in the British consular court room in Yokohama. Flowers and his deputy were, in theory, to act as assessors or assistants in the proceedings. Since the Japanese magistrates were new to Western style jurisprudence, the consul had considerably more influence than the usual assessor under British law. The Japanese deemed this situation undesirable and onerous and established their own court soon after the Restoration.[73]

With the exception of British subjects, the Japanese courts did not have the authority to compel citizens of the Treaty Powers to appear as witnesses in Japanese courts. By the mid 1870s, the Japanese court was beginning to gain authority and claimed jurisdiction over all non-Treaty-Power foreigners in Japan. By 1873, some Western concepts of law had been incorporated into the

Japanese legal code. Also, work had started on a comprehensive Civil Code which would later come into law in the 1890s. By 1877, the Japanese court processed cases involving Westerners smoothly with little assistance from British or other Treaty Power officials.[74]

When the Western merchants used the Japanese court system to resolve their disputes with Japanese merchants, the lack of enforcement of the courts' decisions was a problem from the point of view of the merchant. Even if the merchant succeeded in obtaining a verdict against a Japanese merchant, procuring the settlement was not always possible: the Western merchant was unable to collect from the defaulting party. When Westerners sued other Westerners, compliance was enforced by filing another case asking for the court to compel payment. As the Japanese could easily leave the treaty port area, Western merchants regarded the responsibility of enforcement as being on the Japanese government. However, in the early period under the Bakufu, the government was unable to effectively enforce verdicts on defaulting Japanese merchants.

LAWYERS AND LITIGATORS

Besides court officials, lawyers were a part of the Western judicial system. Although minor cases were presented by the litigants themselves, major cases involving large sums of money required the legal expertise of trained lawyers.[75] In the treaty port, lawyers could practise in any Treaty-Power court: it was accepted practice that so long as a lawyer belonged to a Bar, he was allowed to practise law in any court in treaty port Japan. Among British lawyers, the distinction between solicitors and barristers was largely overlooked. Since cases were adjudicated using Western law, initially all lawyers were Westerners and defended both Japanese and Western clients. In the 1870 case of 'Moolataya Yuzo' [Murataya Yuzo] vs. Kingdon, Schwabe and Co. in Her British Majesty's Court in Kanagawa, the Japanese plaintiff's case was pursued by a Western lawyer by the name of Barnard.[76] By 1875 however, a Japanese lawyer, Tatsno Tomoitchiro [Tatsuno Tomoichiro], pursued his client's interests at the US Consular Court in the case of Chuisuke [Chusuke] and Takenoouchi [Takenouchi] Kanjiro vs. The Pacific Mail Steamship Co.[77]

The Western merchant community, even with its active litigation, did not always have a harmonious relationship with its lawyers. The editors of *The Japan Weekly Mail* published a series of articles in the autumn of 1870 that complained about the lawyers in the treaty ports. The fees of the litigators were called 'extortion' and 'unfair and illegitimate profit'.[78] The writers of the articles charged that legal fees were 'three to five to six hundred per cent over those chargeable in England or America by the ablest Counsel'.[79] These high fees, from the point of view of the writers, would result in the merchants regarding law as an adversary, not a protector; in their mind, a social evil. They appealed for qualified men from Oxford and Cambridge to come to Japan and replace their own lawyers.[80] A particularly telling example of popular attitudes among the treaty ports residents is the anti-Semitic cartoon from *The Japan Punch* which depicted lawyers as Jews seeking profit.

Sometimes the cause of these friction was based on personality conflicts. The most obstreperous attack was reserved for the aforementioned Barnard. The weekly newspaper published an essay in which he was castigated for being a 'chronic disturber of the peace'.[81] When Barnard left Japan, the press printed a gloating article celebrating his 'evaporation'.[82] Other lawyers were criticized for their eccentric behaviour. One Western lawyer in Yokohama used to arrive in court dressed as a samurai, complete with two swords.

The one conclusion that can be drawn from this analysis is, not so much about the actual 'justice' or 'fairness' of the courts, but about the perceived fairness and efficiency of the consular court system. Japanese officials, it is safe to conclude, regarded the courts as an anathema that was part of the system of unequal treaties. The Meiji government worked to rid the country of these courts by rapidly adapting and translating French legal codes for Japan. By the turn of the century, a complete Civil Code had been promulgated. Japanese merchants' perceptions of the courts, on the other hand, are largely unknown. But, they were active users of system of law that was alien to their own.

The mechanics of processing civil complaints was quite often a judicial afterthought. For example, British port civil law was most prepared for conflicts between Japanese and Western merchants, when in fact, the majority of complaints were between Western merchants. Japanese law for merchants in the enclave, perhaps less surprisingly, had little legal provision for civil complaints and only had a set procedure for criminal complaints such as theft or fraud.

Western merchants were generally uniform in their belief that a Western style system of private law was a requirement for international trade. However, each consular court, whether British, American or otherwise, had its own inconsistencies and particularistic characteristics that influenced its legal system. The British system, as we have seen above, was completely different from the other Treaty Powers in its established legal norms, expertise, and professionalism. Although British subjects may have been satisfied with the basic functions of the court, they clashed on points of law (as well as fact) as in the King case. In the case of US merchants who were discontented with the system of merchant-consuls, as well as with the personal behaviour of adjudicators. Those using the American courts perceived them as less fair and transparent than British courts.

The legal systems that were available to Japanese and Western merchants for contractual redress were not coherent entities. Although the consular courts have been criticized for their role in perpetuating imperialistic Western agendas, the reality was that the judicial system in place at this time could not be taken as a monolithic entity. The methods and authority granted to each court also differed; whereas British courts were part of the system in China, the US courts, despite having consuls in China, were far more fragmented. The Japanese legal structure, at this early juncture, was still in a transitional state. It had neither the authority nor the maturity to handle the merchants' disputes. Redress in these systems was not always adequately reached due to problems in the enforcement of the verdicts. Treaty-port law, far from being comprehensive, was but one tool of contractual redress.

6

IN PURSUIT OF A BARGAIN
Information, Good Faith and Contracts

I allude to the utter want of good faith evinced [by] the greater part of the native traders. . .There is no REDRESS for a foreign merchant for wrongs done to him by a Japanese trader, except such as he obtains for himself by force.

> 'A BRITISH MERCHANT'
> in a letter to *The Japan Times*, 8 September 1865

[British] Merchants of Japan, if these be your practices – 'what will they say in England?'

> 'ONE OF THE PUBLIC'
> in a letter to *The Japan Times Overland Mail*,
> 12 February 1869

WITHIN THE TREATY PORTS, agreements failed for all the usual diverse reasons. The goods did not meet expectations, shipments were late, the price of goods fluctuated, hidden costs destroyed narrow profit margins, and simple greed drove merchants to default to better opportunities. Yet among the disagreements between the merchants, certain patterns arose, suggesting a structure and shape to Japanese-Western merchant interactions. Many of the problems experienced by merchants were the result of the lack of adequate information – not only was information costly, it was not always accurate or available. For example, translators were not always available or particularly skilled. In one case, the original contract was written in German, a language which few, if any, Japanese merchants spoke at

115

the time. This lack of information made tailoring contracts difficult, yet at the same time, because the merchants were unfamiliar with one another and at times, worked in an environment of mutual distrust, the situation demanded written contracts. Thus, the agreements they made were rigid, and at the same time, vague. This uncertainty within the contract itself left room for interpretation by each party, but both parties did not necessarily agree on these unwritten rights and duties perceived as inherent in the contract.

Both the Japanese and Western merchant had cause to complain of the other's venality and dishonesty. This chapter proposes to examine the problems that occurred when merchants attempted to trade using open ended contracts. A selection of cases will be used to illustrate the problems that arose from trading in this environment. These cases were typical of the period, and were chosen on the basis of the amount of detail, the issues pursued in the claim, and for their completeness. Because of missing issues in newspaper runs, the details and conclusions of some cases were lost. All cases described below derive from the complete records of a court hearing. Open-ended contracts for goods will be examined in detail this chapter. Contracts for labour and services will be discussed in a separate section at the end of this chapter because such services did not use written contracts. The role of good faith – that is, whether or not it mattered if a contract was breached intentionally for personal gain – will be addressed. In addition, the cases discussed in this chapter will be used to investigate the treatment of 'bargain money', or down payments, and how this money was used to secure compliance with a contract.

CONTRACTUAL FAILURE: THE ACCUSATION OF FRAUD

Contractual disputes were a heated topic among merchants in the treaty ports because the civil complaint of contractual breach was tied intimately to the criminal charge of fraud. Although, in theory, all the Western courts recognized the separation between civil and criminal disputes, the merchants often did not. Disputes between Western and Japanese merchants immediately ensued from the inception of the treaty ports and continued through the period. Contractual breach was far from uncommon. Two years after the opening of Yokohama (1861), British merchants had lodged $30,000 worth of claims against Japanese merchants.[1] Roughly 0.6% of the total dollar value was contested; however, this estimate is based upon suspect trade data.[2]

Complaints by Western merchants of Japanese fraud were not without basis. In 1859, Francis Hall, merchant in Yokohama and partner in Walsh, Hall, and Co., reported an early instance of fraud. A 'silk brocade' vest, under careful scrutiny, was shown to be backed with paper and not silk.[3] Other examples of fraud by Japanese were as simple as increasing the weight of the goods by stepping on the scale while weighing goods.[4] By the 1870s, the Japanese had gained a worldwide reputation as cheats and frauds.[5]

Ernest Satow, a British diplomat who started his career in Japan as a junior interpreter, also made some comments on the prevalence of fraud. Satow was, among Western diplomats, one of the more willing to see events from a Japanese perspective. He eventually kept a Japanese mistress and acknowledged his Japanese family.[6] He wrote in his memoirs that by 1862, three years after the opening of the ports, although both Japanese and Western merchants were guilty of dishonest activity and contractual breach, the 'balance of wrong-doing was greatly against the native and the conviction that Japanese was a synonym for dishonest trader became. . .firmly seated in the minds of foreigners [Westerners]. . .'[7]

Another example of alleged fraud is Jardine Matheson and Co.'s problems with the firm Takasuya.[8] When the ports first opened, William Keswick and Thomas Gower, Jardine's representatives in Japan, had ordered silk from the firm. The Japanese firm complied with its previous contracts in which the British company had entrusted cash to Takasuya, and the latter acted as an agent and purchased silk inland. In the early 1860s, relations with the West had deteriorated, the instability in the treaty ports, in addition to the constricted supply, greatly increased the volatility of silk prices. Takasuya found itself bound to the lower prices that it had contracted with Jardine before the price rise. Takasuya began to sell the silk, bought with Jardine's money, at the new higher prices and kept the profit. Takasuya continued to sporadically deliver silk at the agreed price. From Takasuya's perspective, the firm met with its obligations and managed to take advantage of the higher prices. By 1863, the scheme had collapsed for Takasuya. In addition, the firm had problems with further changes in the silk market as well as with their own agents who had absconded with some of the silk and money. Takasuya owed Jardine $92,000 and the merchant responsible, Takasuya Seibei, disappeared into the interior silk growing areas.[9]

Jardine tried to recover the debt by means of official and unofficial avenues of redress. An official complaint was made in 1866 to the Japanese authorities but Jardine was informed by the Governor that Takasuya and his firm had other creditors, and it appeared unlikely that Jardine could recover any money. As Western merchants were forbidden by the treaty to go into the interior, Jardine went to the trouble of hiring a Japanese agent to investigate Takasuya and his holdings. The agent found that Takasuya held eleven properties, and it appeared to Jardine that Takasuya was far from destitute. The list of his assets was submitted to the authorities, but little action was taken. In 1867, the debt was written off. In this incident, legal and commercial pressure proved ineffective outside the enclave.

Japanese merchants used a number of methods to cheat the Western merchants. Silk was sold by weight, and some Japanese merchants cheated by weighting the inside of the skeins of silk with debris such as metal and small stones.[10] When Arai Rioichirō, a Japanese businessman, travelled to New York in the 1870s in an attempt to organize the first direct Japanese shipments of silk to the United States, he met with entrenched resistance. When he called upon one New York merchant, he was shown an 'example' of Japanese silk: a silk skein loaded with debris and metal to increase its weight. Another less obvious method was to use heavy paper labels to make the silk appear heavier. Other shipments did not match the quality stipulated in the contract. For example, high quality silk was sometimes placed on top of the box with the bottom filled with lower quality short thread. Arai, tarred with the same brush, was angrily asked to leave.[11] As a merchant with long-term goals to establish the silk import business in the US, he found his compatriots' pursuit of short-term windfalls to be detrimental to the establishment of trust-based business relationships.

The Japanese did not have a monopoly on fraud and contractual breach; Western merchants also committed various acts of shady practice. One common complaint was that Japanese merchants were sometimes not paid for their labour. When some of the residents of Yokohama were building a synagogue in 1872, the men who had hired the Japanese carpenter Koigiro left Japan without paying the $211.75 owed to him.[12] In another case, a Japanese merchant, Shibia Seigoro, was not paid by the British merchant Edleman for silk worth nearly five thousand dollars. The confusion in this case was a result of under-specified inspection procedures of the silk combined with a personality conflict which escalated the dispute. In one instance, Edleman lost his temper and struck the Japanese merchant on the ear.[13]

Some Western merchants exploited differences in trade procedure, only adding to the climate of distrust. The lack of good faith was not exclusive to Japanese merchants. Masuda Takashi, who later became head of Mitsui Bussan, a major business conglomerate, was a young Japanese merchant in the Yokohama enclave. In his memoirs, Masuda described the problems in the silk trade and wrote that Japanese merchants began to regard the Western merchants as acting in bad faith over sample issues.

Masuda delineated the problems in silk dealing by describing the sequence of events in a typical silk deal. A Japanese wholesaler would receive a shipment of silk, and would take a sample of the silk to Western merchants. A deal would be made which was sealed with the clapping of hands. At this point, from the point of view of both merchants, the deal was closed, and the Japanese merchant, in theory, could neither change the price of his goods nor breach his contract. The Japanese merchant's next responsibility was to bring the goods into the Western merchant's shop. There, the Western merchant house reserved the right to inspect (*haiken*) the silk and kept the silk in his warehouse for three to five days. If the silk did not match the sample, the Westerner could return the silk without penalty. For the Western merchant, his contract was tentative (*kari-keiyaku*), whereas the Japanese merchant's contract was absolute.

It is interesting that Western merchants did not distinguish between fraud and breach of a contract – a broken contract was seen as fraud. Fraud is a criminal, not civil offence, whereas breach of contract is a civil offence. When the issue came to court, it was treated as civil matter, but in the correspondence and the press, contractual disputes were often referred to as fraud. Such language may have been a result of a lack of legal knowledge, or a ploy to attract the attention of diplomatic officials. It might have also been a reflection of the seriousness with which merchants and the press viewed the problems of contractual compliance in the ports. In addition, it is unclear from the merchants' letters if they recognized the distinction between 'fraud' and 'breach of contract'.

SUPPLY, DEMAND, CONTRACT, AND TRUST

Clearly both Japanese and Western merchants, at times, had complaints about the other party. The treaty port was sometimes an environment of mutual distrust. In addition to the political and economic instability, the market was untested, the players unknown, and parties could default on their agreements with few consequences. When commodities were limited, contracts were breached, at least in the silk and silkworm egg market. No single social or legal institution could compel either the Japanese or Western merchant to deal honestly with the other. Furthermore, the differences in trade practices were viewed with suspicion by both parties. Only personal affinity, incentive, greed, and profit bound the merchants together.

The high Western demand for the limited quantities of Japanese silkworm eggs focused much attention on the necessity of contractual compliance and trust. The fluctuations of prices in Yokohama tested the patience of the Japanese and Western traders, as well as the agreements made between them. Because of the silk blight in Europe, Western merchants in Japan worked to procure silkworm eggs from Japan to re-seed the destroyed French and Italian silk industry. Initially, the export of silkworm eggs was illegal in Japan, but under Western pressure, this restriction was lifted. The majority of Japanese silkworm species were hardy and reproduced prolifically, thus making them desirable in Europe. Silkworm eggs were sold in 'cards'; moths were encouraged to lay eggs, about half millimetre in size, onto stiff paper. The silkworm eggs naturally adhered to the paper backing, and the paper was then sold as silkworm egg cards. The eggs came in two types. White eggs, and the finer quality, and therefore more expensive and sought for, green eggs. The eggs would hatch to produce the worms which would eventually produce the silk cocoons. The cocoons were treated and were then reeled for silk thread.

A September 1865 letter in *The Japan Times* from a Western merchant writing under a pseudonym summarized many of the perceived frustrations of trading with Japanese merchants in this environment, in which contracts were routinely breached.[14] In 1865, only a handful of Japanese merchants were licensed to sell the eggs. In the particular instance described in his letter, the unnamed merchant obtained the name of a licensed silkworm egg dealer from officials in the Japanese Customs House. An agreement was reached between the merchants, and bargain money was exchanged. Furthermore, because trade in silkworm eggs was restricted, the signed contract was registered at the Japanese Custom House, and stamped with a Consular Seal – presumably the official British seal. Demand for silkworm eggs was huge. The letter-writer described crowds of Western buyers all waiting at the quayside trying to obtain eggs. In this particular instance, the Japanese seller allegedly defaulted on the contract and sold the eggs to another Western buyer at a higher price, after assuring the initial buyer that he would not do so.

The Western merchant implied in his letter that Japanese merchants and Japanese officials worked in collusion with one another to obstruct trade and the smooth function of contracts. As evidence, he cited that he was informed of the Japanese merchant's breach by Japanese Custom officials, who visited his office to tell to him the contract would not be fulfilled. The merchant described another experience in which he argued with a Custom House official over a business matter. Unable to get results, he went to his consul to complain, but the consul remained 'unmoved and unshaken'.[15] According to the writer of the letter, he complained that registering the contract with Japanese and Western officials had little or no effect in discouraging contractual default. In the Western merchant's view, however, ultimate responsibility lay with the Japanese merchants and authorities: 'We willingly concede the extreme difficulty our own authorities have in enforcing with the native authorities their plainest obligations. . .'[16] The writer of the letter expressed anger and dismay at the manner in which the sellers of silkworm eggs defaulted on their agreements: 'In this position several merchants of Yokohama found themselves. . . compelled to see cards which had been bought with their advances, sold for the sake of extra prices to their competitors, or else themselves to buy them at a half to a whole Itzeboo (*Ichibu*) more than the price at which they had contracted them.'[17]

The Western merchants of this period had the normative expectation that the courts should resolve civil disputes. The angry Western merchant concluded that Japanese merchants were not to be trusted, and justice could not be had from either Japanese officials – because they were in collusion with Japanese merchants – or from Western officials, who were powerless in the face of Japanese obstruction. The writer of this letter expressed further discontent because the ports lacked an institution that would protect his interests and force contractual compliance. The letter concluded with the observation that justice could not be had except by force.

A few months later, *The Japan Times*, commenting on a silkworm egg legal dispute described in the section below, expressed a similar theme in which the court was cast in the role of reformer as well as adjudicator of trade disputes within the treaty port. The editorial's tone was not as disillusioned and embittered as the previously mentioned letter to the editor, but both shared the view that the courts, in that environment, should uphold agreements made between merchants. The article argued that by the Western courts meting out 'even handed justice' and by prosecuting Western defaulters of contracts, the Japanese would learn from the court the importance in which Western merchants upheld the sanctity of contract.[18] Ironically, judging by the civil legal conflicts between Westerners, such examples and sanctions by the court had little effect on the Western merchants' own commercial behaviour.

However much the Western powers may have been convinced of the inevitability of free trade in Japan, for Japanese merchants, this course was neither obvious nor certain. As illustrated above, Japanese merchants had a reputation of being unreliable trade partners not only in the enclave but in the West. The putative reasons behind such sharp practices have ranged from the lack of commercial expertise to moral defects among the Japanese. However, if we examine the incentives of the Japanese merchants to cooperate with the Westerners, the lack of incentives for contractual compliance are key to understanding the Japanese merchant's behaviour. Some Japanese merchants in the bakumatsu period sought short-term gain and did not foresee any long-term relationship with the Western merchants. Hence the propensity for default.

TRADING WITH STRANGERS

One of the problems with trading in the treaty port was that small differences in trade procedure could lead to serious, sometimes dangerous, disputes. The 1870 case of the People of the United States on the information of G. Blass vs. Kimura Jinzo is of interest because it not only described in detail a simple transaction – the purchase of some coats and hats for personal use – it also illustrated how a transaction could go wildly wrong.[19] This was a criminal case for attempted assault. It was also a direct result of a misunderstanding over a relatively simple commercial transaction. Even in 1870, more than ten years after the opening of the first ports, the trade procedure for a simple transaction caused considerable confusion for both parties. This case was heard in a United States Consular Court under the jurisdiction of Colonel T. Scott Stewart in Hyogo. The legal case itself dealt with the straightforward issue of whether or not Kimura Jinzo attempted to committed assault.

The underlying issue was one over the bargain money: the Japanese defendant, new to the port, was unfamiliar with the concept of bargain money and the practices of the treaty port. In the spring of 1870, Kimura Jinzo, a nineteen year old military officer of Kagoshima, came to the treaty port of Hyogo from his home. Within days of his arrival, he went into Bush & Co., a general store, where he chose two black coats and two hats. He asked the Western man attending the sale to lower the price of the goods down from 40 *ryo* to 30 *ryo*, and '[he] said he would do so, and made a contract to sell at that price'. Kimura did not have the full amount on his person, and stated that '[the] shopman asked if it was a bargain'; presumably implying an open ended contract. The clerk then asked for the bargain money, but the young man misunderstood, and stated that he had little money. The shopkeeper has seen money in Kimura Jinzo's pocket, and took the money, 2 *ryo*, off his person, out of his pocket, and retained it as bargain money. Although it is unclear from the testimony whether there was a full formal written contract, it appears unlikely that a formal document was ever exchanged. The shopkeeper's receipt given to the Japanese functioned as evidence of the agreement. Kimura Jinzo asked for the money back but was refused. According to the defendant's testimony, he assumed there had been some sort of misunderstanding with the shopkeeper, and left the store.

Kimura Jinzo returned to his quarters and attempted to raise the remaining 28 *ryo* for his coats and hats, but could not raise the funds. He returned to the store and informed the shopkeeper that although he had agreed to buy the clothing, he was unable to pay for it and wished to have his bargain money back. The shop keeper refused, and the Japanese officer complained loudly. A few days later, Kimura Jinzo returned to the shop again, and repeated his request that the shopkeeper return the bargain money. The shopkeeper stated that he would not return the bargain money because the Japanese man had defaulted on the agreement and had refused to take delivery. After that point there was some debate about whether Kimura Jinzo drew his sword, or whether the shopkeeper threatened the Japanese officer with a pistol. In the end, the court acquitted Kimura Jinzo because there was a lack of adequate evidence about who had threatened the other first. It should be noted that the court made a judgment on whether there had been an incident of assault. It had not passed judgement on the pair's trade practices.

In either case, the conflict arose from a misunderstanding and a lack of knowledge on Kimura's part of contractual procedure, albeit a simple one, between himself and the shopkeeper. Furthermore, the communication barrier made information exchange difficult, which exacerbated the situation. Although the transaction was simple, the terms of the contract over the bargain money – it would not be returned if the buyer defaulted – were not made clear to Kimura Jinzo. When he initially left the store after he made the deal, he clearly did not understand the concept of bargain money. Because of the language difficulties, rather than asking the shopkeeper for further clarification (more information), the young Japanese officer left the premises, and only understood the terms of his contract when he inadvertently ran afoul of them. Although the officer interrupted the court proceedings with heated outbursts throughout the course of the trial, possibly indicating a short-temper, there was no evidence that Kimura Jinzo entered into the store in order to cause a disruption. In this case, the seller of the good dictated the terms of the contract, and the buyer accepted the terms. However, because of the high costs for information, the contract was neither explained nor verified to the buyer.

SAMPLE SALES

In order to streamline the trading process and to circumvent language difficulties, a seller would sometimes show the buyer a sample. In a cloth deal, the seller might show a buyer a square of cloth, and promise to produce a bolt of the same colour and quality. A contract using such a method specified the quantity of the good and indicated that the shipment would 'match' the sample, with some general descriptive terms identifying the fabric as lawn, canvas, or velvet. In other cases, the seller might provide a potential buyer a taste of the tea for sale, or show the buyer a skein of silk. Samples could be large or small – there was no standardized sample size or value. In some cases, samples were a single skein or a single item, other samples were entire bales of silk or multiple items. In some sales, the buyer was allowed to keep the samples as part of the sale. For example, if merchants sold a quantity of silkworm eggs, the buyer was sometimes allowed to keep the sample eggs as part of the first shipment. Japanese and Westerners both used samples. Westerners used samples to sell goods from the West, and similarly, the Japanese merchants used samples to sell goods from the interior. Western merchants also used samples for sales within the their own community.[20]

Samples had a problem associated with them. The definition of what constituted a 'match' of the sample was unclear. For example, a hypothetical order for mattress ticking cloth may match a sample in quality and quantity, but may be of a different colour.

To a Western merchant, the colour of the ticking may be an inconsequential detail because mattresses were generally covered by sheets. For a Japanese merchant, who had intended to use the cloth for garments or some other such use, the pattern and colour would be a crucial detail. Especially in a period before assembly lines and interchangeable parts, the issue of what constituted an adequate match was a source of dispute. To further confuse matters, both Japanese and Western merchants exploited these ambiguities as an excuse to escape unprofitable obligations. When a dispute occurred, what were the rights of the buyer and seller? In these cases, it was particularly difficult to ascertain who was the defaulter in order to assign fault for the failure of the agreement.

Sujibayashi Naokichi vs. Chipman, Stone & Co.[21] of 1876 was one such case in which the definition of what constituted a 'match' in sample was tested. This case was heard in the United States Consular Court under Consul General T. B. Van Buren. The case was over three written contracts for various lamp parts, which all contained a penalty clause for the defaulter. The defaulter was to pay double the amount of bargain money. The plaintiff sued for the return of the bargain money of $180 and asserted that Chipman, Stone & Co. had breached the contracts with him because the shipment was late. Thus it was of importance to identify who defaulted on the agreement. The defendant admitted that the shipment was late, but by only a 'trifling exception' and denied that the shipment did not match the sample. Some of the debate centred around issues of the colour of the lamps, hinge versus screw burners, the provenance of the lamps, and type of lamp chimneys. In the case of the lamp colour – some of the lamps were green instead of the sample's white – the defendant claimed he had already taken a reduction in price when the plaintiff came to take delivery. The defendant described the price cut as being 'victimized'.

The court ruled in favour of the defendant on the basis of the defendant's testimony that the goods matched the sample. Also, the court treated each of the succession of contracts as separate agreements, and the fact that plaintiff demanded all the goods together was counted against him. The court accused the plaintiff of bad faith; particularly damning in the court's opinion was the fall in the price of lamp chimneys in the Yokohama market. The court stated that:

> The real motive of the plaintiff in thus refusing may probably be found in the fact that the market price of chimneys in Yokohama was lower, when the goods arrived, than the price agreed upon in the contract. . . My experience here leads me to believe that many of these contracts are entered into on the part of the Japanese in the hope and expectation that some trifling difference may be found in the goods, or some breach committed by the other party; to afford them the opportunity of speculating in damages or in a large reduction of the price of goods.[22]

The court, furthermore, stated that the case was frivolous on the part of the plaintiff and ordered him to pay a fine of $30, as well as all the court costs. The issue of good faith was a crucial part of the court's reasoning. The court's decision was based on the fact that the plaintiff stood to lose money if he honoured the contract. Moreover, if in fact the Japanese merchant had a genuine grievance, information had been lost in forming the contract. The criterion of a sample 'match' to a shipment was not clear to either of the parties.

SELLERS DEFAULTING

In cases when Western sellers defaulted, Japanese merchants contracted for goods from Westerners, which for various reasons failed to appear. Japanese merchants would sue for the return of bargain money or to have the courts compel the Western merchants to sell goods to them at the given price. In the case of Aburaza Ihei and Isuruya Kanezo vs. Glover & Co., the 'Native Merchants' sued to compel completion of a contract over lead.[23] This case was heard in January of 1866 in the British Consular court by F. G. Myburgh, the British Consul of Yokohama. This case is also notable because it involved a third party who was to receive the disputed goods. Like the case against Kimura Jinzo, the problems in this case resulted from the lack of information and a misunderstanding over the terms of the contract. The dispute principally arose from an estimate given by Glover & Co. which was taken as a term of contract by Aburaza Ihei and Isuruya Kanezo, rather than as a description.

In this case, the buyers, Aburaza Ihei and Isuruya Kanezo,

concluded a contract at their offices for 3000 piculs[24] of lead with the sellers, the British firm of Glover & Co., in October of 1865. A Chinese compradore, Achong, employed by the Japanese merchants, verbally negotiated the actual terms of the contract with N. P. Kingdon, who was the representative of Glover & Co. Another Japanese merchant, Kamaya Sayhitchi (Seihichi), recorded the agreement in the Japanese merchants' contract book, although not in Kingdon's presence. It appears that both parties did not sign a formal contract in both languages. According to the plaintiff, the agreement was for 3000 piculs of lead at $4.50 a picul (a total value of $13500), which was to be delivered within 35 days. As soon as the negotiations were finished, the Japanese merchants paid $500 dollars in bargain money. According to the plaintiff's account, some days following the agreement, Glover & Co. delivered 1000 piculs of the lead, and the Japanese merchant then paid an additional $400 in bargain money, as the initial payment was an insufficient amount.

On the other hand, Kingdon asserted that no quantity had been specified, and the agreement was for the Japanese merchants to take 'all' the lead inside the Glover & Co. compound, about 2,200 pigs,[25] within 30 days. In Kingdon's testimony, he claimed that he noticed a discrepancy in the length of the contracts from the initial verbal agreement and the final version: 30 days would have allowed him to remit the sale on the next mail ship, whereas the written contract stated that the deal would be completed in 35 days, thus he would have had to place the payment on a later ship. Kingdon claimed that he had complained to a Western clerk about the matter. Moreover, he asserted that Aburaza had taken delivery of only 800 piculs of lead. Kingdon's staff acknowledged that they received the additional bargain money, but the total sum was well below the 10% customary in the treaty ports. According to Glover & Co.'s staff, there had been some misunderstanding about the total weight of the lead, of which there was about 2000 piculs.[26] Four days after the 35 days had elapsed, Aburaza had not paid the balance nor taken the remainder of the lead. He confronted Aburaza about the discrepancy over length of the contract and the fact that the Japanese merchants had not yet taken delivery of the lead. According to Kingdon's testimony, one of the two Japanese merchants acknowledged wrongdoing over the length of the contract, and offered him 25 cents more per picul for the remaining lead. Furthermore, 'he was kneeling down at the same time holding me by the knees, and trying to induce me to make a fresh contract'. These statements were neither corroborated nor disputed by the plaintiff because the court case ended before they made any further statements.

After making the initial arrangements with Glover & Co., Aburaza had concluded a separate contracted to sell 2000 piculs of lead to S. Stephenson. Interestingly, Kingdon, a Western merchant, sold the goods to the Japanese merchants, who then sold the goods to another Westerner, Stephenson. The Japanese merchants acted as an intermediary (using a Chinese negotiator) between two Western merchants. Aburaza was short of funds at this point and asked for an advance of the lead sale from Stephenson. Stephenson did not refuse, but insisted on accompanying Aburaza and his colleagues to Glover & Co. to pay for the lead. Aburaza went to collect the lead from Kingdon, to then sell to Stephenson. However, because of the confusion in the weight, only 800 to 1000 piculs of lead were available from the Glover & Co. compound, and Stephenson would not accept the delivery: he would only accept a delivery with a total weight of 2000 piculs. Because the contract could not be fulfilled, Aburaza and his colleague paid Stephenson $1,800 in compensation.

The courts ruled in favour of Glover & Co., stating that the plaintiffs were responsible for knowing the terms of the agreements which they concluded. Moreover, the contract had expired with timely notice. The court's decision was in favour of the defendant on the basis of the plaintiff's lack of good faith. They had not taken any actions towards paying for the balance of the goods while under the term of the contract. On the other hand, the assessors of the case, two treaty port residents, dissented from the court's decision in favour of the plaintiffs. Because contracts were routinely extended, the treaty port assessors may have sided with the buyer and may have considered the terms of the court ruling unduly stiff.

The main conflict of the case was a result of a misunderstanding that arose from the language barrier rather than bad faith. The total weight of the item sold was not made clear, the Japanese merchants did not realize the estimated weight of 2,200 pigs of lead was below 3000 piculs. A 'picul' was a generally standardized unit of weight, (about 60kg) whereas a 'pig' indicated a rough block of cast metal of indeterminate weight. The defendant was not aware that the buyer had not understood the true amount of the good sold, and had assumed that he had made himself clear. Thus, because of the communication barriers, the terms of the contract remained vague, but at the same time, the terms of the contract that each party perceived became fixed and inflexible; when it came time to unravel the matter in court, it was difficult to negotiate around these assumptions bolstered by these communication barriers.

INFORMATION AND NEGOTIATION

Information was so expensive in the treaty ports that in some cases, even after the cases went to court, negotiations still continued. Resolution by formal adjudication has traditionally been regarded as a measure of last resort: usually, all other avenues of redress have been exhausted. In 1864, the case of Yeseja Hudzo (possibly Iseja Hyuzo) vs. Macpherson and Marshall, the issue of a breach of contract in good faith became an issue.[27, 28] The case was heard in the British Consular Court by Consul C. A. Winchester. In this case, the defendant accused the plaintiff of bad faith, and yet, throughout the trial, both parties made offers that still left open the possibility of resolving the issue.

Generally, actors are unwilling to pursue future relations with individuals suspected of bad faith. If, for example, a contract was breached due to unavoidable delays, such as shipwreck, then the business relationship between the defaulter and the other party was potentially reparable. On the other hand, if a contractor defected to another dealer with a better price, and thus defaulted on the agreement, then the business relationship with the initial dealer was generally broken. In this case, the Japanese merchant's, that is the plaintiff's, motivations for bringing the suit were questioned.

The details of the case are straightforward: Yeseja Hudzo made an agreement with Macpherson and Marshall to buy about 300 piculs of iron wire. According to the Japanese merchant, he received 50 of the 300 piculs, and in his view, it did not match the sample shown to him by the Western merchant. The two parties concluded a contract that stated that Yeseja Hudzo would purchase 108 piculs of a given quality of iron wire at $22 per picul. They also agreed that he would purchase 216 piculs of another quality of iron wire at $17 per picul. Macpherson and Marshall's shipment was to arrive within five days or the contract was void. In addition, another term of the contract was that the wire had to be cleared from customs and through Macpherson and Marshall's offices within ten days of its arrival.

Yeseja Hudzo asserted that the wire was useless and sued for $3376, the cost of the contract. The basis of the plaintiff's rejection of the goods was that the wire was at the bottom of the ship and had become damaged beyond repair: Hudzo complained that the wire was not equal to the sample because it broke when bent. In addition, it took 17 or 18 days to land the total shipment, therefore breaching the contract. In compensation, Hudzo had asked for 50 piculs of wire to be exchanged for that of a better quality but Macpherson and Marshall allegedly refused. Hudzo then claimed he agreed to accepting the wire, but requested that the remaining 250 piculs be the same as the original agreement. Furthermore, the plaintiff alleged that Macpherson and Marshall had refused to inspect the shipment of wire. In the course of the trial Macpherson and Marshall denied that the wire was substandard and brought some examples of the actual wire into the court. They demonstrated that the wire was not damaged and was equal to sample shown to the plaintiff. Moreover, by bending and twisting the wire, they illustrated that it did not break.

Notable in this case is the description of how each party tried to negotiate with the other for a mutually acceptable solution within the context of the court proceedings. When it had become clear that the wire would not suit the plaintiff's purposes, the Japanese merchant made another offer in the course of the court proceedings in which he stated he would take 100 piculs of the best quality wire and use the bargain money ($500) to pay for it, but Macpherson and Marshall refused to accommodate him and rejected the offer. Macpherson and Marshall also pointed out that the market price of wire had been $22, and had gone down to $15. They implied bad faith on the part of the plaintiff, who stood to lose money if they fulfilled the contract. Furthermore, they accused Hudzo of trying to 'wiggle out' of a bargain because of the fall in the price of wire. Yet, at the same time as accusing the plaintiff of bad faith, Macpherson and Marshall made an offer in which if the plaintiff deposited the remainder of the money within 4 days, he would be allowed to select another quality of wire which was not equal to the sample shown to the plaintiff. Macpherson and Marshall offered that they would set aside the wire for inspection by an assessor. It is unknown if Macpherson and Marshall's offer was accepted by the plaintiff because, in the end, the court ruled against the plaintiff on the basis that there was no evidence of breach of contract.

The difficulty in obtaining information caused a number of problems. The court in this case was used as a forum for negotiation because it allowed for easy communication in a structured manner. In theory, the court functioned to adjudicate on a particular issue; it was to discern whether Macpherson and Marshall were liable for the cost of the contract with the plaintiff. If the defendants had wished to negotiate with the plaintiff, they could have presumably done so before the law suit. Yet in this case, they chose to bargain in the courtroom. In short, in the face of a language barrier, once a contract is established, the terms are fixed and not open to negotiation as in the case of 'normal' contracts because communication costs are too high. In this particular case, the court, even with its costs, was used as a mechanism for trade.

INFORMATION AND DECEPTION

In the case of Yamatia, Sagamia, and Yuroshia vs. E. Alpiger, which took place in October 1865, the issue of silkworm eggs and contractual default was examined in some detail.[29, 30] Although this case occurred one month after the publication of the irate merchant's letter mentioned earlier, it was unlikely that the defendants of this case and the letter-writer were the same person. The writer of the letter to the editor of *The Japan Times* clearly identified himself as British, but the defendant of this case, E. Alpiger, was Swiss; hence the trial was adjudicated by Consul R. Lindau in the consular court of the Swiss Confederation. The problems that occurred in executing the contract were many, but resulted primarily from the high cost of information and to some extent deception and fraud on the part of Alpiger. One of the original contracts was in German, a language that the Japanese merchants did not understand. Alpiger had not provided a literal translation of the contract to the Japanese and, at the time, there were few, if any, Japanese who understood German. Compounding the issue was Alpiger's apparent prejudice, paranoia, and greed, all of which did not add to a conducive business environment.

This case lends another perspective to the image promulgated by Westerners that all Japanese merchants were unscrupulous traders who defaulted on their contracts. A group of Japanese merchants, who had been trading in the area for seven years, entered into an agreement in which the defendant engaged the Japanese merchants in a deal to buy 20,000 silkworm egg cards. The Japanese merchants were to supply the eggs by September first: the contract was to expire on 18 October. In this contract written in German and Japanese, the defendant was to take a shipment of four sevenths green eggs and three sevenths white eggs, both matching in quality to the sample. In this case, the Swiss merchants paid the Japanese a 2,500 *ichibu* advance to assist the merchants in the purchase of the goods. It is unclear whether this advance was bargain money or whether the merchants asked for the money to pay for the cards from another party – most likely a combination of both. In the text of the trial, the initial payment was explicitly referred to as an 'advance'. In the judgment of the case, the initial payment was termed as 'bargain money.' In the commentary on the case published in the newspaper, an editorial referred to the money as 'bargain money'.[31] The Western merchant took delivery of 176 cards. Later, for unnamed reasons, Alpiger requested the return of the advance, and furthermore charged the Japanese merchants interest for the four months and fifteen days they had kept it. The Japanese merchants not only returned the money, but also paid the $70 interest. The 176 cards that Alpiger initially took were now unpaid for. At this point, in the Japanese merchants' opinion, the contract had been breached when Alpiger took back the money; Alpiger on the other hand stated that he had had every intention to fulfil the contract.

On the day that the contract was due, the Japanese merchants duly presented Alpiger the silkworm eggs as per the contract. The Swiss merchant chose 311 cards from the 13,500 cards shown to him. The price, as per the contract, was 2 *ichibu* a card, although the market rate was about three-and-a-half *ichibu*. Alpiger, furthermore, refused to pay for the cards he selected, remarking in the trial that he did not pay for the eggs in order to compel fulfilment of the remaining contract. The court reprimanded Alpiger and stated that he had no 'right to suspect their good faith' because the Japanese merchants had illustrated their readiness to fulfil the contract when they arrived with cards the day the contract was due. He stated that he had rejected the other eggs cards because they did not match the sample. In his view they did not match the sample because the cards did not have a printed seal on them. Without the seal, in the Western merchant's eyes, the sample did not match. The consular court rejected this argument, considering it a 'futile pretext'; the court remarked that the defendant could have hired someone to have the entire shipment of cards stamped for a few *ichibu*. The plaintiffs suggested that the Swiss merchant broke the contract because the market price of white eggs had dropped. When the courts questioned him further, the defendant stated that he refused to pay the plaintiffs so that 'he might have a guarantee against the Japanese, who very often kept bad faith, besides, it was always very difficult to get redress from the native authorities and he wished himself to take care of his own interests'.

Adding to the issue, when one of the Japanese merchants tried to get his attention, Alpiger struck him once with his walking stick because 'he was very busy and was going out of the house. . .that to get rid of him he had struck him'. Alpiger was unrepentant, and alleged that he was well within he rights to strike a Japanese in the confines of his house. In his closing statement, he stated 'I should have given him fifty [blows], I ought to have killed him!!'

In the course of the court proceedings, the translations of the contracts were compared. One of the main problems in the contract was that one of the copies of the contract was in German. The merchants made the initial agreement, and then Alpiger drew up a contract in German. Alpiger had supplied a *draft* copy in English, which he also understood. The translator was hired to translate this document into Japanese so that the Japanese merchants could have a written copy of the document. The translator was an acquaintance of the Japanese merchants, and his English abilities were apparently not adequate for the task at hand. Alpiger orally (*viva voce*) explained the particulars of the contract to the Japanese and the translator duly wrote down the items as the Japanese contract. The Japanese contract roughly specified the amount, price, and dates of the contract. According to testimony, the cards were to match the sample, but no provisions were made in the written contract on issues such as quality. The contract was accurate, however, although certain details were omitted; details such as the stamping and labelling of the cards were allegedly orally discussed through the translator but were not written into the Japanese document. One omission was quite serious. The German contract specified that in the case of non fulfilment, the Japanese were to pay an indemnity of one *ichibu* per card – about 50% of the contract's worth. When the Japanese merchants signed this document, they signed a different document from their Japanese copy. The court commented that Alpiger demonstrated 'great negligence' in not providing the translator with a literal copy of the contract in English for the Japanese.

The court ruled in favour of the plaintiff and awarded the Japanese merchants 3,488.70 *ichibu* in damages. The damages included the money, with interest, owed by Alpiger for the 176 sample cards and 311 cards he had retained and 2498.00 *ichibu* in damages for non-fulfilment of the contract. The court, in its judgment, repeated its charge that Alpiger was 'negligent' in his duties as a merchant in allowing the Japanese merchants to sign a German contract which differed from that of the Japanese contract. In addition, the court declared that Alpiger voided the contract when the bargain money was returned. The court also noted that the Japanese had shown their good faith and intention of fulfilling the contract when they appeared with eggs during the period in which the contract was in full force. In addition to this civil dispute, the court demanded that Alpiger pay a fine of 120 francs with costs for assaulting the Japanese.

Although the letters to the editor, articles, and communication to diplomats often complained of the Japanese merchants' bad faith in the silk trade, within the context of this case, the treaty port Westerners did not side with Alpiger, but sided with the Japanese merchants. For example, to further obstruct the court proceedings, Alpiger took issue with the fact that the plaintiffs, Yamatia, Sagami, and Yurusia were not actually the parties with whom he signed the contract. He stated that he would not honour the contract because an employee of the firm, and not the head, negotiated the contract, and therefore the contract, in his assessment, did not exist. The Japanese merchants rejected this assertion. As the plaintiffs were the agents who ultimately furnished the eggs, they stated that they did not believe that such an action was out of order. Five Western local merchants, including a member of the local Municipal Council, signed and submitted a letter to the Swiss Consul, refuting Alpiger and stating that a *banto* was an adequate representative for business transactions; dealing with the head of the house was not necessary. One of the signers, N. P. Kingdon, testified that he was not aware of any Japanese merchants repudiating an agreement made on their behalf by their clerks. With this turn of events, Alpiger demanded the Swiss Court to collect a 20,000 *ichibu* indemnity from the Japanese to protest this action of the Western merchants. Alpiger's reasoning, it seems, was not entirely sound. Not surprisingly, the court rejected this request. The court did not have authority over Japanese subjects, and the request was, in itself, unreasonable because the Western merchants, not the Japanese, submitted their views to the case.

This idea that the institution of contract and credit had priority over affinities within the treaty port community, even at the expense of personal ties and affinities, was echoed in *The Japan Times* editorial on this case.[32] The article used strong phrases such as 'maze of fraud' to describe Alpiger's actions. It stated that the court should prosecute Alpiger to the fullest extent of the law. 'Credit is the life of Commerce,' continued the article, and it argued that there was a dearth of credit in the treaty ports because of a lack of 'confidence' and 'honesty' in business transactions with Japanese merchants.[33] He commented explicitly, 'He thus clearly broke the contract and absolved the Japanese.' The writer condemned the Western merchant for being 'chicane' and commented that Alpiger did not 'evidently [possess] any quality which enters into the composition of a merchant'. It commented that the Western merchant community would not always be biased by their experiences with 'untrustworthy' Japanese merchants or by simple prejudice. Rather, they supported the efficient functioning of credit and contract.

Silk, silkworm eggs, and silk filament comprised the bulk of early Japanese international trade. The silk trade and related goods were also commodities in which Western merchants complained of unfulfilled contracts. In the case of silk, the contracts were not fulfilled because Japanese merchants supplied substandard goods, in addition to the usual contractual wrangling such as excess storage fees, storage cost, or simple default.

Japanese silk as an export commodity got a decided boost from the French silk blight in 1852. The blight destroyed not only the silk growing industry in France, but also all the ancillary industries of weaving, dyeing, painting, not to mention all the associated sewing industries. Although some raw silk from Italy helped lessen the effects of the shortage, by 1860 the disease had spread to Italy, and throughout Europe silk was in short supply. The opening of Japan was fortunate for the French silk industry, as it meant a supply of raw silk of requisite quality. Japanese silk was not seen by consumers in the West as fine in quality as France's, but served nevertheless as a substitute until the French industry recovered. In 1860, the first full year of trade, about 2.2 million dollars worth of piece and raw silk goods were exported from Japan.[34] By 1863, the amount of silk exported swelled to almost 7.5 million dollars.[35]

Léon Roches, the French envoy in Japan, was instrumental in securing silk. French expertise in shipbuilding was traded for improved access to the silk trade. The silk market may have been perceived as a windfall by silk merchants, especially those who sold the silkworm eggs. The French were eager to resurrect their silk industry and pressed the Bakufu to lift the prohibition on the export of silkworm eggs. Obviously, eggs exported to France would effectively seed the competition. The Japanese at some point would have to compete with European silk producers. Japanese merchants may have concluded that building confidence and relationships was not vital under the circumstances.

From the Bakufu's perspective, the commercial consideration was subordinate to military and security assistance, namely expertise in building a Japanese naval force.

The silk market in Japan had its share of problems. Japanese merchants adulterated their silk with debris, but Western merchants, eager for raw silk, bought the silk knowing some of it to be of poor quality. During the first years of the enclave, due to the restrictions on silk exports, Japanese merchants did not have a regular or reliable supply of silk. It was entirely possible for one Japanese merchant to have silk while all other merchants were empty handed. This was especially true in the early 1860s when the Bakufu diverted silk for domestic consumption, and merchants paid for smugglers to bring bales of silk. Few merchants had any silk to sell. Thus the unscrupulous sort of Japanese merchant had a double incentive to supply substandard goods. It was a windfall opportunity and there was no other competition to which the Western merchant could turn.

The differing expectations of the merchants created an environment in which merchants found it difficult to build trust. Western merchants came to Japan with the expectation that Japan would, after the opening of the ports, henceforth trade with the West. Some Western merchants were opportunists who intended to make their fortunes and leave. Other firms intended to trade on a long term basis in the Japanese market. Many Japanese did not expect the Westerners to stay, and thus had no incentive to act in good faith. Even among those that traded with good intentions, the differences in trading methods combined with the seemingly lack of good faith of the Westerners, resulted in an environment of mutual suspicion. Western merchants defaulting on deals on the basis of contractual terms – sample mismatch – only exacerbated matters and fuelled distrust in the other party.

Such behaviour was not unique to the Japanese; twentieth century Mexican shoe manufacturers exhibited similar behaviour when faced with such a windfall situation. In World War II, US shoe producers stopped making shoes for domestic consumption and started making military issue boots for the war effort. Mexican shoe manufacturers took up the slack and produced shoes for the 'civilian' market. The Mexican shoe manufacturers reacted differently to US buyers than to their own market. In short, they acted to maximize as much short term gain as possible by sending sub-standard goods. Ultimately, the war ended, and the domestic shoe production reverted back to the US. Older producers recount that during the war they could sell sandals that were defective or looked bad. In the short term, this meant large profits for the commercial wholesalers who exported, but in the long run it meant a lack of confidence in Mexican producers and limitations on exporting Mexican footwear.[36] In an extreme case, a shoe manufacturer recalled that his grandfather did not bother with shoes at all, and shipped boxes filled with rocks.[37]

Ironically, silk turned out to be a long-standing export commodity for the Japanese, and not a windfall at all. With Louis Pasteur's discoveries in bacteriology, the silk blight was contained and by the 1870s European silk growing began to recover. By this point, even with the lack of confidence in Japanese merchants and trade methods, Japanese silk had established itself in the United States, and quality control procedures were instituted. The world's consumption of silk increased, and by the eve of World War I, Japanese silk exports were well above 100 million US dollars a year. The slump in the post World War I economy, World War II, and the invention of synthetics such as nylon eventually shrank the Japanese silk industry, but Japanese silk had been a major export product for nearly half a century.

THE IMPORTANCE OF BEING EARNEST

The 1876 case of Nakajima Saisuki[38] vs. W. P. Mitchell[39] was another case in which a Japanese successfully sued for damages stemming from a breach of contract. This case was adjudicated by the British, and each side hired professional lawyers to pursue their claims. The plaintiff claimed $2,700 paid to the defendants as bargain money as well as damages which resulted from the breach of contract. A particularly striking aspect about this case was the extensive and thorough paper trail of contracts and receipts maintained by the Japanese merchant. The problem stemmed from bad faith. Both parties held each other at arm's length, and because of their lack mutual confidence, the contract was not carried out. Both parties adhered to the literal wording of the written contract, which could not accurately reflect the circumstances. This insistence on form resulted in a lack of flexibility, which caused losses on both sides.

On 14 May 1876, W. P. Mitchell, a trader whose offices were in lot 95 in Yokohama, went to Tokyo and visited the plaintiff to sell a shipment of 15,000 cases of kerosene. Two days later, the plaintiff travelled to Yokohama and entered into a provisional contract at $2.67 and 1/2 cent per case, to be delivered by the 22nd of the month. Whilst in Yokohama, the merchants all boarded the ship and inspected the goods. By 20 May, the parties signed a final version of the contract. The arrangement was such that Nakajima would pay 20% of the purchase price in cash, and the rest was to be paid for with a security from the Prince of Sawa. After viewing the goods, Nakajima had met with the representative of the Prince of Sawa, and in exchange for title deeds to his house, Sawa had agreed to become the guarantor. Nakajima paid Mitchell $700 in bargain money and in turn received a receipt. To further complicate matters, Nakajima made an agreement with a third party, a merchant by the name of Mano Shedetoshe, to sell the kerosene.[40] In this contract, Nakajima was responsible for 5% of a $39,750 contract if he failed to fulfil it.

On the day the contract came into force, the plaintiff went to collect his goods, but Mitchell told Nakajima that the goods were not ready for delivery. Witnesses attested to gales and generally poor weather which made landing the goods from the ship impractical. The next day, Mitchell arrived at Nakajima's hotel and informed him that there had been complications in processing the goods. The defendant requested that Nakajima take the goods in two lots instead of the previously agreed single lot. It was impossible land the total shipment because the wharf area could only contain about 10,000 cases of oil. Although this was not consistent with their agreement, Nakajima acquiesced to the changes, and the next day went to the port to collect the kerosene. Only 2000 cases were available, not the 7500 or so that Nakajima expected, and Mitchell explained that he needed $2000 more to pay for custom duties. Eventually, Nakajima agreed, and drew up a new document stating that he paid $2000 in addition to the bargain money and was to receive cases of kerosene the next day.

When Nakajima protested about the arrangements, Mitchell allegedly said, 'Not according to the written contract, to the understanding we had at the time of making the written contract.'[41] The exact number was not specified in order to allow for flexibility in the agreement; no one had known how many cases could be landed in one day. The availability of dock space, boats, workers, and weather all affected the number of the boxes that could be landed in one day. In his testimony, Mitchell asserted that he never gave unqualified acceptance of the letters which contained the contracts, rather, he placed emphasis on 'other agreements, verbal ones' that had been made.[42]

On the 25th, Nakajima went to the *hatoba* (wharf), to inspect his goods. Only 2000 cases had been landed and of these 100 of the cases were damaged in his estimation, and he requested that they be replaced. Nakajima handed Mitchell a $2000 cheque and in turn received a receipt. According to Nakajima, he thought he was now free to take the 2000 cases of kerosene. Mano, who had bought the oil from Nakajima, was now in Yokohama ready to take the oil to Tokyo. He had arranged to take the oil by boat across the bay to Tokyo, and started load the oil onto his boat. They succeeded in loading 100 of the cases when a Western merchant, identified as 'from lot number 28', stopped them. He announced that the oil belonged to him and they had no right to take it. Because Mitchell's and the Western merchant's addresses were different, Nakajima assumed that the merchant had nothing to do with his deal with Mitchell. Mitchell arrived on the scene and explained that the man from lot 28 was a partner in the deal, and furthermore, he would not allow Nakajima to take delivery of the goods until he received the security from the Prince of Sawa. That is, he wished for Nakajima to pay for the total shipment of 15,000 cases before he received the 2000 cases on the hatoba. By this point, it had become late, and Mitchell had to hire a 'European' night watchman to protect his stock left overnight on the quay, thus increasing costs.

There was no mention in the contract or the additional document that Sawa's guarantee had to be produced when the Japanese merchant took delivery of the 2000 cases. From Nakajima's point of view, because this was contrary to the formal contract and the agreement signed when he handed Mitchell the $2000 advance, he refused to pay. Mitchell alleged that he and Nakajima had a verbal agreement to bring the Prince of Sawa's guarantee. When Nakajima rejected this assertion and asked for the cheque to be returned, Mitchell refused the money and oil. A witness described the merchants shouting with angry words being exchanged. Nakajima allegedly resolved to go to the British consulate to complain. Mitchell sent his clerk after Nakajima to settle the matter amicably. When the two parties met, Mitchell announced that he had been to see the Prince of Sawa and the latter had refused to be Nakajima's guarantor: Mitchell accused Nakajima of breach of contract. Without the security, Mitchell announced that he would sell the oil by auction the following day. The threat was duly carried out and the oil for which Mitchell had paid $2.47 and 1/2 cent per case, was sold at a loss at about $2.10 to $2.30 per case. Mitchell claimed $1300 of loss from Nakajima's breach.

The plaintiff demonstrated that the assertion that Nobutane, the Prince of Sawa, refused to back Nakajima was likely to be false: Nakajima produced papers that confirmed the agreement. The Prince himself later testified in court and brought documentation that he was willing to back Nakajima. Sawa asserted he had told Mitchell that Nakajima would give the Western merchant the security when he was satisfied that the deal had gone through. The case for the defence produced a paper which purportedly claimed that Sawa would not guarantee Nakajima's debt. In Mitchell's view this was proof of a breach of contract. However, the letter apparently said that Sawa would give his security when the contract was completed and the 15,000 cases were delivered. It appears that there was yet another misunderstanding: Sawa had not told Mitchell that he would not back Nakajima; rather, he stated that he would retain his security until the contract was completed to Nakajima's satisfaction. In addition, Sawa himself did not make any of the financial arrangements and had used an agent for his dealings with tradesmen.

At around this time, Nakajima had engaged G. Ness as his lawyer to aid him in resolving the various issues. Nakajima then handed the lawyer the 20% and the letter of security from the Prince of Sawa. The lawyer then attempted to resolve the issue with Mitchell, with little result. Mitchell demanded $800 for losses and expenses, otherwise he would hold Nakajima for breach of contract. Mitchell announced that he had every intention of fulfilling the contract, and that Nakajima had breached the agreement. The lawyer personally vouched for Nakajima's willingness to resolve the issue.

Mitchell had retained a Japanese translator named Totska[43] throughout the trades who acted an interpreter and translator for both parties, but it appears that the confusion continued. Ultimately, the court ruled in favour of the plaintiff, awarding him $2,700 dollars with interest. Costs were to be borne by the defendant. However, the damages that Nakajima had incurred from non-fulfilment were not granted. In November of 1876, Mitchell appealed the case on the grounds that the verbal understanding was not treated as evidence in the initial trial. The court again ruled in favour of the plaintiff, and rejected Mitchell's arguments. It expanded on the idea of good faith — both men stood to lose from the agreement and gain from the delay of the shipment, but Mitchell had made the first move and asked to modify the agreement.

SMALL CLAIMS AND THE MARKET

As seen above, merchants pursued civil cases with one another for a multitude of reasons for amounts ranging from a few dollars to hundreds of thousands. These larger, more complicated suits provided descriptions of medium and long term relationships between Japanese and Western merchants. The cases give hints into the formation and dissolution of deals worth thousands of dollars, over weeks, months, and sometimes years. Yet, the drawback of focusing on large deals is that they were not the only transactions in the treaty ports. In the early days of trade, most merchant 'houses' were small one-man operations, working on a constrained budget. Many such houses folded during economic recessions in the late 1860s and early 70s. Furthermore, the Japanese merchants who traded with the Westerners were not all from large merchant houses such as Mitsui; some were small independent dealers and workmen selling their goods and labour. For the majority of traders, the majority of their transactions were small and simple. They were not the product of a long term relationship but were spot deals. By examining the lawsuits for relatively small sums of money, we have the opportunity to examine the issues and everyday problems that plagued treaty port merchants.

Small scale contracts are defined here as those under one hundred and fifty dollars. This is a somewhat arbitrary number as there was no legal definition of 'small claims' type dispute in the treaty port courts. At the time, the only legal distinction that existed, at least in the British consular courts, was at the one thousand dollar level.[44] However, most cases below the one hundred dollar level were cases in which agreements for trade were made without written contracts or bargain money: $150 seems to be natural line of demarcation for simple contracts. A receipt of bargain money received functioned as evidence of an open ended contract. Although some small contracts did use bargain money, for the most part, the merchants functioned with little or no formal written contracts in these transactions.

At first glance, the small cases appear to be insignificant: the reports of the cases were short, no more than a few column inches long, at most. Diplomats complained these petty cases took up all their time, and clogged the consulate workload with paperwork. The amounts were sometimes small. For example, Nakagawa Mankichi sued Jaffray for 13 3/8 dollars. In the majority of the cases, the plaintiff stated a claim that the defendant was indebted to him, and expressed a wish to be paid. In the seventeen years covered in this volume, the majority of the cases are from the period following the Meiji Restoration. This increase in the number of small claims cases was probably a result of a combination of factors. Increased knowledge of Westerners, and the increased numbers of Westerners increased in the treaty ports. With more business, it could be safely said, there were more disputes. If a lengthy case was in session, it tended to monopolize the time and resources of the court and affected the number of small scale disputes. For example, in the autumn and winter of 1875, the case of Itō Hachibei vs. Walsh Hall and Co. dominated the British Consular court. In this particular case, the consular court suspended the hearing of the case for a few days to pursue other claims, but in most instances, cases were heard through to completion without interruptions.[45]

These small claims cases did not involve particularly complex issues; cases within the Western community were similar to the mixed cases in their simplicity. In cases such as Weigand vs. Harryman for $27.25 and Chang Chow v. C. Lester for $12.00, the plaintiffs requested that the debts be paid, which the judge granted. In other cases when the defendant denied the debt, or claimed indebtedness of a smaller sum, the judge would listen to both sides, examine receipts or account books, and then render a judgment. The procedure was nearly identical for mixed small disputes. In the case of Senjiro vs. J. Watson, Senjiro sued Watson for $19 for provisions he had purchased on behalf of the defendant; Senjiro stated that he had not been paid. Watson argued that this claim was false, and stated that he had books that demonstrated that he had paid Senjiro. When the court was adjourned the next day, his books proved not to be definitive, and Senjiro was awarded his claim.[46] A few cases dealt with promissory notes and other trade intruments, but the majority at this level were straightforward.

These transactions were straightforward, unlike bargain money cases; essentially cash for goods and services. Why then, did the parties need to go to litigation at all? The occurrences of these small disputes in a population of a few hundred seem to suggest that Japanese and Westerners had problems transacting business with each other, and that there was a lack of shared business expectations. In most of these cases, it appears there was little to misunderstand. Intermediary institutions such as banks − or incentives such as reputation to compel payment − may have been weaker than those in their own communities. Furthermore, information was not disseminated effectively through formal and informal venues between Japanese and Western merchants. As described in a previous chapter, the boundaries that surrounded the social and business community were semi-permeable; both parties could easily escape their social and legal obligations. No one law, moral code, or network bound the Western merchants to the Japanese merchants, nor Western merchants to one another.

The occurrence of both Western and Japanese merchants pursuing small claims for fairly trivial sums over similar issues suggests that the legal suits for these small sums were not a result of

Japanese misunderstanding the function of contracts. The courts appear to have treated these rather minor complaints in much the same way. There is no evidence that the Japanese used the courts any differently than the Westerners when it came to small claims. Another similarity with both sets of cases was the majority of these small claims cases were centred on generic goods and services. The agreements were not as highly specified as in bargain money agreements. Both groups had cases over issues involving servants, assistants, other such labour that could easily be had at a similar price, and for generic goods such as comestibles, newspapers, refreshments, and horse feed. For example, the cases pursued against William Curtis by five different Japanese were over debts owed for poultry, a measure of coal for home use, some amount of goods delivered to him, and a bill for some work done.[47]

In addition, the existence of merchants pursuing multiple claims from the same defendant seems to suggest a degree of consistency in their claims. If a resident was a bad risk, a number of merchants pursued their debts against him. For example, among the cases, certain Westerners and Japanese make repeat appearances as both plaintiffs and defendants. P. Bohm was an individual who seemed to have persistent legal troubles. In 1876, he was the defendant in a series of cases ranging from $25 to $246.66 pursued by Japanese and Westerners. He was also a plaintiff in a 1872 case in which he sued a Western resident, C. Esdale for an $8 subscription to *The Japan Gazette*.[48]

One might surmise that Japanese and Western merchants brought these small scale disputes because the courts were a forum in which the communication was easy. In addition, the courts had interpreters and translators which helped in taking the guesswork out of the dispute, thus resolving them cheaply. Jurisprudence required that each side was given some time to express their grievances, thus providing structure. Furthermore, the small – and by and large petty – disputes may appear to be byproducts and externalities of Japanese merchants acclimatizing to the methods and practices of Western contracts. When compared to the contractual disputes for thousands of dollars, disputes over a dozen or so dollars seems out of place.

Interestingly, there was one difference between Japanese and

Western small cases. Through to 1880, there were few records, if any, of small claims cases pursued by Western sellers against Japanese buyers in court. In general, claims against Japanese sellers for breaches of contract averaged over a thousand dollars. At the same time, records of claims by Western buyers against Japanese under 100 dollars simply did not exist, except when pursued as a portion of a larger claim. Whereas Westerners and Japanese both were plaintiffs against Westerners, Westerners generally sued only other Westerners for small claims. This curious state of affairs may have been a result of the structure of the court and the market. Initially, it might have taken more time and effort to sue in Japanese courts than in Western ones. The barriers might have been higher, although Westerners, like Japanese pursuing claims in Western courts, did not have to deposit fees with the Japanese courts. The entry barriers in terms of fees for Westerners were low. Another possibility is that the market was such that Japanese merchants did not purchase easily interchangeable goods and services from Westerners; rather, the contracts and agreements made between Westerners and Japanese tended to be highly specific in terms of goods and quantities. Whereas the Westerner may have hired a Japanese servant or hired a Japanese labourer, it was unlikely that a Japanese would have bought groceries from a Westerner or hired a Western rickshaw driver; for such goods and services, they would have hired a Japanese or bought goods from Japanese merchant. Westerners hired other Westerners and Japanese for labour and easily interchangeable consumer goods, but Japanese did not hire Westerners or buy many Western consumer goods. Whilst this is historically true, the lack of small claims cases against Japanese also indicated this state of affairs.

CONCLUSION

This trading environment was, for various reasons outlined in the previous chapters, one of mutual distrust. The courts attempted to reinforce the idea that contracts should be complied with, even in the event of a loss. In short, a key issue was the good faith of each party. Western merchants also sought good faith, and as evinced by their commentary of the Alpiger case, they supported the Japanese merchants because they upheld their agreements. Yet, although the norm expressed by the court was that contracts ought to be upheld, both Western and Japanese merchants continued to display opportunism throughout the period.

Because of this unstable atmosphere, Western merchants insisted on bargain money when they made agreements with the Japanese. Bargain money had a twofold purpose. It tied the buyer to the contract, and the contract became a legal entity. As consideration, bargain money allowed for the possibility of legal recourse when the merchants could not resolve their commercial disputes. The threat of legal action may have played a part in the contractual compliance. At the same time, information was expensive and limited, so trade agreements – whether oral or formal written contracts – were left vague to allow for some of the eventualities that occurred in the course of trade. However, this 'flexibility' in the form of vagueness, caused problems when parties did not share the same expectations. When changes and modifications could not be made because of the communication barrier, problems resulted. In order to resolve the issue, both parties referred to the contract, a document (if it even existed) which did not and could not accurately reflect the dynamics of the business transaction. To exacerbate the problem, when the dispute went to court, the courts were bound to rule on the formal contract agreed upon by the two parties. The legally enforceable contract in an environment in which information was costly may have been, in some instances, an instrument which obstructed the efficient flow of trade in the treaty ports.

PROMISE, AGREEMENT AND CONTRACT
Itō Hachibei vs. Walsh, Hall & Co.

In fact, the whole business seems to have been conducted on a principle of mutual childlike trust and confidence worthy of the millennium.

General T. B. Van Buren of the US Consular court delivering judgement on the case of Itō v. Walsh, Hall & Co.[1]

I N 1871, a Japanese merchant named Itō Hachibei and a Western firm, Walsh, Hall & Co., embarked upon a partnership. In the course of their business relationship, significant sums of money, well over a million dollars, changed hands. In one transaction, Itō used $500,000 Mexican dollars of Walsh, Hall & Co.'s money. When Itō returned the sum to the Western firm, the Japanese merchant and his escorts took a wagon load of 380,000-400,000 niboo gold coins (*nichibukin*) to Walsh, Hall & Co.'s god-own. This sum of money was handed over to the Western merchant with little ceremony. Later, one of the assisting Japanese merchants stated: 'I did not get a receipt for the money. It was raining, and there was considerable confusion at the moment, and as we were continually doing business with [them] the idea of a receipt never came into our minds.'[2]

The fact that a Japanese-Western transaction of a wagon-load of gold proceeded without an explicit contract and documentation, such as a receipt, is surprising; it exhibited a significant level of trust in an environment which the trade practices were unfamiliar and the market untested. In addition, legal remedies were neither accessible nor transparent. Japanese merchants pursuing a complaint against a Westerner would have had their cases heard by a Western consular court. In the opposite circumstance, the case would been heard in a Japanese court with Western legal advisors. Both forms of legal redress would have been unfamiliar to the merchants. In addition, the professionalism of both Japanese and Western courts, with the possible exception of the British court system, was suspect. Given the volatile economic and political environment of newly 'opened' Japanese treaty ports, one might expect that merchants would have demanded explicit documentation to protect their interests, especially in view of the risk and the difficulties with the legal remedies. Yet throughout the business dealings between Itō and Walsh, Hall & Co., they did not use formal written agreements and persisted in doing business on an *ad hoc* basis; all the transactions were based on verbal agreements.

Eventually, the relations between Itō and Walsh, Hall & Co. soured in 1875 and resulted in a legal case at the United States consular court. The plaintiff of this case, Itō Hachibei, brought a suit against Walsh, Hall & Co. in September of 1875. He claimed the sum of $108,715.42 from Walsh, Hall & Co. as a balance of an account and interest connected with transactions he had with the defendants. Walsh, Hall & Co. denied any indebtedness and counter-claimed that Itō owed them the sums of $16,222.55 and $16,483.60, as the balance of accounts.[3]

The court records of this case reveal the prosaic details of deal making in treaty port Japan in explicit line-by-line testimony of the plaintiff, defendants, and witnesses. By using the information contained in the court documents, combined with other Japanese and Western sources, the timeline of events, in which we see the formation and dissolution of a business relationship, can be reconstructed. In this business relationship, as the above incident illustrated, the merchants traded with one another without depending on formal written contracts or documentation. If formal contracts were made, they were cursory at best. In addition, they relied on familiarity and interpersonal relationships to resolve disputes, instead of resorting to authorities or formal agreements.

BACKGROUND ON THE CASE OF ITŌ HACHIBEI AND WALSH, HALL & CO.

This chapter is based on the court proceedings of the United States consular court published in *The Japan Weekly Mail* and other local newspapers of the treaty ports. The events described in the case took place almost five years prior to the court proceedings. As the defendant of the case was an American firm, General Van Buren presided as judge of the US consular court, with the assistance of two assessors. Itō Hachibei was a Japanese subject, but he retained the services of F. V. Dickins, a Western lawyer. G. P. Ness represented the defendant. The case transpired from September 1875 to January 1876 and there are records of 52 sittings. Court transcripts were published in *The Japan Weekly Mail*, a weekly news magazine, in a regular local 'Law and Police' column. This column published all legal cases tried by any consular court, all Japanese legal cases in which a Westerner was a plaintiff, and a list of police arrests and incidents. In this particular case, a complete transcript was published of all testimonies; however, the lawyers' questions were not printed. With a few exceptions, the lawyers' arguments and the judge's comments were paraphrased.

There are several problems in working with this source. One is a result of working with a small local press. At times, the periodicals were seemingly thrown together at the last moment. *The Japan Weekly Mail* contained numerous misprints, and also, variable spelling of non-Western names. For example, Walsh, Hall & Co.'s Chinese compradore is referred to as Sy Coy, Sin Coy, or Zin Coy. As there was no consensus on transliterating Japanese, Kumagai Shoske was occasionally called Kumagi Shoski or Kumagai Shoski.[4] Also, when referring to a Japanese individual, the paper sometimes referred to him by his first name and, at other times, his last.

The case itself was long and convoluted with many names, dates, deals, and details. Furthermore, the chronology became particularly confused with witnesses giving misleading statements, either for self-protection or for personal gain. In this chapter, conflicting testimony has been clearly noted. In order to better follow the case, a brief summary of the case and the major issues is given below. This civil case was a debt allegedly owed to Itō by Walsh, Hall & Co.: Itō claimed he was owed $108,715.21 by the defendants and wished to recover ¥100,035 of securities given to Walsh, Hall & Co. On the other hand, Walsh, Hall & Co. denied that they were indebted, and claimed that Itō owed the two sums of $16,222.55 and $16,483.60, as the balance of accounts. These amounts were a result of transactions between the plaintiff and defendant five years prior to the court proceedings. In September 1871, Itō Hachibei and Walsh, Hall & Co. had entered upon a partnership to exchange dollars for profit. Itō had given ¥100,035 to Walsh, Hall & Co. as a security. Exchange transactions went badly, and the partnership lost money. After this point, the testimony of the plaintiff and defendant diverged. The former stated that the partnership entered into rice deals to recoup losses, but the defendants denied the partnership and argued it had ended after the initial dollar transactions. Walsh, Hall & Co. asserted that they only advanced money to Itō for the deals, but the losses were Itō's alone. The appropriateness of the use of Itō's securities that had been left in trust with Walsh, Hall & Co. became another major issue. Throughout Itō and Walsh, Hall & Co.'s five year relationship, the securities had remained under the control of Walsh, Hall & Co. In the course of the many transactions, money was borrowed by Walsh, Hall & Co. for Itō using Itō's securities. Itō claimed that he had not authorized such use of his securities.

Another major factor in this case was the personal relationship and obligations that Itō had with his Walsh, Hall & Co. contact, Robert W. Irwin. Although the defendants and Irwin himself denied the allegations, there had been some exchange of favours in an attempt to recover the losses incurred in the business deals. In addition, and not denied by Walsh, Hall & Co., the defendants consistently gave favourable terms for loans and transactions to Itō to secure his services for other deals and for the sake of ongoing amicable relations.

BACKGROUND OF ITŌ HACHIBEI

Itō Hachibei, the plaintiff of the case, was and remains very much a historical 'mystery'. In the 1870s, he appears to have been wealthy, influential, and involved in one of the largest civil cases in treaty port Japan — after which he disappeared from the records of treaty port trade. Itō was connected to major merchants and officials of the period. For example, one of his daughters married Viscount Shibusawa Eiichi,[5] and another married the governor of Kanagawa. Although the literature, particularly Japanese scholarship, is rich with the biographical details of Itō's merchant contemporaries, nothing has been previously written about him in English or Japanese scholarship. Itō's career was not an enduring one. He was not, for example, listed in any of the official Meiji merchant rosters, possibly because his primary occupation was money lending.

Itō was very much a man of the period and location. He was a man from outside the capital and its networks, but nevertheless acheived a measure of success in business by taking advantage of the political and economic instability of the period. Like Minomura Rizaemon, his contemporary at Mitsui, he was a man from nowhere.[6] Whereas Minomura worked for the established house of Mitsui, already centuries old at this point, Itō started his own enterprises, made a fortune, lost a fortune, made another one, lost it again, and then disappeared in the span of less than thirty years. He moved himself geographically from a small rural village, into the centres of political and economic power in Edo, and eventually extended his reach to Yokohama where he became one of the first Japanese merchants of the period to form partnerships with Westerners. Financially, he traded and created numerous enterprises, which ranged from a ceramic ware store, and janitorial management, to complex arbitrage deals in Japanese coin and eventually dollars.

As he was a merchant who made his fortune in the treaty port environment of pre-Meiji and Meiji Japan, a brief digression to describe Itō's life is warranted. Although Itō probably achieved more success than most of his merchant peers, many merchants like Itō came to trade with the Westerners in the treaty ports from outside traditional merchant networks. Much of the information on Itō comes from the source, *Onna hyakuwa* (A Hundred Stories from Women of the Bakumatsu Meiji Period), which was an extraordinary series of oral histories collected by a Taishō-era reporter, Shinoda Kozo. Shinoda interviewed an unnamed female servant in service with the Itō house for one of the chapters, 'Aburabori Itokei no Hachinin Musume' ('The Eight

Daughters of the Itō House in Aburabori').[7] Although the bulk of her description centred on the domestic arrangements of the Itō house, the speaker was remarkably astute as to Itō's business dealings and biographical details.

In the maid's description, Itō came across as quite a colourful and flamboyant character. Itō was originally from the country-side near Kawagoe, in what is now Saitama Prefecture. He was born probably in the late 1820s or early 1830s, and was said to have been 'adopted', or made a *yoshi*, twenty times.[8] 'Yoshi' referred to the practice of families adopting young men as apprentices to eventually take over the family business. Young men were 'adopted' once, or a few times at most. While it may be a colourful exaggeration, twenty times was an unheard of number, and points to the uniqueness of Itō's personality. To be 'adopted' so many times is as unusual as someone today marrying twenty times. At this point in Itō's life, he went by the name of Ikusaburō. As he was a commoner, he did not have a last name. Like many Japanese men, he took various names throughout his life, depending on his age and business.

Eventually, Ikusaburō was successfully adopted by Itō Hachibei Sendai and married the eldest of Sendai's two daughters. Sendai's business, Tachi-ise-ya in the Kyobashi area of Edo, was part ceramic goods shop and part money lender to various domains. His father-in-law was nicknamed 'Honest Hachibei (Sendai)' ('Shojiki Hachibei'), because he was said to have been amiable and well liked. Perhaps because of these very traits, his business was not at all prosperous. Sendai was not skilful at recovering debts from the domains, and when he died, the house was in a state of semi-penury. After Sendai's death, Ikusaburō adopted the name of the family head and became Itō Hachibei.

His first course of action as head of the household was to resurrect the house's finances by recovering the domain loans. Using his former experience as a banker, he investigated the terms in which Sendai lent money to the domain. The debts were thought to be irrecoverable as the initial lender, Sendai, had died. The debts were referred to as 'dead horses' as the capital could no longer work for the Itō house. Of this, Itō evidently said, 'It's important to get the dead horse to fart',[9] and travelled to the various domains and where he personally recovered the sizable fortune of 10,000 *ryo*.[10] He then divided the Itō businesses, and used income from the ceramic shop to provide for his family. The capital from the money lending business became a separate enterprise which he expanded by hiring clerks.

However, in 1855, soon after his success, an earthquake and fire completely destroyed his warehouse, shop, and house. By chance, a servant had saved a box of records of his debtors. Using these documents, he raised enough money to build a modest house in the Hamamatsu-cho area in Edo. The house was near the temple of Shiba no Zojyoji which was associated with the house of Mito, one of the most powerful domains in the Tokugawa Bakufu. With the ceramic shop destroyed, he bought the rights to manage the cleaning of the temple. This enterprise employed a staff of about twenty people and provided a steady income. He once again separated his business and the profits from the cleaning enterprise which supported his family. Using various personal connections, he arranged to be employed by the Mito domain in their money lending business at the temple. Due to his skills and ability, he was promoted and became a manager of Mito's money lending enterprise.

This association with the Mito domain became the backbone of his future success. While employed in this capacity, he allegedly used the Mito name and his status as an employee of Mito domain to further his own money lending business, and was said to have made an immense profit. In 1865, he started a company, Beikoku Soba Kaishyo, which specialized in grain and rice speculation.[11] This enterprise was a success. In addition, he speculated in copper on the advice of Kawasaki Hachirōemon, who was employed in Mito's copper coin mint. By the eve of the Meiji Restoration, he had become successful enough that Mito *ronin* targeted him as a source of ready cash. The *ronin* demanded a 10,000 *ryo* 'donation' for the Tokugawa cause. Itō, unlike most merchants, curtly refused. The *ronin* jailed Itō and threatened him with decapitation. His wife and son, upon receiving news of his incarceration, convinced Mito officials to release Itō and ultimately paid the ransom. As he left his cell, Itō was said to have boasted, 'I have a 10,000 *ryo* neck'.

In the memoir in Ubukata Toshirō's book, *Meiji Taisho Kenbun* (Seen and Heard in the Meiji and Taisho Era), Itō Hachibei again appears as a freewheeling, free spending individual. In this account, he donated 30,000 *ryo* to the Bakufu cause and, according to this account, financed the Battle of Ueno. This account also described Itō's early trades with Westerners. In one deal, he cheated them by replacing oil with water. In another deal, he replaced his merchandise with rice straw. According to this account, Western merchants lodged complaints against Itō. Itō escaped any serious consequences by claiming to the Bakufu that his shady practice had patriotic motives. By cheating Westerners, he reasoned, he made Japan stronger.[12]

Itō rebounded from the collapse of the Bakufu, in order to endure another setback. After the Meiji Restoration (1868), he closed down his money speculation business, and obtained an appointment as a government lending clerk (*Kashitsuke goyo gakari*) and also a position as a senior clerk (*joseki goyo gakari*). He worked at the official lending place of the Meiji government which was located at the old estate Sakai Uta in the Koami-cho area of Tokyo. At the time of the Meiji Restoration, the new government sought 'donations' from wealthy merchants to defray the expenses of transporting the Imperial House from Kyoto to Tokyo (formally Edo). In a Meiji government document, Itō Hachibei was listed as the donor of 46,000 *ryo*, an enormous sum in its day. His bequest was also the second highest donation, second only to the house of Mitsui, the largest commercial house of the period.[13] Itō, who had thirteen years earlier literally risked his neck for 10,000 *ryo*, donated almost four and a half times as much to the new Meiji government. Itō probably contributed the money as he was in a tenuous position due to his previous service to the Mito domain, which was on the losing side of the war for Restoration.

Even after donating this sizable sum, Itō's business flourished, enough that he managed to buy a large house that once belonged to the Mito domain. The mansion housed both his family and businesses. The maid described his front business room as being large enough to accommodate up to fifty employees. She also noted a formidable weapon collection in the hallway behind the office. (Under the old regime, commoners were forbidden to bear weapons.) His family at this time had grown to eight daughters and one son, the former of which was seen as ruinous

156

in a time in which substantial dowries and bride goods were essential. In addition, he had four concubines and an army of servants. The house was managed by O-Kayo, the manager of his concubines, under whom the household flourished.

He consorted with notable men of his day and became known as a man about town, spending his fortune freely. The maid described wealthy merchants such as Tanaka Heihachi visiting and enjoying Itō's hospitality. Itō was remarkable in that he made his fortune even though he remained outside the traditional merchant guild establishment. His network of contacts included powerful merchants and officials. To further his influence, he succeeded in marrying his daughters to prominent men with much ceremony and expense.

At this time, the late 1860s and early 1870s, he became involved with speculation in dollars. He made frequent trips to Yokohama where he instructed his clerks to buy and sell, among others, currency, coal, and rice. He over-extended himself and was unable to cover his losses, and after losing his legal case against Walsh, Hall & Co. in 1876, the house collapsed; Itō was bankrupt. After persevering through poverty, fire, threats of decapitation, war, and a new government, Itō did not survive the rigours of international trade. The mansion was sold, the furniture sold or given away, and Itō closed his business. The maid stated that the house never recovered, and in the course of this research, no further records of major deals by Itō were found. However, in Ubutaka's account, Itō managed to recover: in his old age, he reportedly complained, 'I've become a beggar. I only have 20,000 *ryo*.' Yet, at the time, 20,000 *ryo* was a sizeable fortune.[14]

BACKGROUND OF WALSH, HALL & CO.

The defendant of the case, Walsh, Hall & Co., was an American firm that traded in Japan. Walsh, Hall & Co., was one of the first 'Japan firms', that is, a firm established in Japan rather than in China or elsewhere. Walsh, Hall & Co. was the first Western firm to come to Yokohama from Kanagawa.[15] As one of the leading American firms in Japan, it also maintained offices in Nagasaki and Kobe. The firm, founded in 1859 by Dr George Hall and the two Walsh brothers, John Greer and Thomas, functioned as a commission house dealing mainly in camphor, gold, silk and tea. Francis Hall, unrelated to Dr George Hall, joined the firm in 1862, and led it through a period of prosperity.[16] Under Francis Hall, the firm shipped cargoes of silk to the United States and pioneered shipping tea to the West Coast. In addition, the firm fostered close business and personal ties with Iwasaki Yatarō, the founder of Mitsubishi. Walsh, Hall & Co. also employed Masuda Takashi, the founder of Mitsui Bussan, for one year. After the departure of Francis Hall in 1866, Walsh, Hall & Co. shifted its focus from a trading and commission house 'to a firm active in the industrialization of Japan'.[17]

The 1870s was a difficult period for Walsh, Hall & Co. In this decade, the firm extended its operations into dollar speculations, munitions, rice, ships, manufactured items and machinery, of which not all were profitable. The house expanded and employed American, British, Japanese, and Chinese staff. With Iwasaki Yataro, the firm began a paper making venture in Kobe using Western continuous paper making machines in 1875. That same year, the firm also sold machines to the former lord of Hiroshima, Asano Nakagoto, for his paper making company.[18] In addition to contending with Itō's lawsuit, an economic depression in Asia drove the firm to attempt to sell its offices in Kobe.[19] Also in 1875, Robert Walsh's wife died, and he returned to the States with his children. Robert Walsh, Thomas and John Greer's brother, had come from the US to assist in the business: his departure left Walsh, Hall & Co. short handed. By the 1880s, the business had recovered, and the paper making factory was making a profit. In 1897, John Greer Walsh died, and his brother sold the remaining interests to Mitsubishi and left for London, thereby closing the firm.[20]

ROBERT W. IRWIN OF WALSH, HALL & CO.

Robert W. Irwin was Itō Hachibei's key contact at Walsh, Hall & Co. with whom he did business – Irwin was also one of the defendants of the case. Robert Irwin became a partner at Walsh, Hall & Co. in 1870 and worked at the firm until 1874.[24] Irwin himself was a British subject. In 1875, he and E. Fisher started another firm at lot 14 in Yokohama. Both Fisher & Co. and Walsh, Hall & Co. were general commission houses and had similar business practices. Masuda Takashi, a Japanese merchant and founder of Mitsui Bussan, had considerable personal affection for Irwin. He devoted a chapter in his memoirs to him, praising him for his skill and character.[22] Irwin worked with Masuda when the latter was employed as a clerk at Walsh, Hall & Co. Irwin later handled all Mitsui Bussan's foreign trade when he was a partner at Fisher & Co. In addition, Irwin also handled the military contracts of Inoue Hajime's company, Senshyu, at Fisher & Co.[23] To fill these orders, the firm expanded and established an office in London, headed by Irwin's older brother. By 1878, Irwin had left Fisher & Co. to become Mitsui Bussan's man in London. Irwin also became a diplomatic representative of Japan to the Kingdom of Hawaii. In that capacity, one of Irwin's major achievements was organizing the immigration of Japanese farm labour to the Hawaiian sugar plantations.[24]

As will be borne out in the description of the court case, Itō and Irwin met frequently in a business capacity. The unnamed maid reported that a Westerner, whom the staff nicknamed 'Foxy' (*Kitsune*) Arupin, was a regular and popular visitor to the Itō house.[25] 'Arupin' was most likely 'Irwin': 'Irwin' transliterated into Japanese is 'A-ru-in', but the 'u-i' combination is extremely awkward in Japanese so a 'P' might have been added to ease pronunciation. The maid stated that 'Foxy' Arupin worked for Ame-ichi, (Walsh, Hall & Co.), and later for Mitsui Bussan. No other Westerners of that period, whose name sounded like 'Arupin', matched that description. The 'Foxy' part of the nickname is somewhat more elusive. The name may have alluded to his colouring but this is difficult to verify. Another possible explanation may have derived from that fact that foxes in Japanese mythology were magical creatures who were crafty and occasionally treacherous. As the deals with Irwin were one of the contributing factors to the fall of the house of Itō, the maid may have been alluding to Irwin's charming and, in her eyes, perfidious nature.[26]

According to Itō's maid, Itō and Irwin also met in a social capacity. Itō Hachibei himself spoke no English,[27] but Irwin, spoke pidgin Japanese well enough that he did not always require the services of an interpreter to do business. She recounted one particular incident when Itō was entertaining Irwin. Irwin had a mistress, a Yanagibashi geisha named O-Cho-san, Miss Butterfly. One of Itō's favourite concubines was named Miss Tiger, and Irwin suggested that they swap mistresses. Itō responded, 'A Butterfly for a Tiger? Who loses in this deal?'[28] From this exchange, one could surmise that Itō and Irwin had a relationship that extended beyond mere business pleasantries.

CHRONOLOGY OF EVENTS

The partnership agreement

The events covered in the trial were business dealings that took place in 1871. The transactions were carried over to 1874, although 'friendly relations ended in 1874'.[29] Itō and Walsh, Hall & Co. first did a coal deal in 1871. The transactions went smoothly enough so that in 1871, Kumagai Iske, the *banto* (clerk) of Walsh, Hall & Co. approached Itō about doing a deal with Walsh, Hall & Co. to buy and sell foreign money. The details of the deal were as follows: the Meiji mint was about to be established, so the price of money already in circulation was expected to rise. Walsh, Hall & Co. wanted to speculate in this market with a number of short time contracts buying and selling money. Also present at this initial meeting was another merchant, Hachimoto Benzō, a friend of Kumagai. Itō and Hachimoto agreed to a second meeting in which he met directly with Irwin.

A partnership deal was reached in which all the profits or losses were to be split: 2/3 to Walsh, Hall & Co. and 1/3 to Itō. Hachimoto Benzō testified that Irwin originally offered half the profits or losses, but Itō, in a gesture that was later to his gain when the losses began to mount, protested that such a split was unfair because Walsh, Hall & Co. was supplying the bulk of the capital. Uchida Zenjirō, a Yokohama merchant who specialized in the silver market, was to act as a go-between for the two parties. Because Itō lived in Tokyo, after the money transactions were completed in Yokohama, the books were to be returned to the Yokohama offices of Walsh, Hall & Co. where Irwin was to monitor the transactions. Hachimoto Benzō was act as inspector to both parties because, as Itō stated, 'Benzō has the reputation in Yokohama [of] being an honest man'.[30] Sy Coy, Walsh, Hall & Co.'s Chinese compradore, was to assist in the sales.[31] Itō's capital contribution was about $20,000, or 20,003 *ryo*, but no agreement was made on how much each party was to contribute. Itō placed in trust a 100,085 yen security with Walsh, Hall & Co. which was requested by Kumagai.

The partnership agreement for this deal was mainly verbal, and no official document was signed. Itō stated in his testimony that he signed a contract that delineated the arrangements. Walsh, Hall & Co. denied any knowledge of such a document. Itō rejected this assertion and produced a Japanese copy of the contract written on the inside flap of the cash book which Irwin had retained. Irwin, who could not read Japanese, testified that he had not known that the writing inside the book had been a contract. Furthermore, Irwin asserted that the document of the partnership arrangement was merely a description of the agreement, but not a written formal contract.[32] Both parties agreed that the partnership began in September 1871 and agreed that the exchange business was to carry on for a few months. If the business was successful, the partnership would continue. Irwin testified that 'The agreement was only a verbal one. There was no writing whatever [sic]. There was an understanding that the defendants could retire at any moment.'[33]

Trading: September to 12 October 1871

Both parties' chronology of the activities from September to October 1871 agreed. During this time, dollars, fronted by Walsh, Hall & Co. were traded in short-term time contracts at the Yokohama general trading area. At this time, Japanese currency had not been standardized into yen, and various forms of currency were in circulation, each with a floating value. Currencies were exchanged at the 'Shosha', literally, the 'trading house'.

The Shosha was probably pidgin for Yokohama Tsushō Kawase Kaisha (Yokohama Trading and Exchange Company) which essentially functioned like a bank and a silver and bill exchange house. Yokohama merchants established the company under the administrative guidance of the government in 1870. Yokohama merchants had established it on a licence granted by the government. It was authorized to issue bills of silver to Japanese merchants. It was capitalized nominally at 200,000 *ryo* and was at lot number three in the Japanese portion of the treaty port enclave. The Shosha was reorganized into Dai-ni Kokuritsu Ginkō (The Second National Bank) in 1874. Its business transactions were with Japanese merchants only and it functioned also as a clearinghouse.[34]

In this speculation, traders bought dollars and Japanese currency at the trading house in two ways: in cash sales (in the local pidgin: *jiges*) or short-term time contracts (*sake-mono*). The time contracts lasted a matter of a few days. In a time contract, the *banto* would get a certificate (*kitte*) from the *Shosha* after depositing a sum of money, which was essentially an agreement that the transaction would be completed at a fixed future date, at that day's rate. When the appointed day arrived, the merchant would take the kitte to the Shosha, complete the exchange, and receive a complete account of the sale.

In these joint transactions, Walsh, Hall, & Co.'s compradore Sin Coy handled these trades and took orders from Irwin. Although the cash sales portion of the venture made a profit, the losses sustained from time contracts due to the volatile value of the dollar made the speculations a failure. Other speculators had similar strategies, and the scarcity of the dollars that the partnership had envisioned necessary to turn a profit never occurred. The transaction books were kept by Irwin at Walsh, Hall & Co. offices.

One of the dollar transactions involved a Japanese merchant named Nakamura Sobae. He would later become involved with some rice transactions which became ensnarled in the court dispute. Itō stated that the dollar transactions with Nakamura Sobae were part of the partnership. In this transaction, the partnership agreement was as follows: 1/2 profit or loss to Nakamura, the remaining 1/2 to be split between Walsh, Hall & Co. and Itō, 2/3 to Walsh, Hall & Co., 1/3 to Itō. The group traded $481,000 worth of transactions of which Itō claimed to have advanced some of the capital. These short term time transactions were based on the assumption that all *nibu* (*Nichibukin*, a smaller denomination of *koban* gold coin) would be cleared from the market. If the exchange was met with niboo currency, they would lose money. If the exchange was met with dollar cheques, they would gain a profit. In this case, the *nibu* coins were not cleared from the market, and the group made more losses. It was this money from the dollar transactions that was loaded onto a wagon and taken back to Walsh, Hall & Co. in the rain. As stated above, the Japanese merchants did not get a receipt due to the 'poor weather'.

Trading Losses

After a month of trade and the subsequent losses, Itō and Walsh, Hall & Co. suspended trade, after which no formal accounting of the profits and losses was made. Walsh, Hall & Co.'s *banto*, Kumagai Iske, testified that that the partnership was dissolved at this point,[35] and from then on, all transactions with Walsh, Hall & Co. money to Itō were loans.[36] Itō, on the other hand, maintained that a partnership existed, as some of the money advanced by Walsh, Hall & Co. was without commission or interest. Also, Walsh, Hall, & Co. retained his securities at their offices. This key difference was the root of their legal dispute.

In addition, Itō testified that the Irwin had a personal reason to keep the partnership open. Itō stated that Irwin wished to continue trading in order to conceal the losses made in the initial month of trade. In late 1871, Itō pressed to have accounts settled, but Itō alleged that Irwin requested a delay: 'Mr. Irwin said "Mr. [J. G.] Walsh will be displeased, and it will affect my position".'[37] In return, Irwin promised to do future 'great business'[38] with Itō, and recoup the losses with the profits. Itō agreed and stated that Irwin promised that if they did not make any future profits, they would then settle accounts and deduct payments so Itō would sustain no loss. Itō was to be advanced more money on the strength of the initial partnership agreement for further currency transactions. The terms of any money borrowed by Itō for his own activities was set at 12% per annum. Itō maintained throughout the trial that most of the subsequent deals between Walsh, Hall & Co. and himself were part of the initial partnership agreement. Furthermore, according to Itō's statements, the partnership was extended in order to cover the losses made with Irwin's deals with Itō.

The issue of 'false entries' in 1871

Itō had argued that Irwin had colluded with him so that they both could recover from the initial dollar losses. Irwin supposedly extended the partnership in order to find a new profitable deal, and Itō in return did not press for a final accounting of the losses. In Itō's case, further proof of Irwin's personal entanglement were the so-called 'False Entries' entered into the accounts. Itō's claim of $108,715.61 had included the money covered by Itō in these false entries. Pressed by Irwin, Itō alleged that after the dollar trades in October 1871, Itō had written false entries in his account book to make the transactions appear more successful than they were. He testified that he had entered the amounts as a personal favour to Irwin instead of pressing for a settlement in which the losses were to be divided. An account book contained the receipts and payments of the exchange business. Irwin had written notes in it, indicating that he had, at the very least, looked at the books. Two false entries were made in the account book totaling 200,000 *ryo* and $239,000. Itō testified that Irwin was worried about the impact that the losses would have had on his position at Walsh, Hall & Co.; J. G. Walsh had returned from a trip to the US in the fall of 1871. On the other hand, members of Walsh, Hall & Co. alluded to a conspiracy by Itō and his staff, and Irwin denied knowledge of the entries.

The accounting procedure became another issue in the court case. In the books supplied in court as evidence, the two account entries in question were marked with only a half seal, rather than a full seal. Seals, or *hanko*, were equivalent to a signature, and were a mark of authenticity; for an account entry to be official, it must have had both a half seal and a full seal. A half seal, *warefu*, was used only as a tally – without a full seal it was not offically part of the account book. A Japanese lawyer was supplied by the plaintiff's legal defence as a kind of expert witness to explain the legality of the *hanko*. Although denied by Irwin, W. H. Talbot, a trained accountant, certified that the accounts were accurate, barring a few calculation errors and the false entries.[39]

False entries in the account book required collusion because the books had to pass inspection of many parties, including clerks and inspectors. Hachimoto Benzō testified that he believed Irwin had acted fraudulently when he requested the false accounts. Hachimoto initially refused to make the entries, as did Itō. Eventually, as a favour to Irwin, they testified that they had listed the entries as 'Adzukari Adzuke' (or *azikan azuki* retained money), and Irwin promised to repay the sum, which in Itō's accounting, Irwin partially paid in instalments. Itō and Hachimoto Benzō rationalized their actions by calling the entries normal, but incomplete, transactions as Irwin promised to come through with the money. Because the amounts were not fully paid, Itō stated, 'If the entries had been corrected there would have been no lawsuit like the present one.'[40] Irwin, in his testimony, confronted Itō's testimony with entries from Walsh, Hall & Co.'s official accounts.

Further Transactions and the Lost $40,000 Check

At the end of the dollar trade, business transactions between Itō and Irwin did not cease. In late 1871, the financial speculation ceased, but the securities deposited by Itō into the care of Walsh, Hall & Co. had still not been returned. At the time of this agreement, Itō stated that he believed he was owed about $100,000 by Walsh, Hall & Co. On the other had, Irwin claimed that Itō owed Walsh, Hall & Co. at that time $239,000. Itō, either acting on behalf of the partnership or for his own interests, borrowed money from Walsh, Hall & Co. on a number or occasions. One particular $40,000 'cheque' (advance) apparently became lost in the transactions and became an issue in the court case. The 'cheque' referred to by both Itō and Irwin appears to be used as a bill, rather than a cheque in the modern sense. Both Itō and the defendants agreed that Itō had borrowed $40,000 in late 1871. However, Itō asserted that he did not use the money: the transaction he had planned fell though. Itō reported that he returned the cheque, but did not get a receipt as the clerks were busy at the time. Subsequently, Itō stated that he visited the offices of Walsh, Hall & Co. on numerous occasions, as well as sending his son to settle the business. Because Walsh Hall Co. had never recovered the cheque, no receipt was given to Itō. Walsh, Hall & Co., on the other hand, testified that they had no record of Itō returning the cheque.[41]

Rice Speculation with Nakamura Sobae

Further evidence on the issue of when the partnership ended was provided by the rice speculations with Nakamura Sobae.

According to Itō, Irwin had suggested that they enter into this new speculation in order to cover their losses of late 1871. The scheme was based on the rumour that exports would be deregulated that year. They reasoned that if they bought large amounts of rice, they would make a profit when the demand for rice increased. Itō claimed that with Nakamura Sobae, he and the defendant entered into a secret partnership. Hachimoto Benzō testified that he alone facilitated the deals with Irwin in Yokohama. Like the initial partnership, no written document was produced. The secretiveness of the deal was warranted, according to Itō, because the spread of news of an impending rice export could affect their profits.[42]

In addition, Itō indicated that he believed this deal was an extension of the original partnership agreement; they entered into the speculation in order to re-coup the losses from the foreign exchange business. The securities that Itō had deposited with Walsh, Hall & Co. still remained in their offices. Walsh, Hall & Co. advanced capital to Itō, and some of the transactions were without commission or interest. In order to finance rice sales, advances of $125,000 and $15,000 from Walsh, Hall & Co. were used, as well as some of the money from previous exchange transactions.[43]

Irwin, on the other hand, denied altogether the existence of a deal with Itō and Nakamura. To support their case, a Walsh, Hall & Co. accountant produced account books contained no indication of a partnership between Itō and Nakamura. Irwin stated that the Walsh, Hall & Co. money used by Itō was advanced to him for trade on his own account – all risks and profits Itō garnered were his alone. Irwin testified that Itō was trying to save his own business with the rice speculations, using money loaned to him from Walsh, Hall & Co. If this was in fact the case, the money was clearly advanced to Itō on favourable terms: in late 1871, Itō borrowed a further $20,000 and 5,000 *ryo* from Walsh, Hall & Co. for the rice business with Nakamura Sobae but gave no security for the funds.

Unfortunately for all those involved, the rice speculation was not a success. The liberalization of rice exports did not occur until 1872 and the rice speculations all sustained losses. A number of trades were made with Japanese rice brokers, some of whom testified that they did not have any dealings with any Westerners. However, this in itself was not an indication that there was no deal between Nakamura, Walsh, Hall & Co., and Itō. The actual currency transactions for the initial dollar trades were done by Walsh, Hall & Co.'s Japanese staff or by Itō's group. To further confuse matters, at some point after the dollar trade, Uchida Zenjirō, who worked with Itō and Irwin, became an independent rice broker and had been part of the rice trade machinations. Uchida's relationship to the rice deals remained unclear: Uchida may have had some incentive to testify that rice transactions were part of the original partnership.

The Mito Han Deal and Other Transactions

Whether or not Itō and Walsh, Hall & Co. were in a partnership, they continued to have business relations after the rice deals. For example, in December 1871, Itō borrowed $10,000 in drafts and in 1872, he borrowed $25,000. In the period of 1872-4, Itō's financial state deteriorated and he borrowed frequently from Walsh, Hall & Co. when he found himself short of funds. Walsh, Hall & Co. continued to accommodate Itō with favourable terms. In some of the transactions with Itō, Walsh, Hall & Co. charged neither a commission nor interest on the cash. Itō continued to borrow from Walsh, Hall & Co. until the his last transaction in January 1874 for $5000. Until this point business relations were, in Itō's words, 'exceeding pleasant'.[44]

Up until the court case, Itō and Walsh, Hall & Co. arrived at an arrangement in which both profited. The preferential treatment of Itō by Walsh, Hall & Co. was exchanged for Itō's expertise and influence. This was particularly evident in the machinations in a Mito domain deal on which Itō and Walsh, Hall & Co. both testified. Itō had been involved in the financial workings of the Mito domain for some years. After the Meiji restoration, the new government began the process of dismantling the old domains and their finances. Walsh, Hall & Co. had facilitated a loan from Itō to Mito han of 40,000 *ryo* which was later increased to 50,000 *ryo*; the Mito domain was indebted to Itō. In 1872, Walsh, Hall & Co., through Irwin, collected the debt from the Meiji Government for Itō without commission. The money collected was used to clear some of the debt that Itō had with Walsh, Hall & Co. According to John Greer Walsh, the company forfeited a commission worth $18,000 as a favour to Itō:[45] Walsh, Hall & Co. kept the money and deducted the sum from Itō's account: 'It was done merely as a matter of friendship to save Itō from bankruptcy, loss, and disgrace.'[46] By late March 1872, by Walsh, Hall & Co.'s calculations, Itō owed $9,902.46. Hachimoto Benzō borrowed $3000 more on Itō's account, bringing the total to $12,902.46[47]. Irwin stated that he waived interest on the account as yet another favour to Itō.

At this point another deal was made with Itō: Irwin testified that he offered to waive the remaining debt of $12,902.46 and pay Itō a further $10,000 for his assistance in the deal. Irwin stated that he intended for Itō to use his influence over his son-in-law, the governor of Kanagawa, to recover a debt owed to Walsh, Hall & Co. by the Japanese government for money the company had advanced in connection with a land reclamation project on the Yoshida Shinden site.[48] According to Irwin, Itō attempted to recover the funds but ultimately failed. With this outcome, the deal was withdrawn.

The Issue of Securities

The issue of the misuse of Itō's securities was another factor; each party had conflicting notions on their appropriate use. As stated above, Itō had deposited the bonds with Walsh, Hall & Co.[49] According to Itō, the securities were to be kept in trust; no further use of them had been authorized by him: 'The securities were placed in the hands of the defendants to be used in case my contribution of 20,000 *ryo* was insufficient.' Itō stated that he thought handing Walsh, Hall & Co. the bonds was the same as keeping them in his strong box or in a bank. Both parties agreed that the securities were never returned after the end of the dollar transactions; in fact, they were still in the possession of Walsh, Hall & Co. at the start of the trial.

In addition, there was some debate on the securities themselves: Walsh, Hall & Co. had never verified that the securities that Itō had pledged were worth the value he stated. The bulk of the securities were *hansatsu*, or bonds issued by the various domains. To complicate matters, there was some debate on whether the value of the bonds had changed between 1871 and 1875.

In October 1872, Itō invested in another dollar speculation. Irwin testified that Itō had asked to borrow from Walsh, Hall & Co. $25,000 on his account, but Walsh, Hall & Co. did not have the cash at that time. Itō's speculation was based on some insider information and rumours on the activities of the Japanese Finance Ministry's currency operations.[50] Irwin testified that at this point he had believed that the partnership with Itō had ended in October 1871, and produced accounts and bank documents that supported his claim. Any further deals, though financed by Walsh, Hall & Co., would be Itō's responsibility.[51] Walsh, Hall & Co. borrowed $25,000 from the Deutsche Bank using Itō's securities, and charged Itō the interest rate of the bank. Walsh, Hall & Co. took a 3% commission.

On this particular transaction, the securities could not be produced at the start of the trial because they were held as a security on the loan that Walsh, Hall & Co. had taken out. Itō testified that he regarded this as a breach of confidence. In his view, the securities were only to be used in event of a dire emergency. Irwin, on the other hand, claimed that there had been a verbal agreement in which Itō's securities could be pledged by Walsh, Hall & Co. for $25,000 from the Deutsche Bank, and provided letters from the bank to support his claim that Itō had authorized loans made on the securieties.[52] Clearly, Walsh, Hall & Co. and Itō had not defined the terms of usage of the securities.

Account Settlement

This generally good relationship came to an end when T. Walsh did not provide a one million dollar loan for a government bond speculation suggested by Itō. Itō stated that he spoke to Irwin about the deal and the latter had agreed to bring the matter up with T. Walsh. Unless the previous account of about $12,000 was settled first, T. Walsh refused to grant the loan on account of the large amount and the risk. Walsh, Hall & Co. still tried to accommodate Itō and offered to lend instead a smaller sum of $25,000 borrowed from a bank. Kumagai Iske, Walsh, Hall & Co.'s *banto*, alleged that Itō, Hachimoto Benzo and Nakamura Sobae requested another loan of $600,000. The request was refused by Walsh, Hall & Co., but the plaintiffs protested. Walsh, Hall & Co., in response, granted a no-interest loan of $481,000 on the following conditions 1) the money was to be returned in three days, and 2) Itō had to make good on all the losses in the exchange transactions. Walsh, Hall & Co. did not have the capital for the loan and borrowed it from a bank for Itō. Kumagai Isake claimed that the loan was made, not as an extension of the former partnership, but as a gesture of goodwill so that Itō could make up the losses from the prior speculations. Kumagai Isake also alleged that because this deal had followed the currency speculation, Itō was aware that it was not part of the original partnership.[53] In yet another differing account, Hachimoto Benzō claimed that accounts were settled with himself, Taketani, and Irwin present: Itō was not present. Benzō concurred with the account balances reached by the group but did ask for more time to pay – he requested that the payment be delayed as he needed more time to obtain the requisite funds.

All parties agreed that it was after Walsh, Hall & Co.'s refusal of the one million loan on Itō's terms that the relationship soured. Itō rejected the firm's counter offer and stated he regarded this refusal as tantamount to Irwin reneging on the earlier agreement to enter upon a speculation to recoup the losses sustained in the dollars and rice trade. Itō described himself as annoyed and inconvenienced, and Irwin described him as a 'devil',[54] especially when Irwin stated that he would not assist Itō in the suit. At this point Itō started insisting that the accounts should be settled. When Walsh, Hall & Co.'s calculations did not agree with Itō's accounts, he initiated court action.

THE VERDICT: COURT SUMMARY AND JUDGEMENT

The case approached a close in December 1875 with Itō's lawyer, Dickins, threatening to withdraw. The counsel for the plaintiff cited various nebulous reasons which included Itō admitting a debt to Walsh, Hall & Co., problems with the accounts, and witnesses.[55] The court encouraged him to persevere, and Dickins represented Itō to the end of the case in January 1876. Dickins may also have been motivated by another factor; namely, Itō was low on funds. By 8 November 1875, court costs had risen to the point that Itō was asked to deposit $700 in addition to the $300 he had initially deposited.[56] Itō could not produce this amount, and the case was delayed for a few days in order to allow Itō to borrow the money.

In January 1876, General Van Buren, the judge of this case, ruled a verdict in favour of the defendant. The court found that Itō was indebted to the amount of $31,291.59 to Walsh, Hall & Co. Upon repayment, Walsh, Hall & Co. was ordered to return the securities. In addition, Itō was to pay court costs. Two assessors, whose assent would block any further appeals, concurred with court's verdict.[57]

To arrive at this judgement, the court considered the following questions:

1st — Did the partnership terminate on 12 October 1871?

2nd — Was the balance of accounts agreed to on 22 November, and a final balance afterwards settled and accepted by both parties as the amount due by Plaintiff to defendants, [sic] viz: $12,902.62?

3rd — Is there any fraud or mistake, sufficient to set aside this agreement, if made, on the 22nd of November?

4th — Was the $40,000 loan, made 12 November, paid back?

5th — Were the securities described in the petition, deposited with the defendants in the partnership transactions, or used to secure repayment of loans made to Plaintiff?

6th — Was there any partnership between Plaintiff [and] defendants in the rice speculations?[58]

The court's ruling was based on the assumption that the formal partnership ended in October 1871. From this assumption, the majority of the questions became academic. Itō had agreed in his court testimony that as of November 1871, he had owed Walsh, Hall & Co. $12,902.62. No testimony was given in which fraud or mistake was shown to nullify the contract. The testimony about the false accounting entries was given by the plaintiff as evidence of motivation for the partnership's continuation. It was not a 'fraud or mistake' that would legally nullify the partnership. As for the $40,000 missing cheque, as Itō could not prove that he had returned the cheque, the court found in favour of the defendants. The amount of $40,000 was included in the settlement amount. The issue of the appropriate use of the securities was never clearly resolved. The court ruled that the securities were not misused when Walsh, Hall & Co. placed them with a bank as a loan collateral for Itō. However, the court also stipulated that the securities were to be returned upon Itō's payment of his debt. As the court had decided that the original partnership had ended, the court ruled that no partnership existed for the rice speculation. Thus, the losses from the rice speculations were seen by the court as Itō's responsibility alone.

It is difficult to make an assessment on the 'justice' of this trial as all parties seemingly gave misleading and conflicting testimony to suit their own ends. However, as an American court in the nineteenth century, the court officers, witnesses, and lawyers all displayed their own biases and prejudices. For example, all Western witnesses were allowed to stay in the court room and listen to the proceedings. On the other hand, Japanese witnesses were asked to leave so as not to be tempted to collude: 'His Honour. . .without throwing any imputation unpon [sic] the Japanese character, thought that Japanese witnesses, by being present whilst others were being examined, were very apt to get a hold of the same tale.'[59] All major Japanese witnesses, such as Hachimoto Benzō, were asked whether they were paid to give favourable testimony to Itō. When Benzō was ill and could not appear on a particular court date, the court rejected a Japanese doctor's testimony and considered it insufficient. The plaintiff was ordered to pay a Western doctor to examine Benzō and testify in court on his illness. In another incident, a Japanese lawyer giving information on the legal inadmissibility under Japanese law of *warefu* or 'half seal', was asked whether a jinricksha (rickshaw) man could be 'a coolie one day, and a lawyer the next'.[60]

THE INFORMALITY OF TRADE

The purpose of this chapter is to illustrate the informality with which Japanese and Western merchants traded with one another. In this particular case, a fortune was traded, literally, on the strength of a verbal agreement. Furthermore, the two men who made it did not fluently speak each other's language. Throughout the entire trial of Itō and Walsh, Hall & Co.'s interests with one another, neither side produced a single formal contract acknowledged by the other party. The original partnership arrangements, for example, were informal. Money was exchanged without a receipt: both parties agreed that Nakamura

Sobae returned a wagon load of money without getting a receipt. No documentation was produced in court on the Walsh, Hall & Co. deal over the Yoshida Shinden land. Unlike the $40,000 missing cheque, these informal deals did not cause problems. Itō may well have been misleading the court about the return of the $40,000 cheque. However, he made the argument that he never received a receipt for the cheque because Walsh, Hall & Co. were busy. Also, both the defendant and plaintiff testified that they initiated informal business arrangements.

Another feature of this case is that of alliances were based on business dealings, not nationality. Many histories of the treaty port draw a distinction between Westerners and Japanese, and often present the relationship as a contentious one; that is, Japanese merchants were seen as a discrete entity in competition with Western merchants. This is not to say that this is an inaccurate description of Japanese and Western merchants: each group had a distinct set of advantages and obstacles to contend with in the treaty ports. However, in the business deals described by this case, the lines of distinction were based on business relationships. For example, Japanese clerks of Walsh, Hall & Co. remained loyal to their firm. Independent Japanese business men, such as the rice brokers interviewed towards the end of the trial, did not give favourable testimony to Itō.

Another major issue in the case is the extent to which interpersonal relationships were valued by both the Japanese and Western businessmen. Social capital, in this case, was a highly valued commodity. Business was done on the strength of mutual promises. If we assume that Itō and the staff of Walsh, Hall & Co. were not merely foolhardy, the arrangements were vague to serve some purpose. The lack of formal written contract may have allowed for flexibility in the transactions. As the market for dollar speculation was extremely volatile, the parties needed flexibility in their arrangements; formal arrangements, such as one with a set start and end date of the partnership, would only serve to hamper the transactions. Negotiating every detail of the deals might have taken more time and resources than the parties were willing to expend. Many of the transactions required rapid decision making. Both parties may have planned to depend on the strength of relationship to resolve disputes, instead of resorting to the authorities.

Also notable in this case is the importance placed on the relationship between Itō and Irwin. As asserted by the defendant's counsel, the issue of Irwin's special deals with Itō, ranging from the false entries to future profit in order to defray past losses, may have all been entirely fiction. Ness, Walsh, Hall & Co.'s lawyer, in his closing arguments asserted that 'The plea of fraud that had been raised by Itō in regard to these balances, which had been called false ones by Itō, was an Eastern idea.'[61] Some evidence did support the defendants' claims that Itō and his collaborators were perpetuating fraud. Irwin claimed that Itō offered him 30% of whatever he recovered if Irwin assisted him in the trial. Irwin refused, and he reported that Itō seemed annoyed that Irwin had rejected his request.[62] Another issue was over a letter that Itō had allegedly written admitting that he owed Walsh, Hall & Co. money. This letter, exhibit 14 in the case, was written by Itō.[63] However, Itō seems to have attempted to manipulate events so that the letter appeared to originate from Walsh, Hall & Co. Taketani Hanjirō, an interpreter for Walsh, Hall & Co., testified that Kumagai Shoseke falsely testified about not knowing the origins of Exhibit 14. He also stated that Itō offered money for misleading testimony.[64] Other problems with Itō's version of events lay with possibly forged evidence: Irwin pointed out discrepancies in the accounts, and asserted that exchange rates were manipulated in Itō's books so that it appeared that Walsh, Hall & Co. owed Itō money. In addition some documents supposedly written by him were not recognized by Irwin as his own.[65]

Of course, Irwin may have been misleading the court for his own ends – for example, the documents may well have been written by Irwin. Some of Walsh, Hall & Co.'s witnesses, such as Kudzusaya Chijirō, were exposed as unreliable or untrustworthy men.[66] Also, Irwin himself testified that until the breakdown in the relationship, he regarded Itō and his colleagues as 'honest men'.[67] In addition, witnesses testified that Itō would not knowingly commit fraud. The case also brought to light the problems within Walsh, Hall & Co. itself; the process of authorizing deals was not at all transparent. In particular, some unauthorized use of the Walsh, Hall & Co. seals occurred in daily transactions. A *hanko*, or seal, would render a document legally admissible in Japan, much like a signature in the West. For example, Kumagai Shoseke (Shoski), Kumagai Isake's son, had a Walsh, Hall & Co. seal made in order to transact business for Walsh, Hall & Co. However, Walsh, Hall & Co. did not know of its existence. It does not appear that Kumagai Shoseke intentionally misused the seal. He testified that he made the seal for convenience and to facilitate Walsh, Hall & Co.'s transactions with Japanese merchants.[68] We can surmise that Walsh, Hall & Co.'s employees transacted business with little supervision.

Ultimately, the losses of the Itō-Walsh, Hall & Co. partnership did jeopardize Irwin's position at the firm, just as he allegedly feared in Itō's testimony. Although the exact reason is not clear, Irwin's relationship with John Greer Walsh was reportedly not a happy one, and Irwin left the firm after Walsh's return from the US. At the time of the trial, Irwin had left Walsh, Hall & Co. and was at lot #14, working as a partner in Fisher & Co.[69] The dispute may have been a contributing factor in the deterioration of relations within the firm. Interestingly, at the time of the trial in the British consular court, Irwin's firm Fisher & Co. was a defendant against a 'Mr. Middleton' over a debt.[70] Irwin as well as J. M. Smith, another former Walsh, Hall, & Co. employee, testified in both trials. Like the Itō case, this case was also about some confused financial arrangements in which few formal contracts were made. Unlike this case, Irwin and Fisher & Co. lost the case.

It is also interesting to examine Itō's testimony on his business relationship with Irwin; namely, he placed great importance on the personal favours that they made to one another. As discussed above, Itō may have been giving misleading testimony, but even if he was, he told a story that he believed would be credible in court – either because this description of events was true, or because it was plausible. In Itō's testimony, he had one relationship with Irwin, and another relationship with Irwin's firm. That is, Itō emphasized the importance of Irwin's motivation for the false entries and the continuation of partnership because it benefited his colleague Irwin. The benefit to Walsh, Hall & Co. was tied to the benefit that Irwin received from the deal.

Let us assume for a moment that events transpired as Itō described them; Itō and Irwin had a deal with Irwin to continue the partnership with further speculation to recoup losses. In the event that they found new speculation in which they turned a profit, both parties gained: Irwin would be in the good graces of his employers, and Itō would have recovered his losses. If this agreement had in fact been made by Itō and Irwin, it appears they did not make contingency plans in case the speculations went sour. Stewart Macaulay observed similar behaviour among auto parts sellers in twentieth century Wisconsin. Lawyers who advised businessmen complained of legal problems resulting from the vagueness of their agreements. When bargaining, the business community often talked of pleasant generalities on what was to happen, but failed to reach agreements on any of the hard, unpleasant questions of contingencies until they were forced to do so by a lawyer.[71]

When the speculations were a failure, both parties stood to lose: Irwin would lose favour in his employer's eyes and Itō would be in further debt. In the course of the actual deals, the losses drove Irwin to cut his losses, leaving Itō with what amounted to the proverbial 'hot potato'. If the speculation were successful, all parties stood to gain. Both parties appear to have made an agreement with little thought to the consequences of the deal going sour.

Both parties stated that after Walsh, Hall & Co.'s refusal of a loan for the government bond speculations, the relationship deteriorated. If a partnership existed, Itō embraced a wider view of 'partnership'. Although Itō claimed to have a contract which outlined the partnership, he referred to the agreement in vague terms. If the transactions went well, the partnership would continue. It seems ironic that Itō, at the start of relations, was the trader who insisted on drawing up a formal document. Irwin, on the other hand, perhaps covering himself legally, explained the deal as an agreement which he terminated after the dollar losses. Walsh, Hall & Co.'s official position in court was that any responsibilities and liabilities that occurred outside the time bracket were to be borne independently. Clearly the rice and currency deals did not go well. However, Itō, at least in court, took the prospect of success as the basis for the continuation of relations. Irwin's offer of loans and future recovery of losses suggested to him that the contract was in abeyance, but not terminated.

If we were to accept Itō's assumption that an indefinite partnership existed, this threw further relations into a gray area in that moneys from Walsh, Hall & Co. were no longer loans, but rather quasi-interpartnership transactions. Both sides attested that they had cordial relations after the financial losses. Moreover, most of these other transactions were not part of the partnership; Itō borrowed money for his own projects, and there was no dispute over the responsibilities of the profits and losses. Yet, three unofficial deals, all contested by the other party, were seen by Itō as part of the original deal to recoup losses. In addition, Walsh, Hall & Co. gave Itō access to funds for these projects on extremely favourable terms. That is commissions and interest were reduced or waived altogether.

Itō alleged that the money loaned for the rice speculation was part of a partnership deal. Irwin stated that there was no partnership and this was a separate transaction. As there was an explicit end date to the contract at least in Walsh, Hall & Co.'s view, the court supported Irwin's argument. In the last speculation attempt, he asked for a loan but was refused. Itō's fury suggested that he thought Irwin was not fulfilling a personal obligation to him. As described above, Itō and Irwin had enjoyed a cordial relationship, close enough, to put it crassly, to suggest swapping mistresses. It appears that this deal superseded any agreement made to Walsh, Hall & Co., especially as Itō allegedly did him the personal favour of creating the 'false' transactions. Irwin's unwillingness to continue the partnership with further transactions was tantamount to a betrayal – a defection.

Walsh, Hall & Co., furthermore, used the argument of personal favour as well. They claimed that they extended various loans to Itō Hachibei in order to spare him – a 'trusted' business partner, a friend and colleague – the ignominy of ruin. Thus, the risks stemming from the informality of the deals were balanced with personal favour. Each party had different expectations of this partnership but vagueness on the exact amount owed by each party allowed each party to continue trading relations. They were, in a way, bound to each other because of this debt. Mutually beneficial opportunities were sought out as a result of the quasi-partnership. In short, from Itō's claims, we can see two different promises; the promise Irwin personally made to Itō to cover for the losses and the one made with Walsh, Hall & Co. to suspend the accounts and borrow at low interest.

In the court's ruling, however, these personal obligations were essentially ignored and the letter of the contract, in as much as there was one, was used as a basis for the judgement. The court decision simplified the issues to questions that could be answered 'yes' or 'no'. If we examine Gen. van Buren's judgement, Irwin was absolved from any wrongdoing. The gray areas of the business relationship were not addressed in the court. Irwin and Itō traded and worked together on a regular basis and in the process made highly specific agreements with one another. In fact, the agreements became so personalized that they became impossible to accommodate with Walsh, Hall & Co.'s interests. Itō and Irwin attempted to make agreements that bound their interests together, but ultimately, they failed with spectacular results.

TOWARDS IMPLICATIONS AND THEORY

No greater responsibility ever rested with Foreign Representatives than with those who first came to Japan. Their position was one of honor, and should have been carried out in fidelity and justness, and we should now be reaping incalculable benefits [from] commerce [and] prospering, but the records prove that they were selfish, divided and that their main object was to lower the Japanese to the position of stubborn brutes in order to gratify personal spleen, when unable to combat them on with ideas of right and fairness. That there has been something radically wrong in our Diplomacy none will deny.

The Japan Herald, 31 May 1862

I N A . G R E I F ' S study of medieval Maghribi traders, he showed that these traders did not default on contracts with one another because they had internalized the 'fear of God'. Greif also makes a convincing argument on the economic motivation behind their 'honest' behaviour – namely, the fear of damage to their reputations and the need for coalitions.[1] Treaty port merchants on the other hand, were unlike the Maghribi because they were not a tightly knit group with the same cultural assumptions. In situations like this, law is often seen as the forum to resolve disputes and create social order. However, as we shall see, the courts in the treaty ports had uncertain authority. In addition, in this particular case, law, it appears, was not equipped to enforce future contracts or produce norms. In a market without a shared business culture, law in itself is not sufficient in creating commercial or social order. This chapter seeks to raise issues and give some shape to the implications of the behaviour of treaty port merchants to law.

ASSUMPTIONS AND OPPORTUNISM

In the case of the merchants of the treaty ports, although they came from a variety of business cultures, their behavioural assumptions in trade relationships were not necessarily disparate. One could assume that both Western and Japanese merchants acted out of bounded rationality. As evinced in the bargain money trades and the long term relationship between Itō Hachibei and Walsh, Hall & Co., both Japanese and Western merchants did not verify or understand all details of their agreements. Assumptions were based on personal experience, and affinity, rather than reliable information, sometimes drove the deals. However, the assumptions based upon their experiences trading among their own business communities did not necessarily apply to their foreign counterparts. Such false assessments could lead to conflicts within the treaty ports.

Both Japanese and Western merchants complained that opportunism was rife. If we were to believe the Western objections, only the Japanese were guilty of this trait; it was alleged that the Japanese made contracts they never intended to keep, and substituted shoddy inferior goods instead of delivering the correct order. Westerners accused the Japanese merchants of making contracts and using the courts to collect damages as a means of speculation. On the other hand, in Japanese diaries and letters, merchants assert that most Westerners were thieves and frauds who withheld the true market value of silk and tea in the West in order to keep treaty port prices low. They also claimed that Western merchants exploited the 'inspection' process to 'wiggle' out of unprofitable deals. Furthermore, Westerners accused one another of venality, fraud, and a general lack of 'commercial morality'. In short, both Japanese and Westerners used guile, deceit, or withheld information for personal gain – the very definition of opportunism.[2]

The contractual breaches may have been a result of some Japanese merchants regarding business transactions with Western merchants as 'windfall opportunities'. In the case of the merchants in the treaty ports, such deals were essentially single shot games. In such games, there was a strong temptation to defect. The merchants might have had low expectations of future transactions: some Japanese merchants may have not been willing to invest the time and energy to build relationships with Western merchants.

In the early period, most Japanese could not foresee that the Japanese treaty ports would remain open. Violence between domain leaders and Westerners and all Japanese associated with them only served to underscore the official Bakufu policy of isolation. The official Bakufu position, in the early period, was a policy of expulsion of the foreigners. During the reparation crisis, Western diplomats with the exception of US envoy Harris, left Edo for Yokohama. This gesture was made in protest and conveyed the Treaty Power's displeasure with the Bakufu's handling of the attacks on Westerners. The result was not as Western diplomats envisioned. Some Bakufu officials saw the withdrawal of diplomatic staff as a sort of victory for the doctrine of isolation. For merchants whose trade had already been disrupted this retreat only fed the rumours that the Westerners were leaving Japan. Early relations were characterized by violence and uncertainty; not an auspicious start to trade relations.

Even after it became clear that the treaty ports would remain open, the borders of the treaty port were permeable to the Japanese. The treaty port borders were a sort of paradox; the restrictions on travel were both a barrier and at the same time a sieve. Western merchants were sealed into the treaty ports in that they could not go into the interior to verify information, check crops, or goods. In the same way, Japanese merchants could not leave Japan to verify the same type of information in Western markets. Yet, these Japanese merchants were relatively free from penalty if they chose to default from their contracts. If a disagreement or debt arose that they could not pay, they could leave for the interior and escape their obligations. Rural merchants who had few permanent interests in the Yokohama or Edo merchant networks could easily leave the area. Japanese were in a position to create their own 'windfall'. Accrue enough wealth and debt and disappear. The Japanese government did not pursue Japanese defaulters. Western merchants could default in the same way as the

Japanese merchants; they too could leave the treaty port and escape their obligations. They could take the next ship leaving port to China or the West. Once they left the port area for another country, the local authorities were effectively powerless to pursue them.

Asset specificity varied from deal to deal within the treaty ports. In some cases, such as the case of Itō Hachibei vs. Walsh, Hall, & Co., it was evident that both Itō and Walsh, Hall, & Co. invested considerable amounts of capital and time in their relationship and in their complex and confusing contracts. This deal and the agreement associated with this deal was asset specific. Some bargain money cases were also asset specific. Other deals were not and were simple, sometimes instantaneous, spot contracts for goods and services that could be had by any number of individuals in the port area.

Not surprisingly, one merchant's perception of contractual 'fraud' may well have been the other's perceived obligations, as was often the case in treaty port contract disputes. In the example of silk deals, in the inspection of the goods described by Masuda, some Western merchants used trade procedure to escape their contractual obligations. For a Japanese merchant such as Masuda, the main objection lay in the perception that the contracts were unequal. A Western merchant often kept silk that was unpaid for in his warehouse, thus making the Japanese merchant's bargaining position weak. At the same time, the Western merchant could breach the contract without repercussions.

The inspection itself may also have been seen by 'honest' Japanese merchants as an expression of a lack of trust, which in turn added to the perceptions and expectations of mutual antagonism. From the 'honest' Western merchant's perspective, the inspection allowed him to protect his business from the possibility of the Japanese merchant's fraud. Adding to this situation, some 'dishonest' Western merchants used the inspection period to contact buyers by telegraph in China (and the later the West) to verify whether the silk could be sold at a profit. If they could not, they stated that the silk was '*Pe-ke*' – pidgin deriving from the Malay word meaning 'no good' – as it did not match sample. Masuda noted that such a charge was often an excuse to unload silk rather than a real objection to the goods.[3] Under such conditions, a Japanese merchant might well have decided that Western merchants were untrustworthy and chosen to default himself to protect his interests and seek short term windfalls.

In other cases, details and descriptions were at times seen as a *term* essential to the fulfilment of the transaction. For example, the colour of a lamp – white instead of green – resulted in the re-negotiation of one particular contract. To one merchant, the colour was a trifling detail; to the other, a crucial detail which determined the saleability of the item. In other cases, because the contract was vague, or because changes were not incorporated into the actual written contract, merchants sometimes used the letter of the contract to escape their obligations.

TRUST AND OPEN-ENDED CONTRACTS

One possible explanation of the lack of formal written contracts is that the merchants attempted to build a web of trust relationships. The lack of contracts may have been an attempt to signal to one another that they were willing to take the other's word and sought a trust relationship. If a trustworthy trading partner was found, merchants may have figured the risks were worth the gain or could be otherwise absorbed in the prices. Both Western and Japanese merchants in their home markets made complex transactions without contracts or with only cursory contracts. Constantly referring to contract may have struck the merchants as not only evidence that their counterpart did not trust them, but also indicated to them that the other party himself was not trustworthy. If trust was not extended, it was unlikely to be returned. Formal enforcement, such as law, was almost non-existent; thus the question, why bother with contracts at all? In the case of the contracts in Treaty Port Japan, it was very much a case in which parties had to have a vested interest for the contract to succeed. This is not to say that parties reneged on every contract that was to their disadvantage. If a contract was to their disadvantage, the contract may have been fulfilled for the promise of future deals.

Returning to the example of Stewart Macaulay's study, such behaviour was also described in the US automobile industry. He illustrates the extent to which a business community avoided legal constructs and solutions.[4] For his work, he defined contracts in two ways: (a) Rational planning of the transaction with careful provision for as many future contingencies as can be foreseen, and (b) the existence or use of actual or potential legal sanction to induce performance of the exchange or to compensate for non-performance. In this model, spot exchanges were excluded but parole contracts could count.

Macaulay found that businessmen tended to trust each other and thus make flexible agreements. On one hand, Macaulay found that many business exchanges in the planning stage did reflect a high degree of contract law usage in four categories – description, contingencies, defective performance, and legal sanctions. But, as he found, this group of businessmen preferred to rely on informal venues of enforcement and interpersonal relations to compel enforcement. Exchanges in non-speculative areas were usually adjusted without dispute and without using legal mechanisms. Macaulay argues: 'Businessmen may welcome a measure of vagueness in the obligations they assume so that they may negotiate matters in light of the actual circumstances.'[5] As a result, he argues the opportunity for demonstrating good faith during the life of the exchange relationship often is present.

Another major point of Macaulay's research was that commercial actors loathed to resort to law – litigation was a solution of last resort. Many businessmen expressed a reservation on using lawyers or an over-preoccupation with legality; this was not seen as 'behaving decently'.[6] Although it is prudent to contemplate the repercussions of non-performance, such concerns were seen as lacking in good faith; the business community asserted a belief that such attention to detail indicated a lack of trust which got in the way of good relations. In the event of a conflict, most businessmen telephoned one another and reached a mutually acceptable solution; a solution which would technically be a 'breach of contract' was called 'changing the order' by the businessmen. If such actions did not work, only at that point were lawyers informed of the situation. All house counsel interviewed by Macaulay said that they were called into a dispute only after businessmen had failed to reach a conclusion in their own way. At first lawyers restricted themselves to advice, and only when there was no hope of peaceful resolution was the counsel's letterhead used. Even if the transaction cost of the threat of legal action was small, the effect on the relationship was seen to be profound. The threat of legal action could potentially provoke a breakdown or 'divorce' of a relationship; a result that most parties wished to avoid.

What are the advantages of avoiding legal entanglements? Most situations do not require formal contracts. In the case of low unit price, high volume, instantaneous exchange, a contract is a waste of resources. Although parties do fail to deal with contingencies, they do make sure that the primary obligation is understood. When mutual commitment, information flows, and flexible response are essential, parties cannot achieve what they want with a simple bilateral exchange. Shared needs enforce the contract over law, and in this way, games of Chicken, Prisoner's Dilemma and the War of the Sexes are avoided.[7] In addition, the cost of the relationship diminishes the more it is prolonged; both parties can potentially accumulate and jointly own information.

A striking aspect of Macaulay's research, also mirrored in work by Lewis, and Beale and Dugdale,[8] is that businessmen persist in avoiding legal intervention. As mentioned above, lawyers grumbled that contracts that could potentially be clarified were left under-defined and open-ended. Lewis' work on relationships with general and sub-contractors reflects this idea in particular; neither party wished for laws that defined bidding procedures, but preferred flexibility instead. One caveat, however; in the case of the automobile industry, the contractors were a close knit homogeneous group who communicated easily – disputes were sometimes defused with telephone conversations.

THE COSTS OF CONTRACTING

The costs of contracting can be roughly divided into two groups: *ex ante*, and *ex post*. *Ex ante* costs are incurred in the planning of an agreement. In the treaty ports, such costs would be the time spent finding a reliable trading partner, the cost of going to tea or drinks together, hiring an interpreter, translating documents, and rickshaw fees to and from various offices. *Ex post* costs result when the agreement does not go according to plan. Damages could occur, and costs incurred to 'fix' the scenario in order to obtain the desired result are such costs, and *ex post* costs can be incurred in policing the agreement. For example, damages might be opportunity costs; missing a ship, missing a buyer, or decreases in market prices. The costs in 'shifting the contract curve',[9] for example, would be the costs of going to court to demand completion of the contract, and the associated opportunity costs.

Governing and checking on existing agreements took effort and organization in a treaty-port environment, whereas in a close knit group, such as Robert C. Ellickson's Shasta county ranchers, gossip and reputation-damaging tactics worked to enforce norms. With a semi-permeable boundary, gossip and information were unreliable methods of forcing compliance: *ex post* costs in this respect became high.

From the empirical evidence, it could be said that treaty port merchants attempted to economize on *ex ante* costs. Contracts, even those over complex deals, were simple – many used no contracts at all. Bargain money sometimes functioned as evidence of a deal, and terms of the agreement were often unclear. Information that should have been understood, such as a term of contract (versus a mere description) was overlooked. This is not to say the treaty-port merchants were niggardly when it came to *ex ante* costs. It appears that it was a situation where bounded rationality ran amuck: both Western and Japanese merchants overestimated the quality of their information and subsequent extrapolations. Hence, they often did not have crucial 'bridge-crossing' information. Although it may have appeared to themselves that they had information, more often than not, they did not. Information that could have been had cheaply in their own communities was now prohibitively high. For example, if addresses for a shipment of goods had been exchanged, each party had to have a clerk read and translate the address. If a merchant had traded with an unscrupulous dealer, the false address may not have been spotted until he returned to his office and showed it to the bilingual clerk.

The result was that *ex post* costs were high. Merchants wrote of checking on deals, worrying about compliance, and ultimately, the costs of going to court. Clearly, merchants were aware of the opportunism in treaty ports. The Western treaty-port press was filled with articles, essays, and letters warning of the opportunism of both Japanese and Western merchants. The published court reports also outlined in detail the deals gone wrong. Japanese merchants were equally aware of the Western merchants' opportunistic behaviour and sharp practice. Yet, somewhat to the merchants' detriment, contracts were loosely formed with little investment in planning to protect their investments.

This state of affairs probably occurred because of the perception of opportunism combined with overestimating the quality of their information. Merchants may have perceived that because opportunism was common, they did not want to expend more time, energy, and money in planning if the other party was going to default; *ex ante* costs were already higher in the treaty ports than those in their home communities due to the high costs of information. If the other party defaulted, the planning costs were lost. In addition, because business practices – the so-called 'Custom of the port' – were not established, planning costs were not only inordinately high, they were not necessarily effective. Flexibility was necessary for working in this environment, and under-defined agreements allowed for future adjustments. Opportunism and defection also allowed for a way out of obligations. Thus, rather than expending the initial time and money to set up an agreement, the merchants chose a policy of 'pay as you go'. Itō Hachibei's problems with Walsh, Hall, & Co., for example, were largely the result of under defined relations.

Furthermore, this strategy was a gamble of sorts. If one chose the right 'trustworthy' trade partner, *ex ante* and *ex post* costs were relatively low. The treaty-port merchants had a fixation on 'character' and 'morals', in much the same way as Stewart Macaulay's American auto parts dealers a century later: '. . . businessmen often prefer to rely on "a man's word" in a brief letter, a handshake, or "common honesty and decency" – even when the transaction involved exposure to serious risks'.[10] If a treaty-port merchant thought that he made a good investment in the other merchant's 'character', he may have been more willing to gamble that his future costs would be low, in addition to low *ex ante* costs. However, in many cases, the signals exchanged by the merchants were misunderstood, and thus resulted in high *ex post* costs.

THE EYE OF THE BEHOLDER

Nevertheless, the stereotype of the untrustworthy Japanese merchant stuck in the minds of the Western traders. In their writings on trade in 'the Orient', Victorians and other Westerners correlated the dishonest behaviour with racial characteristics. One Western text on 'oriental trade methods' from the 1920s stated that 'negative philosophy', inefficient use of time, lack of sincerity, and indiscretion were characteristics of all Orientals, in varying degrees.[11] The text elaborates on the Japanese merchants' trade methods by classifying characteristics into 'credits' and 'debits'. On the credit side, the text described the Japanese as clean, kind, and possessors of refined artistic tastes. On the debit side, the Japanese merchants were judged as vain, possessed of unbusinesslike habits, and were incapable of appreciating abstract ideas.[12] Western merchants, the text admonished, had to understand the Japanese merchants and must 'forgive' them for their characteristics.[13]

Contracts and trade between Western and Japanese middlemen were fraught with law suits in which thousands of dollars were disputed. In contrast, the chit system functioned, more or less, with little recourse to law. Thousands of chits were exchanged with little ceremony or dispute. Contract disputes and friction have been variously attributed to a Japanese lack of a legal 'consciousness' of contract,[14] 'shrewd' oriental characteristics, and the treaty ports attracting dishonest traders. One other explanation for the prevalence of disputes has been that the Japanese market was a undeveloped market which lacked crucial institutions, such as law, to ensure smooth functioning.[15] In addition, the lack of shared norms and the lack of affinity towards one another exacerbated the issue.

From the Japanese merchants' perspective, there were few reasons to trust Western merchants. Japanese and Western merchants had differences in trade procedure and the confusion sometimes bred ill will. One Japanese, as late as 1884, had this dim view of Western traders and their abilities:

> . . .the male adults are in the main, composed of either young clerks or unsuccessful men of business. They repair to Japan in the hope. . .of rapidly making fortunes. They have rarely any

social position, and trust that assumption will cover their ignorance. Many who would be taken for counter-jumpers in Regent Street pose as merchant princes on the Bluff at Kanagawa. . .they ape the customs, while they ignore the manners, of their countrymen at home.[16]

In short, the Western merchants were regarded by some Japanese merchants to be of poor character.

In the same vein, some Western diplomats of the period attributed the fractious nature of Japanese treaty-port trade to the poor character of the Western merchant. Alcock cautioned a consul against too readily accepting the complaints of Western merchants:

From all I hear, both as regards your Port and Kanagawa, I cannot help believing that great and in everyway [sic] unjustifiable provocation is frequently given by the rudeness and violence of the Foreigners themselves. . .[17]

Westerners, due to either disincentives within the contract or because of the friction between personalities, did not, at least by Alcock's standards, comport themselves in a seemly manner. The court records indicate that Westerners sued one another, and in this small community, fractious law suits were a common means of resolving disputes. Japanese merchants also behaved differently to the Western merchants than to one another. Oral and written contracts were routinely breached in deals with Westerners.

There were a number of weak links to this chain. First, the courts were the *only*, or at least one of the few, norm building institutions available to the treaty port merchants. Gossip, tradesmen's groups, social sanction, collective bargaining and other such intermediary institutions and tactics were more limited in the treaty ports because of the low exit barriers. Also, the atmosphere of transience and the resulting low investment in the community did not aid in the creation of substantive norms. Substantive norms are every day behaviour that call for the informal administration of rewards and punishments. It was difficult to actually administrate these rewards and punishments within the ports.

It was also unclear to the merchants whether the norms they

brought with them from their home merchant communities were workable in this new community. For example, Western merchants, similar to many Westerners of the period, had a strong racial bias against the Japanese. Norms were such that non-whites were inferior to whites. Initially the race track had posted a sign which announced 'NO NATIVES will be admitted within the enclosure', and tourists commented on the prevailing anti-Japanese sentiment.[18] Japanese merchants had similar norms; for 250 years, in theory, Japan had been closed, and foreigners were to be repelled from its shores. However, to trade with one another, they had to put aside many of these ideas. In most cases, they held on to these norms – for example, Western banks refused to honour cheques presented by the Japanese – which lead to inefficiencies and externalities.[19] Norms were in a state of flux in the treaty ports. Rewards and punishments that once had value within the merchants' own communities, such as rejecting those of a different race, now had differing and unintended effects in this early multi-cultural community. Yet, in a community with so few norms, they clung dearly to the few that existed.

In a similar vein, J. Landa also examined the idea of non-legal processes facilitating agreements in 'A Theory of the Ethnic Homogenous Middleman Group: and Institutional Alternative to Contract Law'. Specifically, she studied the use of ethnicity as a signal for dependability. She cites the example of 'Ego', a composite Chinese modern merchant middleman. In this study, she uses Van Thunen circles to depict Ego's ordering of reliable trading partners: as one moves from the centre outwards, the degree of embeddedness decreases from kinsman to non-Chinese. In this example, he used a cheap information source – by looking at their face, asking their name and where they came from, Ego used ethnicity to determine the degree of dependability. The most embedded party, in this case a near kinsman, was in his calculus the most trustworthy.[20]

Within the treaty ports, such shorthand had to be discarded by both Westerners and Japanese because no party was particularly embedded. Both Japanese and Western merchants were sojourners and settlers to not only the treaty-port market, but the locale itself. So-called 'aberrant' behaviour and appearance were no longer reliable indicators of trustworthiness (after all, all foreigners exhibited some sort of 'aberrant' behaviour). It seems, of course, that the persistence of racial stereotyping, whether efficient or not, was an old habit which was hard to break, especially in an environment in which useful information was costly.

Among Western merchants this situation was particularly true: Western merchants thought they could discern the 'character' of other Western merchants, and made loose agreements with them. However, the trappings of respectability were easy for new Western treaty-port resident to obtain. A superficial spirit of camaraderie and solidarity developed in the port because, in the end, Westerners all had to co-exist within the confines of the foreign enclave. Entry barriers to clubs and networks were low in an effort to quickly create a community and network out of the firmament of the treaty ports. Merchants needed information so entry into their networks was relatively easy; for example, men's clubs were hardly exclusive and were easy to join, and clubs, such as theatre groups, were often short on members. In addition, if we were to choose to believe the comments of some diplomats, church officials, and tourists, 'moral', especially sexual, standards in the treaty ports were low, and thus a modicum of credibility was well within a merchant's grasp.

GOING TO COURT

It is tempting to assume that courts would enforce trade agreements such as contracts. The idea of 'law and order' is pervasive one. Law is often seen to create order. In the agreements examined in this study, merchants did not comply with their contracts because the courts were effective in enforcing them. The merchants did not fear the sanction of the courts, nor were the court particularly effective in settling disputes.

Rather, merchants, particularly Western ones, had a complex relationship with the courts. On the one hand, merchants regarded them as ineffective. As discussed in Chapter V, the Japanese and various consular courts were neither monolithic nor uniform in professionalism or efficiency. Even among the Treaty Powers the quality of the courts varied widely. Western officials were seen as ineffective due to their work load and lack of sympathy for merchants. Also, the courts were perceived as not always effective in producing results: Western merchants complained that even if a judgment was secured against a Japanese merchant, the Japanese merchants would sometimes leave the treaty port area without paying the courts' ordered debts or fines. Japanese courts were also subject to complaint. From the Western merchants' perspective, the Japanese officials were not to be trusted. Likewise, Japanese merchants variously viewed Western courts as alien, biased, and inefficient. Both Japanese and Western merchants found the Japanese courts for mixed cases to be artificial. Some Westerners did not trust Japanese authority, while some Japanese merchants regarded Western diplomatic 'assistance' in court cases as a bias against Japanese cases.

On the other hand, Western merchants regarded the courts as essential to commercial relations. Yet even with this multitude of complaints, both Westerners and Japanese used the courts with regularity to resolve their disputes. Japanese merchants sued Westerners in Western courts under Western law. Westerners sued one another, and when the Japanese courts were more streamlined, Westerners sued Japanese in Japanese courts with vigour. Why then were the merchants using a system that was purportedly inefficient, biased, and ineffectual to resolve their disputes?

One explanation of this behaviour may be that these courts, with all their flaws, were one of the few forms of dispute resolution available to the merchants. Intermediary venues and institutions did not exist. For example, there were few banking institutions that could be used by both Japanese and Westerners. Non-legal governance structures to which disputes could be referred for dispute resolution or arbitration did not exist. There was no guild, organization, or better business bureau to which to bring their complaints. The Chamber of Commerce and Municipal Council neither had the teeth nor the support of the Japanese merchants.

Furthermore, Western merchants and officials had a fixed belief that the courts were the source of authority and that law was the tool to shape merchant relations. Within America and Britain, it would be safe to say that courts were a powerful source of authority and generally reflected the society's norms. In the treaty ports, the courts were merely a relatively cheap option of dispute resolution in an environment in which transaction costs were high; translators were provided, and deposit of fees were waived for non-citizens.

TOWARD NORMS

Any authority, even an unreliable one, was better than no authority, and thus the disputes went to court. Western merchants pursued their claims in a Japanese court. Civil law was, in their eyes, backwards or non-existent, yet they still pursued cases with vigour under Japanese authority. Japanese merchants, including some who did not trust Westerners, went to court. The pursuing of a case, even under a flawed system, was an attempt at norm building. By appealing to an authority, some roles and rules were to be established.

Because of information costs and the costs of meting out rewards and punishments, there were few mechanisms that created substantive norms. Thus, for the Japanese and Western merchants, law, traditionally seen as the last resort, became an important means of contract resolution. It was too difficult for the merchants to govern their contracts in another language, they were not always willing to let go of their social norms to befriend one another, and the environment was too permeable to use gossip to effectively damage reputation.

Hence, bargain money, the primary means by which deals were sealed in the treaty ports, had a two fold purpose; it gave the buyer incentive to complete the deal, and it made the contracts legally binding under Western law. By exchanging bargain money, if the transaction did not go according to plan, the merchants' deal had some sort of enforceability in the Western courts. Going back to the original gamble between *ex ante* and *ex-post ante* costs, the merchants' calculation, if it could be called that, was that if things went wrong, the courts would sort it out. Because the entry barriers for foreigner suing in court were artificially low (initially, they did not need to deposit nor demonstrate they had the ability to pay costs), if they believed they would win (bounded rationality, again), this course of action was rational from the point of view of the merchant.

Yet, the courts were a short-cut of sorts. Norms created by the courts were handed down from an authority and were not 'naturally occurring' norms created by consensus or out of a common belief of the community. Effective, substantive norms as described by Ellickson are:

> The stuff of civilization . . .these informal rules – which have no identifiable author, no apparent date of origin, nor certainty of attention from historians – are among the most magnificent of cultural achievements.[21]

The norm-making pronouncements of the courts – for example, 'merchants should honour their agreements' – did have an identifiable author, the courts, whose authority could be rejected or accepted. Furthermore, the authority that the merchants turned to for norms had already been previously judged as imperfect and second choice. Indeed, merchants did reject the norms of the courts: Western merchants paid for advertisements and wrote letters in the press claiming that they were treated unfairly by the court. Japanese and Western merchants also voted with their feet. Some never bothered to pay the court ordered sums, and others left the ports. Norms created by the courts could not be easily laid like a veneer over the fractious merchant community.

NORMS AND LAW

One possible reason, of many, why treaty-port court decisions were not easily equivalent to trade norms may lie the fact that the courts based their judgements on Western contract law. Legal rendering of contract law is quite different from the day to day realities of trade. It is easy to forget that contracts and exchanges occur with or without the elaborate codification delineated in law texts or created at the bench: 'It must not be forgotten that [the law of contract] in the "real world" the rules may be no more than chips to be used in the bargaining process on the breakdown of a contractual relationship.'[22] As J. Kay writes, contract law inflicts a certain degree of structure, and therefore artifice, on the commercial exchange:

> When I buy a lettuce from a greengrocer, it is as if I say to the greengrocer's assistant, 'I offer to buy this lettuce at the price displayed' and he or she replies, 'As an authorized representative of the greengrocer, I accept your offer.' Even lawyers do not actually conduct these conversations. But if there is any subsequent

dispute, the courts will act as though such an exchange took place.[23]

In the nineteenth century, the legal framework of orthodox contract law had pretensions of universality, and it was assumed that law reflected the realities of trade. It was also believed that 'community ideas of fairness and justice are as then seen as having little role in contract law'.[24] In addition, contract law's close ties with the then nascent field of economics, lent it an air of axiomatic truth. As one preface to a 1847 contract law text noted, the law of contracts were 'founded upon the great and fundamental principles of right and wrong deduced from natural reason'.[25]

However, the legal contracts did not, and still do not, reflect all the complexities of business transactions. On a purely doctrinal level, contract as a legal entity fail to reflect commercial realities. For example, specific mechanisms of the contract law, such as consideration, are requirements particular to Western, namely, English law, and not to a some 'universal' trade practice. In orthodox legal contract doctrine, because one had the right of refusal, it was not concerned with characterizations, such as market stance or bargaining power, of relationships. Orthodox interpreters of the law also state that no one could be compelled to enter a contract against his or her will or agree to terms that s/he did not find to his pleasing. Classical contract law also does not distinguish the between spot and long term contracts. In this doctrine, both types are seen as the same entity.

A specific problem of equating legal contracts as a reflection of trade transactions is based on the idea of a 'reasonable man'. When contracts broke down, a legal judgement must be made from the standpoint of the 'reasonable man'. In general cases, the implied expectations of the quality and ancillary service associated with a particular good may vary in every culture and subculture. In the specific case of the treaty port, the expectations of a reasonable man were particularly unclear: the 'reasonable' expectations of Japanese merchants may well have been different from Western merchants. A trade relationship in which two parties make an open ended contract is particular in that it involves explicit and implicit agreements: that is, reading and understanding complex signals and shared expectations. To complicate matters, information was costly and the business culture was in its nascent stages. Because treaty-port courts made pronouncements on reasonable expectations and customs that were newly established, or, in some cases, not shared by the entire community, the courts may not have created norms that were accepted by the treaty port.

THE LIMITATIONS OF LAW

In addition to these problems of legal remedies for contract, law is often an expensive and inefficient solution. In the planning stage, Coase's idea of transaction cost comes into play. If parties tried to contract for every contingency, the cost of the contract would be infinite as there are infinite contingencies. In addition, contracts cost in terms of their enforcement and implementation. The state, at tremendous expense, must maintain a justice system with lawyers and judges. In addition to this social cost, a firm loses production time and diversion of resources when it go to court to seek a legal remedy.

In order for a contract to be efficient in complex trade agreements, each party must be aware of the nature of the game and the basic rules in which he or she is situated. That is, the treaty port merchant had to manage expectations. One way of understanding expectations was having information – which was often costly. The rules, as explained above, were not clear in the treaty port. Although economic factors are important, the degree of dependability is significant; thus the choice of partner becomes significant.

In a modern example, R. Lewis' research on general contractors revealed that they do not necessarily take the lowest bid. In fact, general contractors often chose sub-contractors whose reputations and work are well known to them. The choice of sub-contractor/partner was chosen at the same time with considerations of price. In some tendering situations, Lewis reports a maneuvering in prices and contracting in order to secure the most reliable partner at the best price.[26] This idea of choosing a dependable partner that is similarly embedded relates to cross-cultural contracting. Lewis remarks that with international agreements, contractors are less vague and more dependent on legal and explicit contracts. Disincentives and enforcement of submitted bids are built into the tendering process, but flexibility is diminished.[27] In the case of the treaty ports, the reputation and work habits were not always known to either to Japanese or Western merchants; hence, if that information could not be had, flexibility in their agreements was key. In the ports in which weather, political upheaval, fire, and vermin could affect the cargo, business could not be done without flexibility. Hence the reliance on under-defined agreements, even with unknown partners.

In the long run, in order for relations to work, norms as well as law were needed for the efficient transactions. Given no norms, actors will seek norms. If the courts are the only form of norm creating institution, actors, or at the very least, treaty port merchants, turned to law. However, there were a number of problems in depending on law to create business norms. The courts themselves, in this case Western courts and the Japanese courts stylized into the form of Western courts, had problems enforcing entitlements because the courts themselves could not easily discern the entitlement. The courts did not reinforce accepted norms but tried to create them; an ultimately futile exercise in the semi-permeable environment in which the residents had the option of leaving.

CONCLUSION:
THE REPUBLIC OF
COMMERCE

'I wish your worship would take these oaths to the Devil, dear master,' replied Sancho, 'for they're bad for the health and very harmful to the conscience.'

Don Quixote, Part I Chapter X

IT HAS ONCE been remarked that trust 'merely muddies the (clear) waters of calculativeness'.[1] At the same time, contracts, in the real world filled with obstacles and friction of everyday life, cannot function without a degree of trust. The costs of contracting for every possible contingency would be prohibitive. Thus, trust becomes necessary and crucial in making a transaction using an open ended contract. In the Japanese treaty ports, the Western and Japanese merchants met and traded in a complex and uncertain world. Information costs, needed to make business decisions, were prohibitively high. Social sanctions such as damaging reputation through gossip was not always effective in this loosely knit group.

In the group of merchants examined for this study, merchants tended to make under-defined contracts. Also, evidence suggests that merchants tended to make a 'leap of faith' and assume a degree of trust. In the treaty port, trust eased the lack of information, and allowed for flexibility in the business transactions. However, such a system was not always foolproof. As the court records show, there are records of defection on both sides.

In the end, the treaty ports were republics of commerce, bound by economic self interest, with the frequent interference of Japanese and Western authorities. Although the civil law of Western law courts nominally protected the transactions between merchants, in reality it was difficult for the mechanism of law to compel the compliance of commercial agreements made between the merchants. The contractual disputes between Western and Japanese merchants were a low priority for the Japanese authorities. Japanese civil law, as defined in the West, was still in its nascent stages. No monolithic set of laws, customs, or institutions bound the treaty port merchants to one another. There was no network or alliance between them. No social contract dictated good behaviour. Only self interest, personal ethics, affinity, and occasional violence compelled merchants to cooperate and comply with contracts. What can be learned from the denizens of this republic of commerce?

By examining contractual conflicts in the Western and Japanese courts and in the merchant press, journals, and letters, this study has sought to explore the trade methods and lives of the treaty-port merchants: this study sought to shed light on how they did business. Contracts in themselves are strange animals whose spots change depending on one's perspective. Economics, legal theory, sociology, to name a few branches of study, all have differing perspectives on contract, and to further complicate matters, historians examine contracts in their given time and context. The purpose of this study was not the ambitious task of redefining contract; rather, it sought to make empirical observations on how merchants in the treaty ports of nineteenth-century Japan traded with one another.

GENERAL FINDINGS

To summarize, trade in the treaty ports between Japanese and Western merchants was not without friction and problems. Contracts between merchants failed for various reasons ranging from misunderstanding to greed. From the body of evidence used for this study, it appears that merchants traded with one another using under-defined agreements. They were quite often not written, and if they were, the documents tended to state only the essential terms of the agreement. The merchants generally used a system of 'bargain money' in which the buyer made a roughly 10% down payment for open-ended transactions. At times, a receipt for bargain money functioned as a contract. Contracts with numerous and specific terms and conditions seem to have been avoided. There were some instances in which highly specific contracts became an impediment to the transaction because it did not allow for flexibility.

Contracts, in this body of evidence, were honoured because it was in the merchants' interest. Their incentives may have been profit, a perceived moral value, or because they had a long term interests. It appears that the satisfactory discharge of expectations was necessary for those who wanted to continue to work with a given merchant for any extended period of time. Repetition, and the cost of moving from one scene of activity to another must have been the strongest 'enforcers' of the treaty port business morality.

There were two major explanatory reasons behind contracts failing in the treaty ports. The high cost of information and the lack of exit barriers. Because information was scarce and costly, it was difficult to verify the veracity of a merchant's promises. In addition, because both Japanese and Western merchants could easily default on their promises and abscond with their gains, it was not always possible for the merchants to gain either justice or retribution. These two main reasons – among others – resulted in deals with under-defined contracts, which created misunderstandings, which in turn, caused a break down in relations. By extension, successful Japanese-Western merchant relationships resulted not from expertise on a given commodity, but on a combination of reputation, opportunity, and a small measure of luck. Thus, the successful treaty-port merchant was a merchant who had the ability to manage expectations and information.

At the same time, this scrabble for self interest was not seen as always desirable. If we were to believe the complaints to officials and the local press, merchants defaulting on contracts was seen as a problem. Merchants used the courts as a form of dispute resolution, but because there were so few other forms of enforcement, the courts' decision never became the norms of the treaty ports. However, because the court's judgments were based on ill-defined ideas such as the 'custom of the ports', the point of view of a 'reasonable man', and Western law which was not always accepted by Japanese merchants, the courts' decisions did not always reflect the commercial reality of the merchants. It appears that courts were not entirely accepted by either Japanese or Western merchants as source of social norms.

INFORMATION AND TRUST

Why were contracts in the treaty ports fraught with such discord? The contractual breaches and the subsequent disputes were not endemic in either Western or Japanese merchant culture. In the West, in the tightly knit nineteenth century merchant communities in cities such as London or New York, a promise or handshake was sometimes sufficient for business. Within Japan, breaches of even oral contracts among Japanese merchants had been rare.

One answer lay with the fact that contracts, as instruments of trade, were imperfect tools. In exchange for the benefits of specific goods and advance planning, the merchant took on the risk of default. A merchant, for example, could default and not produce the promised goods. At worst, he could leave the port area with the down payment. Even if all transactions went smoothly, an anticipated market could collapse. The barriers to trade and planning were many. Political friction between the West and Japan made the Japanese market unstable, and the prices, and therefore profit, could not be relied upon. In short, some merchants defaulted because they could, and a contract they made could not force them to comply with their agreements.

In order avoid such unscrupulous individuals, a merchant needed information. Because of the language barrier and lack of shared business culture, information-gathering was costly, and contracts often made without adequate information sometimes caused more problems than they solved. It was difficult for the merchants to distinguish between good and bad trading partners. Systems of credit, except chits, were initially non-functional. Establishing trust and finding reliable trading partners took time and effort. Also, traders did not have an agreed authority to turn to for dispute resolution. Western and Japanese

201

merchants had to expend energy and time for basic trade relations.

For example, the language barrier raised the costs of generating the actual contractual document; in the majority of cases, contracts had to be written in Japanese and English in order for both parties to understand the deal. In the first few years of trade, the only European language that the Japanese understood was Dutch, and the Westerners did not understand Japanese, or much Dutch for that matter. Early contracts and other information had to go through a two-fold translation process. Documents were first translated into Dutch, and then Dutch into Japanese, and vice versa.

As stated above, one of the major findings of this study was that contracts made in the treaty ports – whether between Western merchants, or between Japanese and Western merchants – were often under-defined and open-ended. If the contract was rigid, it was treated as a form, and both parties allowed for a degree of flexibility in their trade relations above and beyond the stipulations of the contract. The high cost of information and the constantly changing circumstances resulted in contracts which were often simple and did not delineate contingency plans in case of breach. Also, these contracts were often changed under informal circumstances and not noted in the written version. For example, in the case of Itō Hachibei vs. Walsh Hall & Co., described in detail in Chapter VII, wagon loads of silver coin were exchanged without the confirmation of a receipt and much good will. Throughout the court proceedings, it was unclear whether there was a written contract between the two merchants.

This lack of planning, combined with the lack of a common language and business conventions, resulted in misunderstandings, as manifested by the number of cases in which only a verbal or brief written contract was used in the deal. On the surface, the lack of planning seems irrational or foolhardy. If one was trading with unfamiliar partners, it seems that a rational merchant would insist on a clear contract in which the terms were clearly stated.

However, the real or imagined defects of Japanese and Western merchants were not all irrational. There were advantages of having an under-defined oral contract. Such agreements avoided the high cost of making a contract and at the same time allowed for flexibility. Time was quite definitely money in the treaty ports as hiring translators took both time and money. Time pressure was felt on 'letter days' – days in which mail ships were leaving port, merchants would work through the night preparing orders and letters. Many contracts were oral which was hazardous when neither party spoke the other's language well, and orders were changed and details adjusted as the deals progressed. This practice caused the British consuls to complain that most of their time was spent in processing a never-ending caseload. Time was of the essence in some of the deals. In some currency speculations, a difference of a day may have had serious repercussions on their profit. Moreover, translators themselves were also sometimes in business, so confidentiality was difficult to achieve.

A CAVEAT

From the historian's perspective, one must not overstate the degree of mistrust that existed between the merchants. Newspapers, letters, diaries, and magazine articles written by merchants for merchants often addressed problems and complaints, rather than the day to day details of smooth running operations. Reports of sensational fraud and strong language invariably made better press. Court proceedings were the result of business relations deteriorating. By the time a case reached the courts, both parties had often compiled a list of complaints, some purely fictional. In short, by nature of the sources, there exists a selection bias.

The vagaries of the contract, and the problems that ensued, may be interpreted as the extent to which merchants trusted one another. In reality, the great majority of deals were successful and without incident – of which we have little record. Many deals functioned well on trust and an under-defined document, and promises made in pidgin and sign language.

IMPLICATIONS

If the treaty-port merchants are any example, given an environment in which trade norms are ill defined with two distinct group of actors unfamiliar with one another, they will turn to a flawed legal system. Modern examples may be present day China, Eastern Europe, or certain South East Asian countries. Old norms in such countries, namely those associated with command economies, are shifting towards market oriented ones. Businesses in such countries should not overrely on law to protect them, nor be surprised when actors bring the issues to court, however flawed the 'system'. Law in itself is not sufficient in creating commercial or social order. In order to transact business, they would do well to support intermediary norm creating institutions such as ombudsmen, negotiators, chambers of commerce, and consumer groups. Immediate resort to law, rather than creating more order, can sometimes cause disorder.

Transactions costs can make the creation of substantive norms difficult in treaty-port-type environments. If norms were created by an authority such as the treaty port courts, it was difficult to dispense the informal rewards and punishments associated with maintaining the rules because the courts lacked credibility. However, with no other venue available to them, the courts will be used as source of authority, however flawed. This finding is corroborated in modern studies as well. In Eastern Europe, businessmen used the courts even though they claimed they was inefficient and corrupt.[2]

It has been unfashionable to talk of norms or even the propensity to obey or want to obey authority; the idea of social, political, and economic choice has been one that we would like to imagine as a cherished freedom. However, it is not unlimited. It was unlikely that Puccini's Butterfly would negotiate an advantageous contract for her sexual and homemaking services – her norms, at least within Puccini's imagined universe, were clearly prescribed. In her contractual dispute, she had no court, no intermediary institutions to take her claim. She paid dearly with her life.

The treaty ports accord the historian the opportunity to examine a world in which norms, expectations, and rules were loosely defined. Within this environment one would expect that Economic Man would truck and barter according to his well-ordered preferences. He would be unconstrained by the inconveniences of honour, manners, morals, or custom. He could default on contracts as easily as Pinkerton could leave Butterfly and marry his American bride in *Madame Butterfly*. The reality, of course, was not as simple. Man is bound to society and its rules, as much as to his self-interest.

NOTES

INTRODUCTION

1. G. Giacosa and L. Illica, 'Libretto to *Madama Butterfly*' in *Madam Butterfly (Opera Guide 26)*, Nicholas John, ed. (London: John Calder (Publishers) Ltd, 1990) p. 72. 'I must say, in this country,/ The houses and the contracts are elastic!. . . And so I am marrying in the Japanese style/For the next nine/ Hundred and ninety-nine/ Years. Free, though, to annul the marriage/ monthly!' Translation: R. H. Elkin from same source.
2. G. Giacosa and L. Illica, 'Libretto to *Madama Butterfly*' in *Madam Butterfly (Opera Guide 26)*, Nicholas John, ed. p. 99. 'This will all come to pass, of that I'm certain/ Banish your idle fears for he will/Return I know.' Translation: R. H. Elkin from same source.
3. Arthur Groos' meticulous research did find a historical basis for Pinkerton and Butterfly. John Luther Long's sister, Sarah Jane Correll, had been a missionary in Japan in the 1890s and had told the true story of Butterfly to her brother. According to Groos, Lt. Benjamin Franklin Pinkerton's prototype was most likely Ensign William B. Franklin. Butterfly's identity remains more obscure though Correll states that the real 'Butterfly' spent many nights waiting in vain for her 'husband' to come home. A. Groos, 'Madame Butterfly: the Story Behind the Story' in *Madama Butterfly Program for the Welsh National Opera* (1998) p. 27.
4. John Luther Long first wrote the short story, David Beasco wrote the play based on the story, and finally Puccini wrote the opera based on the play.
5. J. E. Hoare, *Japan's Treaty Ports and Foreign Settlements; The Uninvited Guests, 1859-1899* (Kent: Japan Library, 1994) pp. 21-23.
6. T. Yokoyama, *Japan and the Victorian Mind: A Study of Stereotyped Images of a Nation 1850-80* (London: The Macmillan Press Ltd., 1987) pp. 46-66.
7. E. S. Crawcour, 'Changes in Japanese Commerce in the Tokugawa Period', in Hall and Jenson, eds. *Studies in the Instiutional History of Early Modern Japan* (Princeton: Princeton University Press, 1968), 'The Development of a Credit System in Seventeenth Century Japan', *Journal of Economic History*, 21 (1961), 'The Tokugawa Heritage', in W. Lockwood, ed. *The State and Economic Enterprise in Japan* (Princeton: Princeton University Press, 1965), and 'Economic change in the nineteenth century', in *The Cambridge History of Japan*, vol 5. M. Jansen, ed. (Cambridge: Cambridge University Press, 1993).
8. See for example, Yokohama Kaikō Shiryōkan [Yokohama Archives of History], Irustorashion nihon kankei kiji shu, 3 vols. (Yokohama: Yokohama Archives of

History, 1986), Yokohama Kaikō Shiryōkan and Yokohama Kindai shi Kenkyukai, *Yokohama no Kindai* (Tokyo: Nihon Keizai Hyoronsha, 1997), and Yokohama Kaikō Shiryōkan, *Yokohama Chukagai* [Yokohama's Chinatown] (Yokohama: Yokohama Archives of History, 1994).

9. K. Ishii, *Kindai Nihon Igirisu Shihon: Jyarudin Maseson shyōkai o chushin ni* (Tokyo: Tokyo University Press, 1984). Also notable is S. Sugiyama, *Meiji Ishin to Igirisu Shōnin, Tomasu Guroba no Shōgai* (Tokyo: Iwanami Shoten, 1993).

10. See citation 6.

11. H. S. Williams, *Tales of Foreign Settlements in Japan*, (Tokyo: Charles E. Tuttle Company, 1986), *Foreigners in Mikadoland* (Tokyo: Charles E. Tuttle Company, 1963), and *Shades of the past; or, Indiscreet tales of Japan* (Tokyo: Charles E. Tuttle Company, 1959).

12. Pat Barr, *The Coming of the Barbarians; A Story of Western Settlements in Japan 1853-1870* (London: Penguin Press, 1967), and *The Deer Cry Pavilion: a Story of Westerners in Japan 1868-1905* (London: Macmillan Publishing, 1968).

13. J. McMaster, 'British Trade and Traders to Japan 1859-1869', Unpublished Ph.D. thesis (London: University of London, 1962).

14. See, for example, G. Daniels, *Sir Harry Parkes, British Representative in Japan; 1865-1883* (Kent, Japan Library: 1996). Also, there are number of memoirs published by Westerners in Japan such as R. Alcock, *The Capital of the Tycoon: A Narrative of a Three Years' Residence in Japan*, 2 vols. (London: Longman, Green and Co., 1863), and Joseph Heco and James Murdoch, *The Narrative of a Japanese: What He has Seen and The People He has Met in the Course of The Last Forty Years* (San Francisco: American-Japanese Publishing Association, n.d.), 2 vols., among many others.

15. R. T. Chang, *The Justice of the Western Consular Courts in Nineteenth Century Japan* (Westport: Greenwood Press, 1984).

16. D. F. Henderson, *Village Contracts in Tokuugawa Japan* (Seattle: University of Washington Press, 1975), *Conciliation and Japanese Law* (Seattle: University of Washington Press, 1965), and *International Encyclopedia of Comparative Law*, vol VII (Boston: Martinius Nijhoff Publisher, 1973).

17. J. H. Wigmore, 'Materials for the Study of Private Law in Japan', *TASJ*, 20 (1892), *Law and Justice in Tokugawa Japan, Being materials for the history of Japanese law and justice under the Tokugawa Shogunate, 1603-1867* (Tokyo: Kokusai Bunka Shinkokai, 1941-43), J. H. Wigmore, ed., *Law and justice in Tokugawa Japan: materials for the history of Japanese law and justice under the Tokugawa Shogunate 1603-1867* (Tokyo: Kokusai Bunka Shinkokai, 1967-1987), 9 vols.

18. H. Iwamura, 'Kobe chuzai Eikokoku taishikan saibamkiryoku hoyaku, 1871 kugatsu yori 1872 jyu ichi gatsu made no kiryoku' [Japanese translation of Documents of British (sic) consular court at Kobe, From September 1871 to November 1871], Osaka Keizai Hoka Daigaku Ho Gakkai ,16 (1987).

19. R. Coase, 'A Problem of Social Choice', *Journal of Law and Economics* (1960) p. 1. Coase illustrated his theorem with a rather counterintuitive fable now commonly known as the Parable of the Farmer and Rancher. In this story, a farmer has his crops ruined by a neighboring rancher running cattle over the farmer's fields. The farmer would pay the rancher to take these trespass control measures even if law made the rancher strictly liable. By extension, in this example, making the rancher legally liable for damages would not make him any more careful of his cattle's movements, reduce the size of his herd, or erect fencing.

20. R. Ellickson, *Order Without Law; How Neighbors Settle Disputes* (Cambridge: Harvard University Press, 1991) pp. 280-1.

21. R. Ellickson, *Order Without Law; How Neighbors Settle Disputes*, p. 2.

22. *Ibid*, p. 3.

23. *Ibid*, p. 3.

24. Also see, R. C. Ellickson 'The Case for Coase, and Against Coaseanism' *Yale Law Journal*, 99 (1989) p. 611, and H. Demsetz, 'When Does the Rule of

Liability Matter', *Journal Legal Studies*, 1 (1972) pp. 13, 16; Walter Blum and Harry Kalven, Jr., *Public Law Perspectives on a Private Law Problem* (Boston: Little, Brown and Company, 1965) pp. 58-59.

25. See, for example, H. Nakamura, 'Basic Feature of the Legal, Political, and Economic Thought of Japan' in Charles A. Moore ed. *The Japanese Mind; Essentials of Japanese Philosophy and Culture* (Honolulu: East-West Center Press, 1991).

26. S. Macaulay 'Non-Contractual Relations in Business: A Preliminary Study', *American Sociological Review*, 28 (1963) pp. 55-69.

27. K. N. Llewellyn, *The Bramble Bush: On Our Law and Its Study* (New York: Oceana Publications, 1960) p. 58. See also G. L. Priest and B. Klein, 'The Selection of Disputes for Litigation' in *The Economics of Information*, vol. 1. Levine, David K. Lippman, A. Steven, eds. (Brookfield, Vt: Ashgate, 1995) p. 412.

28. S. Macaulay 'Non-Contractual Relations in Business: A Preliminary Study', American Sociological Review, 28 (1963) pp. 55-69.

29. R. T. Chang, *The Justice of the Western Consular Courts in Nineteenth Century Japan*, (Westport: Greenwood Press, 1984) p. 14.

30. Avner Offer, 'Between the Gift and the Market: the Economy of Regard', *Economic History Review*, 50 (1997).

31. J. O. Hale, 'The Myth of the Reluctant Litigant', *Journal of Japanese Studies*, 4 (1978) pp. 359-390.

CHAPTER ONE: THE TOKUGAWA LEGACY

1. K. Katsu, *Musui's Story*, trans. Teruko Craig (Tuscon: University of Arizona Press, 1988) p. 97.

2. Useful works in English on the late Tokugawa/Meiji period include: W. G. Beasley, *Great Britain and the Opening of Japan* (London: Luzac, 1951), and *The Meiji Restoration* (Stanford: Stanford University Press, 1972), H. Bolitho, *Treasures Among Men: the Fudai Daimyo in Tokugwa Japan* (New Haven: Yale University Press, 1974), A. Craig, *Chōshū and the Meiji Restoration* (Cambridge: Harvard University Press, 1961), H. Hartoonian, *Toward Restoration* (Berkeley: University of California Press, 1970), W. B. Hauser, *Economic and Institutional Change in Tokugawa Japan: Osaka and the Kinai Cotton Trade* (Cambridge: Cambridge University Press, 1974), M. Jansen, *Sakamoto Ryōma and the Meiji Restoration* (Princeton: Princeton University Press, 1961), R. Toby, *State and Diplomacy in Early Modern Japan, Asia and the Development of the Tokugawa Bakufu* (Stanford: Stanford University Press, 1980), and C. Totman, *The Collapse of the Tokugawa Bakufu, 1862-1868* (Honolulu: University of Hawaii Press, 1980).

3. S. Crawcour, 'The Development of a Credit System in Seventeenth Century Japan' *Journal of Economic History*, 21 (1961) p. 345.

4. K. Yamamura, 'From Coins to Rice, Hypotheses on the Kandaka and Kokudaka Systems' *Journal of Japanese Studies*, 14 (1988) p. 342.

5. Takao Tsuchiya, 'An Economic History of Japan', *Transactions of the Asiatic Society of Japan*, Second Series 15 (1937) p. 211. *Transactions of the Asiatic Society of Japan* will be henceforth denoted as *TASJ*.

6. W. Lockwood, *The Economic Development of Japan; Growth and Structural Change* (Princeton: Princeton University Press, 1954) p. 5.

7. Mary Elizabeth Berry, 'Public Life in Authoritarian Japan', *Daedalus*, 127(1988) pp. 149-150. See also, G. W. Sargent (trans.) *The Japanese Family Storehouse* (New York: Cambridge University Press, 1958) pp. 239-244.

8. Conrad Totman, *Japan Before Perry: A Short History* (Berkeley: University of California Press, 1981) p. 197.

9. Thomas C. Smith, *The Agarian Origins of Modern Japan* (Stanford: Stanford University Press, 1959) pp. 50-63. This chapter of Smith's book explains the interdependence of family farming groups in the eighteenth century.

10. C. Totman, *Japan Before Perry*, p. 200.

11. E. S. Crawcour, 'Economic change in the nineteenth century', in *The Cambridge History of Japan*, vol. 5. ed. M. Jansen (Cambridge: Cambridge University Press, 1993) pp. 585-6.
12. *Ibid*, p. 572.
13. E. Reischauer and A. Craig, *Tradition and Transformation*, (Boston: Houghton Mifflin Company, 1989) p. 98.
14. E. S. Crawcour, 'Economic change in the nineteenth century', pp. 571-2.
15. *Ibid*, p. 592.
16. C. Totman, *Japan Before Perry*, pp. 207-9.
17. W. G. Beasley, 'The Foreign Threat and the Opening of the Ports', in *The Cambridge History of Japan* (Cambridge: Cambridge University Press, 1993), p. 276.
18. *Ibid*, p. 260.
19. *Ibid*, p. 301.
20. Paul C. Blum, *Yokohama in 1872, A Rambling Account of the Community in which the Asiatic Society of Japan was Founded*, (Tokyo: The Asiatic Society of Japan, 1981), p. 40.
21. *Ibid*, p. 41. Here the term 'Yoshiwara' refers to pleasure districts in general.
22. *Ibid*, p. 3.
23. See Sadahide's prints *Yokohama Honsho kei Miyozaki-gai shinkaku, Yokohama Honcho* and *Narabi ni Miyozaki-cho saiken zenzu*.
24. Now called Motomachi. Blum, *Yokohama in 1872*, p. 3.
25. M. Paske-Smith, *Western Barbarians in Japan and Formosa in the Tokugawa Oeriod* (Kobe: Thompson, 1930), p. 218.
26. J. E. Hoare, *Japan's Treaty Ports and Foreign Settlements: The Uninvited Guests, 1859-1899* (Kent: Japan Library, 1994) pp. 23-34.
27. Solomon B. Levine and H. Kawada, *Human Resources in Japanese Industrial Development* (Princeton: Princeton University Press, 1990).
28. E. S. Crawcour, 'Economic change in the nineteenth century', p. 601.
29. See J. McMaster, 'The Japanese Gold Rush of 1859', *Journal of Asian Studies*, 19 (1960) for a thorough discussion of the so-called 'Gold Rush'.
30. E. S. Crawcour, 'Economic change in the nineteenth century', p. 602.
31. Shinbo Hiroshi, *Kinsei no Bukka to Kaeizai hatten: zenkogyoka shakai e no suryoteki sekkin* (Tokyo: Toyo keizai Shinposha, 1978) p. 27.
32. W. G. Beasley, 'The Foreign Threat and the Opening of the Ports', p. 291.
33. M. Jansen, 'The Meiji Restoration' in *The Cambridge History of Japan* (Cambridge: Cambridge University Press, 1993), p. 338.
34. W. G. Beasley, 'The Foreign Threat and the Opening of the Ports', p. 271.
35. C. Gluck, *Japan's Modern Myths* (Princeton: Princeton University Press, 1985) pp. 17-21.
36. Adrath W. Burks, 'Administrative Transition from Han to Ken: The Example of Okayama', *Far Eastern Quarterly*, 15 (1995) p. 37.

CHAPTER TWO: TREATY PORTS: BOUNDARIES AND BORDERS

1. J. E. Hoare, *Japan's Treaty Ports and Foreign Settlements: The Uninvited Guests, 1859-1899* (Kent: Japan Library, 1994) p. xi, and O. Edwards, *Residential Rhymes* (Tokyo: Hasegawa, c 1900).
2. *The Japan Times*, 17 November 1865.
3. *Ibid*., 17 November 1865. Original text in French.
4. W. G. Beasley. 'The Foreign Threat and the Opening of the Ports', in *The Cambridge History of Japan* (Cambridge: Cambridge University Press, 1993) pp. 259-61.
5. Hoare, *Japan's Treaty Ports and Foreign Settlements*, p. 6.
6. Jardine Matheson was formally established in 1832 but had been trading since 1828 in China. M. Booth, *Opium; A History* (New York: St Martins Press, 1996) pp. 114-5, 125.

7. This issue is covered in more detail in Chapter V.
8. This trade figure, like many trade statistics collected by diplomats of the period, may be inaccurate.
9. J. McMaster, 'British Trade and Traders to Japan 1859-1869', Unpublished Ph.D. thesis (London: University of London, 1962) p. 23.
10. All dollar values in this work are in Mexican dollars unless otherwise specified. The Mexican silver dollar was the international unit of trade of the period. According to the treaty, Mexican silver was to be exchanged weight for weight in the ports. However, Japanese merchants preferred Japanese coin of which there was short supply. In general, after some fits and starts, in the early 1860s, one gold Japanese coin could be bought from between two and three dollars, depending on the quality of the coin. For an excellent summary of the problems in which early traders faced in obtaining coin, see J. McMaster, 'The Japanese Gold Rush of 1859', *Journal of Asian Studies*, 19 (1960).
    As for the cost of living, an entry level clerk could expect to earn $2,400 per annum, a junior partner at Jardine Matheson stood to earn about $18,000 in 1874. J. McMaster, *British Trade and Traders to Japan 1859-1869*, Unpublished Ph.D. thesis (London: University of London, 1962) p. 175. By 1870, the 'nibus' [probably *nichibu gin*, silver coin] exchanged at 4.3 nibus for 1 dollar. *The Hiogo News*, 19 March 1870
11. J. McMaster, 'The Japanese Gold Rush of 1859', p. 274.
12. M. Paske-Smith, *Western Barbarians in Japan and Formosa in the Tokugawa Period* (Kobe: Thompson, 1930) p. 364.
13. *The Japan Weekly Mail*, 2 May 1885.
14. The Principal Trade Route of the Clipper Ships based on Admiralty Chart 1078, by permission of the Controller of the H. M. Stationary Office [n.d.].
15. J. McMaster, 'British Trade and Traders to Japan 1859-1869', p. 140.
16. H. S. Williams, *Tales of Foreign Settlements in Japan*, (Tokyo: Charles E. Tuttle Company, 1986), pp. 222-3.
17. See for example the partnership announcements contained in *The Hiogo News*, 2 March 1870.
18. Heco and Murdoch, *The Narrative of a Japanese: What He has Seen and The People He has Met in the Course of The Last Forty Years*. vol. 2 p. 235.
19. *Ibid.*, vol. 2 p. 241.
20. *Ibid.*, vol. 2 p. 276.
21. Barr, *The Coming of the Barbarians; A Story of Western Settlements in Japan 1853-1870*, pp. 105-6, 110-115.
22. Anti-Semitism did exist in the treaty port, as evinced by various comments in diaries and letters. The American merchant F. Hall, for example, identified one of his fellow merchant as 'Jew K', and not by nationality or as 'Mr.' and the first initial of a merchant's name, as was his usual custom. He closely followed his comment with a description and costs of K's rather, in Hall's view, plain Japanese mistress. Notehelfer identified 'Jew K' as L. Kniffler. F. G. Notehelfer, ed. *Japan Through American Eyes; Journal of Francis Hall Kanagawa and Yokohama, 1859-66* (Princeton: Princeton University Press, 1992), pp. 80-1. Also, see the anti-semitic cartoon from *The Japan Punch* vilifying lawyers as Jews in Figure 5.1. At the same time, Jewish merchants were not persecuted by their peers, as many of the western merchants remained unconcerned with religious matters, Christian, Jewish, or otherwise. Jewish merchants appear to have been members of the Municipal Council in Yokohama, and allowed into social clubs and activities. Apart from a legal case over non-payment of Japanese labour, there is no record of any community objection to building a synagogue in Yokohama.
23. E. Satow, *A Diplomat in Japan*, (London: Shelly, Service & Co. Ltd., 1921) p. 27.
24. See for example, H. M. Reischauer, *Samurai and Silk: A Japanese American Heritage* (Cambridge: Harvard University Press, 1986), p. 185-6, and Barr, *The Coming of the*

Barbarians; A Story of Western Settlements in Japan 1853-1870, p. 144.
25. H. S. Williams, *Tales of Foreign Settlements in Japan*, p. 21.
26. F. G. Notehelfer in 'Sketch of the Life of Francis Hall' in *Japan Through American Eyes; Journal of Francis Hall Kanagawa and Yokohama, 1859-66*, p. 10.
27. J. McMaster, 'The Japanese Gold Rush of 1859', p. 275.
28. Norman Beecher and Nancy Bartram Beecher, *Fortunate Journey: Our Lives, Our Family, and Our Forebears* (Saline, MI: McNaughton & Gunn, 1993) p. 388.
29. Notehelfer in 'Sketch of the Life of Francis Hall' in *Japan Through American Eyes; Journal of Francis Hall Kanagawa and Yokohama, 1859-66*, p. 61.
30. Paul C. Blum, *Yokohama in 1872* (Tokyo: The Asiatic Society of Japan, 1981) pp. 23, 28-29.
31. Hoare, *Japan's Treaty Ports and Foreign Settlements*, p. 43.
32. *Ibid.*, p. 46.
33. W. E. Griffis, *The Mikado's Empire* (New York: Harper Brothers, 1913) pp. 40-41.
34. Hoare, *Japan's Treaty Ports and Foreign Settlements*, p. 49., H. F. Abell, 'Some memories of Old Japan', *Chambers Journal*, Seventh Series, I (1910-11) p. 681.
35. Williams, *Tales of Foreign Settlements in Japan*, p. 130.
36. Notehelfer, ed. *Japan Through American Eyes; Journal of Francis Hall Kanagawa and Yokohama, 1859-66*, p. 81.
37. T. Saito in *Yokohama Kaikōshiryōkan* (Yokohama Archives of History) ed., Shiyo ga Kataru Yokohama no Hyakunen, *Bakumatsu kara Showa Made* (Yokohama: Yokohama Kaikōshiryōkan, 1989) p. 14.
38. Hoare, *Japan's Treaty Ports and Foreign Settlements*, p. 13.
39. Notehelfer, ed. *Japan Through American Eyes; Journal of Francis Hall Kanagawa and Yokohama, 1859-66*, p. 82.
40. Hoare, *Japan's Treaty Ports and Foreign Settlements*, pp. 181-192.
41. *Ibid.*, p. 29.
42. *Ibid.*, p. 29.
43. Williams, *Tales of Foreign Settlements in Japan*, p. 225.
44. J. H. Wigmore, 'Private Law in Old Japan', *TASJ*, 20 supplement (1892) pp. 129-130.
45. N. Skene Smith, *TASJ*, 14 (June 1937, 2nd series) p. 85.
46. J. H. Wigmore, 'Private Law in Old Japan', *TASJ*, 20 supplement (1892) p. 146.
47. N. Skene-Smith, *TASJ* 14 2nd series (1937), p. 85.
48. J. H. Wigmore, 'Private Law in Old Japan', *TASJ*, 20 supplement (1892) p. 189.
49. N. Skene Smith, *TASJ*, 14 (June 1937, 2nd series) p. 85.
50. *Ibid.*, p. 104.
51. William B. Hauser, *Economic Institutional Change in Tokugawa Japan; Osaka and the Kinai Cotton Trade* (Cambridge: Cambridge University Press, 1974) p. 53.
52. J. H. Wigmore, 'Private Law in Old Japan', *TASJ*, 20 supplement (1892) p. 137.
53. J. G. Roberts, *Mitsui: Three Centuries of Japanese Business*, (New York: Weatherhill, 1991) pp. 48-49.
54. Nagai Minoru (ed.), *Jishyo Masuda Takashi-o den* (Tokyo: Chuo Koronsha, 1989) pp. 115-6.
55. H. M. Reischauer, *Samurai and Silk: A Japanese American Heritage*, pp. 185-6.
56. It should be noted that not all Japanese had such views on westerners: some Japanese authorities and scholars had well detailed knowledge of the political, social, and economic institutions of the west. As D. Keene noted, 'By the end of the eighteenth century, the Japanese were better acquainted with European civilization than any other non-western country.' D. Keene, *The Japanese Discovery of Europe, 1770-1830* (Stanford: Stanford University Press, 1969) p. 123.
57. T. Yokoyama, *Japan and the Victorian Mind: A Study of Stereotyped Images of a Nation 1850-80* (London: The Macmillan Press Ltd., 1987) p. 50.
58. T. Yokoyama, *Japan and the Victorian Mind: A Study of Stereotyped Images of a Nation 1850-80*, pp. 51-2.

59. *Ibid.*, pp. 49, 57.
60. Notehelfer, ed. *Japan Through American Eyes; Journal of Francis Hall Kanagawa and Yokohama, 1859-66*, p. 39 for comments on Japanese children who seem never to cry. See also, T. Yokoyama, *Japan and the Victorian Mind: A Study of Stereotyped Images of a Nation 1850-80*, p. 46.
61. For the definition of Orientalism see the introduction of Edward Said, *Orientalism* (New York: Vintage Books, 1994) pp. 1-28.
62. F. R. Eldridge, *Oriental Trade Methods* (New York, D. Appleton and Company, 1923), pp. 32-35.
63. See for example the case of Itō Hanejirō vs. H. Brigstocke, *Japan Weekly Mail*, August 15, 1874. In this case, Brigstocke, the second officer of the *S.S. Duna* purportedly hit and rendered unconscious a labourer, Itō Hanejirō.
64. Such was the fate of Kyoto merchant Yamatoya Wohe [O-he] in 1863. Joseph Heco and James Murdoch, *The Narrative of a Japanese: What He has Seen and The People He has Met in the Course of The Last Forty Years.* (San Francisco: American-Japanese Publishing Association, n.d.) vol. 2, pp. 13-15.
65. F. G. Notehelfer, ed. *Japan Through American Eyes; Journal of Francis Hall Kanagawa and Yokohama, 1859-66*, pp. 506, 508.
66. Pat Barr, *The Coming of the Barbarians; A Story of Western Settlements in Japan 1853-1870* (London: Penguin Press, 1967) p. 97.
67. F. G. Notehelfer, ed. *Japan Through American Eyes; Journal of Francis Hall Kanagawa and Yokohama, 1859-66*, p. 116.
68. Heco and Murdoch, *The Narrative of a Japanese: What He has Seen and The People He has Met in the Course of The Last Forty Years.* vol. 1, p. 237.
69. Notehelfer, ed. *Japan Through American Eyes; Journal of Francis Hall Kanagawa and Yokohama, 1859-66*, p. 474. See also, Joseph Heco and James Murdoch, *The Narrative of a Japanese: What He has Seen and The People He has Met in the Course of The Last Forty Years*, vol. 1, p. 323.

CHAPTER THREE: REACHING AGREEMENT: THE MECHANICS OF PROMISE AND PAYMENT

1. Nagai Minoru (ed.), *Jishyo Masuda Takashi-o den* (Tokyo: Chūō Kōronsha, 1989) p.115. *Masuda Takashi-o den* is a work that is between an autobiography, biography, and memoir. Masuda did not write this work. In the course of working with him, his secretary Nagai Minoru (who later became an academic) wrote down in the evenings the events and anecdotes he had heard during the working day. Later these writings were published in roughly chronological order. Although Masuda was aware of the work, he died before he was able to read through it.
2. Many thanks to Christopher Woodruff of University of California San Diego for suggesting this idea.
3. Yen-P'ing Hao, *The Comprador in Nineteenth Century China: Bridge Between East and West* (Cambridge: Harvard University Press, 1970) p. 59.
4. M. Paske Smith, *Western Barbarians in Japan and Formosa in Tokugawa Days 1603-1868* (Kobe: Tanaka Printing Co., 1930) pp. 272-7.
5. F. G. Notehelfer, ed. *Japan Through American Eyes: Journal of Francis Hall Kanagawa and Yokohama, 1859-66* (Princeton: Princeton University Press, 1992) p. 71. Hall writes of an incident in which he tries to buy dogs using body language.
6. *Ibid*, p. 80.
7. H. M. Reischauer, *Samurai and Silk: A Japanese American Heritage* (Cambridge: Harvard University Press, 1986) pp. 185-6.
8. Ann Yokoyama, *Yokohama Prints from Nineteenth-Century Japan* (Washington DC: Smithsonian Institute Press, 1990) p. 82.
9. Yen-P'ing Hao, *The Comprador in Nineteenth Century China: Bridge Between East and West*, p.19.
10. *The Japan Herald* (henceforth denoted *JH*), 13 September 1863.

11. *The China Directory*, Japan Supplement 1867, p. 2S (Supplement), 6S.
12. *Ibid*, p. 1S, 6S.
13. *The China Directory*, 1866 p. 233. Also see F. G. Notehelfer's essay, 'Sketch of the Life of Francis Hall', in F. G. Notehelfer, ed. *JapanThrough American Eyes: Journal of Francis Hall Kanagawa and Yokohama, 1859-66*, pp. 3-62.
14. This case is discussed in detail in the following chapter.
15. In the case of Rikichi Hikosuki and Yagishita Chojirō vs. C. A. Fletcher & Co., the Japanese plaintiffs mention buying iron advertised for sale by auction. *The Japan Weekly Mail* (henceforth denoted as *JWM*), 15 July 1874.
16. *JH*, 4 June 1863.
17. F. G. Notehelfer, ed. *JapanThrough American Eyes: Journal of Francis Hall Kanagawa and Yokohama, 1859-66*, p. 158.
18. H. S. Williams, *Tales of Foreign Settlements in Japan*, (Tokyo: Charles E. Tuttle Company, 1986) pp. 48-9.
19. All dollar values are in Mexican Silver dollars unless otherwise indicated.
20. *JWM*, 22 February 1873, and *JWM*, 1 March 1873.
21. *JWM*, 22 February 1873.
22. E. Smith vs. R. Lilley, *JWM*, 13 January 1877.
23. F. Vyse to Alcock, Kanagawa, 6 August 1859 in enclosure to Malmesbury from Alcock, Vol. 3 in Great Britain, Public Record Office. Foreign Office Papers, *General Correspondence, Japan*. (F.O. Series 46).
24. The chit system is no longer in wide use in Japan, expect on the ubiquitous ceramic *Tanuki* (magical raccoon dog) statues. The Tanuki is usually depicted carrying a placard with the character *tsu*, short for *tsucho*, or chit. In popular mythology, these dipsomatic creatures used chits to obtain saké, for which they often did not pay – the privileges and prerogative of being a mythical creature.
25. H. S. Williams, *Tales of Foreign Settlements in Japan*, p. 48.
26. J. Kay *Foundations of Corporate Success; How Business Strategies Add Value* (Oxford: Oxford University Press, 1993) p. 54.
27. G. Morrison to R. Alcock, 5 September 1859, in Great Britain, Public Record Office. Foreign Office Papers, *General Correspondence, Japan*. (F.O. Series 46, reel 5).
28. G. Morrison to R. Alcock, 5 September 1859, in Great Britain, Public Record Office. Foreign Office Papers, *General Correspondence, Japan* (F.O. Series 46, reel 5).
29. F. G. Notehelfer, ed. *JapanThrough American Eyes: Journal of Francis Hall Kanagawa and Yokohama, 1859-66*, p. 434.
30. H. Cortiazzi, 'Yokohama FrontierTown, 1859-66', *Asian Affairs, 17* (1986) p. 7.
31. *JWM*, 4 September 1875.
32. *Ibid.*, pp. 72, 347, 467.
33. *JT*, 8 September 1865.
34. H. M. Reischauer, *Samurai and Silk: A Japanese American Heritage*, p. 185.
35. Consideration need not be adequate; for example, in the case of treaty-port deals, there was no legal reason for consideration to be 10% of the deal. Consideration must have value in the eyes of the law, and it must be legal. A modern example of consideration is the 1 pence coin sent for a music club membership: the 1P is consideration for the agreement that for 5 free compact disks now, one will buy 3 at normal club prices within the next year. See legal discussion of consideration in : P. S. Atiyah, *An Introduction to the Law of Contract* (Oxford: Oxford University Press, 1995) pp. 118-152.

CHAPTER FOUR: DESCRIPTION OF CASES

1. R. T. Chang, *The Justice of the Western Consular Courts in Nineteenth Century Japan* (Westport: Greenwood Press, 1984) p. 121.
2. M. Paske Smith, *Western Barbarians in Japan and Formosa inTokugawa Days 1603-1868*

(Kobe: Tanaka Printing Co., 1930) p. 203.

3. Alcock to Japanese Foreign Ministers, Yokohama, 27 December 1861 in Great Britain, Public Record Office. Foreign Office Papers, *General Correspondence, Japan* (F.O. Series 262, reel 4).

4. *The Japan Times' Overland Mail*, 26 July 1869.

5. *JWM*, 16 October 1875.

6. Tanabe Yasuzaemon vs. Alexander Stewart, *JWM*, 13 May 1876, and *The Japan Gazette*, 10 May 1876. Tanabe's first name is 'Yasuyameno' in *The Japan Gazette*.

7. Bunzo vs. W. Raglan in *JWM*, 14 September 1872. Bunzo pursued, unsuccessfully, $99 of damages for the death of his mother.

8. W. P. Mitchell vs. Nakajima Saisuke, *JWM*, 18 November and 9 December 1876.

9. See the case of Aburaza Ihei and Isuruya Kaneso vs. Glover & Co. in *JT*, 19 January 1866.

10. 'Jaffray' was also spelled 'Jaffrey' in issues of *JWM*.

11. *JWM*, 20 April 1872, and see *JWM*, 14 September 1872.

12. *JWM*, 22 February 1876.

13. *JWM*, 25 May 1878.

14. The following chapter discusses the mechanics of the dispute resolution in the treaty ports.

15. Tanabe Yasuzaemon vs. A. Stewart, *JWM*, 13 May 1876.

16. Suzuke vs. The Pacific Mail Company. *JWM*, 31 October 1874.

17. See for example, see Kanagawa Kencho vs. P. Bohm in the German Consular court, *JWM*, 2 December 1876.

18. *JWM*, 9, 16 June 1877. Also see the law reports of June 1877 in *The Japan Gazette*.

19. *JWM*, 1 December 1877

20. See for example the case of E. Manz [Manzo] vs. A. Campbell, *JWM*, 4, 11 May 1872.

21. The case of Itō Hachibei vs. Walsh Hall & Co. is such an exception. See Chapter 7.

22. *The Nagasaki Shipping List and Advertiser*, 21 August 1861.

23. *The Japan Times' Overland Mail*, 21 August 1861.

24. *The Japan Times' Overland Mail*, 21 August 1861.

25. *JH*, 7 January 1864.

26. See *JWM*, 9 June 1877.

27. *JWM*, 16 June 1877.

28. See the employment contract dispute of Capt. Roper vs. Mitsu Bishi Steam Ship Co. [sic], in *JWM*, 4 September 1875, and *JWM*, 13 May, 9 December 1876.

29. Alcock to Lord J. Russell, vol 4. 4 November 1859 in Great Britain, Public Record Office. Foreign Office Papers, *General Correspondence, Japan*. (F.O. Series 46, reel 3).

30. *The Japan Times' Overland Mail*, 12 February 1869.

31. The issues in this case are similar to those in Itō Hachibei vs. Walsh, Hall, & Co. covered in detail in a further chapter. Both cases had unclear concepts of 'partnership'.

32. *The Japan Times' Overland Mail*, 12 February 1869. See also the quotation at the start of this chapter.

33. *JH*, 1865.

34. *JWM*, 6 November 1869.

35. *The Nagasaki Shipping List and Advertiser*, 21 August 1861.

36. *JT*, 28 April 1866 and 19 May 1866.

37. *JT*, 19 May 1866.

38. *JH*, 14, 17 May 1862.

39. See Chapter VII for a discussion of this case in depth.

40. *JH*, 16 August 1862.

41. *JH*, 26 September 1863.

42. *JWM*, 20 May 1876.

43. E. M. Van Reed vs. Masters and Owners of the British Schooner *Bezaleel*, *The Japan Times' Overland Mail*, 9 October 1869. Also, the case of Knight & Co. vs. W. M. Robinet focused on a shipment of peas on the brig *Regna*. *The Japan Times' Overland Mail*, 9 October 1869.
44. *JWM*, 27 March 1875.
45. Suzuke is most likely 'Suzuki'. *JWM*, 31 October 1874.
46. *JWM*, 10 April 1875.
47. *JWM*, 4 September 1875, and 13 May and 9 December 1876.

CHAPTER FIVE: THE AVENUES OF LEGAL REDRESS

1. *JWM*, 26 September 1874.
2. The Japanese names are reproduced here as they were printed in the Treaty Port press. The treaty-port press at this time did not follow any regular conventions of transliterating Japanese.
3. *JT*, 28 October 1865.
4. P. S. Atiyah, *The Rise and Fall of the Law of Contract* (Oxford: Oxford University Press, 1979), pp. 219-570. Part two of this definitive work on contract, 'The Age of the Freedom on Contract: 1770-1870', is dedicated to how contract reached its apex in the nineteenth century.
5. R. T. Chang, *The Justice of the Western Consular Courts in Nineteenth Century Japan* (Westport: Greenwood Press, 1984) p. 144.
6. *Ibid.*, pp. 143-45.
7. *JWM*, 26 November 1870.
8. J. E. Hoare, *Japan's Treaty Ports and Foreign Settlements: The Uninvited Guests, 1859-1899* (Kent: Japan Library, 1994) p. 54.
9. *Ibid.*, p. 168.
10. *JWM*, 7 November 1874.
11. *JH*, 27 May 1865.
12. *JH*, 14 January 1866.
13. *JWM*, 2 December 1871.
14. See for example the cases of the Law Report of *JWM*, 14 September 1872. In this issue, the Western courts dealt with a sailor found 'drunk and incapable', drunk sailors stealing and attempting to sell the sails of their ship, sailors refusing duty, and an inquest for a drunk sailor falling off a boat and drowning to death.
15. R. T. Chang, *The Justice of the Western Consular Courts in Nineteenth Century Japan*, pp. 28-34.
16. *Ibid.*, pp. 30-33.
17. R. Ellickson, *Order Without Law; How Neighbors Settle Disputes* (Cambridge: Harvard University Press, 1991) p. 70.
18. *Ibid.*, pp. 258-64.
19. J. E. Hoare, *Japan's Treaty Ports and Foreign Settlements: The Uninvited Guests, 1859-1899*, p. 62.
20. J. H. Wigmore, 'Materials for the Study of Private Law in Japan', *TASJ* (Supp), 20 (1892) p. 73. and D. F. Henderson and P. M. Torbert, 'Traditional Contract Law in Japan and China' in *International Encyclopedia of Comparative Law*, vol VII (Boston: Martinius Nijhoff Publisher, 1973), p. 4.
21. Dan Fenno Henderson and P. M. Torbert, 'Traditional Contract Law in Japan and China', p. 4.
22. Dan Fenno Henderson, *Conciliation and Japanese Law: Tokugawa and Modern*, vol. 1 (Tokyo: University of Tokyo Press, 1965), p. 171.
23. J. H. Wigmore, 'Private Law in Old Japan,' *TASJ*, 20 supplement (1892), p. 71-73.
24. Dan Fenno Henderson, *Conciliation and Japanese Law: Tokugawa and Modern*, vol. 1 (Tokyo: University of Tokyo Press, 1965) pp. 128-129. See also, Takayanago Shinzo, 'Wakai shugi ni tatsu Saiban' *Chūō Kōron*, 56 (1941) p. 142.
25. See for example, the dispute between Chube and Nuinosuke in Dan Fenno

Henderson, *Conciliation and Japanese Law: Tokugawa and Modern*, vol. 1, pp. 148-166.

26. R. T. Chang, *The Justice of the Western Consular Courts in Nineteenth Century Japan*, p. xi.
27. *Ibid.*, p. xi.
28. Y. Fukuzawa, *An Outline of a Theory of Civilization*, tr. D. A. Dilworth and G. C. Hurst (Tokyo: Sophia University Press, 1973) p. 183.
29. R. T. Chang, *The Justice of the Western Consular Courts in Nineteenth Century Japan*, p. 135.
30. Lord Malmesbury to Vyse, 7 February 1859 in Great Britain, Public Record Office. *General Correspondence, Japan.* (FO Series 46, Reel, 5).
31. See for example François-James Tyndall de Veer unsuccessful letter to Malmesbury of 26 October 1859 in Great Britain, Public Record Office. *General Correspondence, Japan.* (Series 46, reel 5).
32. E. Satow, *A Diplomat in Japan*, (London: Shelly, Service & Co. Ltd., 1921) p. 157.
33. Alcock to Lord Malmesbury, 20 September 1859 in Great Britain, Public Record Office. *General Correspondence, Japan* (Series 46, reel 3).
34. T. Chang, *The Justice of Western Consular Courts in Nineteenth Century Japan*, p. 7.
35. M. Paske-Smith, *Western Barbarians in Japan and Formosa in the Tokugawa Period* (Kobe: Thompson, 1930) p. 252.
36. China and Japan Order in Council of 1865.
37. J. E. Hoare, *Japan's Treaty Ports and Foreign Settlements: The Uninvited Guests, 1859-1899*, p. 58.
38. *Ibid.*, pp. 73-4.
39. *Ibid.*, pp. 68-70.
40. See further comment on this issue in the appeal case of W. P. Mitchell vs. Nakajima Seisuke, *JWM*, 9 December 1876.
41. J. E. Hoare, *Japan's Treaty Ports and the Foreign Settlements: The Uninvited guests, 1859-1899*, p. 73, and Granville to F. O. Adams, no. 40. 11 November 1871 with enclosure of Hornby to Granville dated 28 October 1871 in Great Britain, Public Record Office in *General Correspondence, Japan.* (Series 262).
42. China and Japan Order in Council 1865.
43. *The Chronicle and Directory for China, Japan, and the Philippines* (Hong Kong: Hong Kong Daily Press Office 1874) p. 115.
44. *Ibid.*, p. 114.
45. *Ibid.*, p. 115.
46. Joseph Heco and James Murdoch, *The Narrative of a Japanese: What He has Seen and The People He has Met in the Course of The Last Forty Years*. (San Francisco: American-Japanese Publishing Association, n.d.) vol. 2 p. 235.
47. R. T. Chang, *The Justice of the Western Consular Courts in Nineteenth Century Japan*, p. 12-13.
48. *Ibid.*, p.11.
49. *JWM*, 16 February 1870.
50. *JT*, 10 November 1865.
51. Joseph Heco and James Murdoch, *The Narrative of a Japanese: What He has Seen and The People He has Met in the Course of The Last Forty Years*, vol. 2, pp. 79-80. See also Williams, *Tales of the Foreign Settlements* (Tokyo: Charles E. Tuttle Company, 1986), pp. 61-63. The assault case is also covered in detail Rickerby's newspaper in *Supplement to JT*, 25 November 1865.
52. T. Dennett, *Americans in Eastern Asia* (New York: Macmillan, 1941) p. 669.
53. Enclosure #2 Alcock to Foreign Minister Lord J. Russell. 23 Nov. 1859 in Great Britain, Public Record Office. *General Correspondence, Japan.* (Series 262). vol. 1, p. 60.
54. F. G. Notehelfer, ed. *Japan Through American Eyes; Journal of Francis Hall Kanagawa and Yokohama, 1859-66* (Princeton: Princeton University Press, 1992), p. 552. See also the comments of F. G. Notehelfer in his introduction to Hall's diary, 'Sketch of the Life of Francis Hall' in *Japan Through American Eyes; Journal of*

Francis Hall Kanagawa and Yokohama, 1859-66, (Princeton: Princeton University Press, 1992) pp. 56-60.

55. *Ibid.,* p. 552.
56. *Ibid.,* p. 552.
57. *Ibid.,* p. 553.
58. *Ibid.,* p. 553.
59. *Ibid.,* p. 553.
60. *Ibid.,* p. 597.
61. J. Heco and J. Murdoch, *The Narrative of a Japanese: What He has Seen and The People He has Met in the Course of The Last Forty Years,* vol. 1, p. 242.
62. F. G. Notehelfer, ed. *Japan Through American Eyes; Journal of Francis Hall Kanagawa and Yokohama, 1859-66,* p. 353.
63. Joseph Heco and James Murdoch, *The Narrative of a Japanese: What He has Seen and The People He has Met in the Course of The Last Forty Years,* vol. 1 pp. 310, 332.
64. J. E. Hoare, *Japan's Treaty Ports and Foreign Settlements: The Uninvited Guests, 1859-1899,* p. 61, and A. P. Porter to Parks, no date [Summer 1869], in Great Britain, Public Record Office, *General Correspondence, Japan.* (Series 262, reel 4).
65. F. G. Notehelfer, ed. *Japan Through American Eyes; Journal of Francis Hall Kanagawa and Yokohama, 1859-66,* p. 58.
66. Joseph Heco and James Murdoch, *The Narrative of a Japanese: What He has Seen and The People He has Met in the Course of The Last Forty Years.* vol. 1, p. 218, and F. G. Notehelfer, ed. *Japan Through American Eyes; Journal of Francis Hall Kanagawa and Yokohama, 1859-66,* p. 383.
67. F. G. Notehelfer, ed. *Japan Through American Eyes; Journal of Francis Hall Kanagawa and Yokohama, 1859-66,* p. 299.
68. Countries such as Austria-Hungary, Belgium, Denmark, France, Italy, Holland, Portugal, Russia, Spain, The United Kingdom of Sweden and Norway, and Switzerland.
69. Pat Barr, *The Coming of the Barbarians; A Story of Western Settlements in Japan 1853-1870* (London: Penguin Press, 1967) p. 85.
70. Joseph Heco and James Murdoch, *The Narrative of a Japanese: What He has Seen and The People He has Met in the Course of The Last Forty Years,* vol. 1, p. 217. and F. G. Notehelfer, ed., *Japan Through American Eyes: Journal of Francis Hall Kanagawa and Yokohama, 1859-66,* p. 35.
71. H. S. Williams, *Tales of the Foreign Settlements in Japan,* p. 41.
72. M. Paske-Smith, *Western Barbarians in Japan and Formosa in the Tokugawa Period,* p. 249.
73. *Ibid.,* p. 249.
74. J. E. Hoare, *Japan's Treaty Ports and Foreign Settlements: The Uninvited Guests, 1859-1899,* p. 83.
75. In the case of D. McKenzie vs. Hansard & Co., over $57 worth of restitution, neither party had a lawyer: *Supplement to JH,* 22 July 1865. On the other hand, in the case of Itō Hachibei vs. Walsh Hall & Co. discussed in Chapter 7, F. V. Dickins, a western lawyer, represented Itō and G. P. Ness represented the defendant. *JWM,* September 1875 to January 1876. In general, cost was a factor on whether to hire lawyers.
76. *JWM,* 21 May 1870.
77. *JWM,* 27 March 1875.
78. *JWM,* 26 November 1870.
79. *JWM,* 26 November 1870.
80. *JWM,* 10 December 1870.
81. *JWM,* 7 May 1870.
82. *JWM,* 2 July 1870.

CHAPTER SIX: IN PURSUIT OF A BARGAIN

1. Alcock to Japanese Foreign Ministers, Yokohama, 27 December 1861 in Great

Britain, Public Record Office. *General Correspondence, Japan* (Series 262, reel 6).

2. Imports and exports in 1861 year had totaled about 5.5 million dollars. M. Paske Smith, *Western Barbarians in Japan and Formosa in Tokugawa Days 1603-1868*, p. 303. As with all early trade statistics collected by consuls, these statistics may not be accurate.

3. F. G. Notehelfer, ed. *Japan Through American Eyes; Journal of Francis Hall Kanagawa and Yokohama, 1859-66* (Kobe: Thompson, 1930) p. 72.

4. Nagai Minoru (ed.), *Jishyo Masuda Ko-o den* (Tokyo: Chuo Koronsha, 1989) p. 89.

5. J. McMaster, 'British Trade and Traders to Japan 1859-1869', Unpublished Ph.D. thesis (London: University of London, 1962) p. 145.

6. J. E. Hoare, *Japan's Treaty Ports and Foreign Settlements: The Uninvited Guests, 1859-1899* (Kent: The Japan Library, 1994) p. 23. Also, the Yokohama Archives of History have E. Satow's personal, often affectionate, correspondence with his children in Japan. The archive is in the process of organizing the papers.

7. E. Satow, *A Diplomat in Japan*, (London: Shelly, Service & Co. Ltd., 1921) pp. 22-23.

8. In Jardine's documents, Takasuya is written as 'Takasia'. In Japanese, his name and firm was Takasuya. J. McMaster refers to the firm as Takashi-ya.

9. J. McMaster, *British Trade and Traders to Japan 1859-1869*, p. 149. See also K. Ishii, *Kindai Nihon to Igirisu Shihon: Jyarudin Maseson shyokai o chushin ni* (Tokyo: University of Tokyo Press, 1984) pp. 31-39.

10. E.g. complaints made against Japanese merchants altering the weight of silk in the case of Shibia Seigoro vs. Albert Edleman, *Supplement to JH*, 14 January 1865.

11. H. M. Reischauer, *Samurai and Silk; A Japanese American Heritage* (Boston: Houghton Mifflin Company, 1989) p. 207.

12. *JWM*, 3 August 1872.

13. *JH*, 7 January 1865. The newspaper contains a misprint and the year is actually printed as '1864'.

14. *JT*, 8 September 1865. See also the quotation at the start of this chapter.

15. *JT*, 8 September 1865.

16. *JT*, 8 September 1865.

17. *JT*, 8 September 1865.

18. *JT*, 28 October 1865.

19. *The Hiogo News*, 2 March 1870. All further case details, unless otherwise specified, come from this source.

20. See for example, Schultze, Reis & Co. v. W. Boyd, in *JT*, September 15, 1865. In this $99 contract dispute over butter, the plaintiff showed the defendant a sample keg of butter.

21. *JWM*, 11 July 1876.

22. *JWM*, 22 July 1876.

23. *JT*, 19 January 1866. All further case details, unless otherwise specified, come from this source.

24. A unit of weight equal to 100 catties, especially a Chinese unit, or about 133 and 1/3 pounds (about 60 kilograms). The word derived from the Malay word 'pikul' – a verb meaning to bear the heaviest load a man can carry.

25. A pig is not a standardized measurement, but refers to the crude block of metal made by pouring molten metal into a mold.

26. There is some discrepancy over the total weight of the lead available in the Glover & Co. compound; it is unclear whether it is 2000 or 2800 piculs.

27. The plaintiff's name was most likely Iseya Hanzo in modern transliteration.

28. *JH*, 11 and 12 November 1864. All further case details, unless otherwise specified, come from this source.

29. This name is spelled Yamati, Yamatia, Yamatai within the newspaper's text of the court trial. This name was probably corrupted and is most likely 'Yamato-ya' as they refer to the plaintiff's establishment as Yamato-ya.

30. *JT*, 28 October 1865. All further case details, unless otherwise specified, come from this source.
31. *JT*, 28 October 1865.
32. *JT*, 28 October 1865.
33. The editorial was probably written by Charles Rickerby, the editor and publisher of *JT* at that time.
34. M. Paske Smith, *Western Barbarians in Japan and Formosa in Tokugawa Days 1603-1868*, pp. 304-5.
35. M. Paske Smith, *Western Barbarians in Japan and Formosa in Tokugawa Days 1603-1868*, p. 329.
36. Patricia Arias, 'La Consolidacion de una Gran Empresa en un Contexto Regional de industrias Pequen-as: El Caso de Calzado Canada'. *Relaciones*, 3 (nd), p. 193. Many thanks to C. Woodruff for the source.
37. Christopher Woodruff: personal e-mail correspondence to Y. Honjo: 4 July 1999. Woodruff declined to release the name of the individual.
38. The name is spelled Nakajima Saisuke in modern transliteration, and he is referred to as Saisuke in the 8 July 1876 edition of *JWM*.
39. *JWM*, 1 July 1874. All further case details, unless otherwise specified, come from this source.
40. The name is probably Shidetoshi or Hidetoshi in modern transliteration.
41. *JWM*, 8 July 1876.
42. *JWM*, 8 July 1876.
43. The name is probably Tosuke in modern transliteration.
44. R. T. Chang, *The Justice of the Western Consular Courts in Nineteenth Century Japan* (Westport: Greenwood Press, 1984) pp. 8-10.
45. Other major cases that dominated the consular courts include the 1865 libel and criminal case involving Glackmeyer and McKechnie: the case was heard in both the British and American courts. In 1876, the Japanese courts were tied up with the case of Edgar Abbott vs. Mitsu Bishi S. S. Co. [sic].
46. *JWM*, 8 March 1873.
47. *JWM*, 19 May 1877.
48. C. Esdale was also another repeat litigant: he was also accused of assault of A. Cayeux. Cayeux apparently insulted Esdale's sister and kicked her son, Esdale's nephew. He was fined two dollars for his transgression.

CHAPTER SEVEN: PROMISE, AGREEMENT AND CONTRACT: ITŌ HACHIBEI VS. WALSH, HALL & CO.

1. *JWM*, 8 January 1875.
2. *JWM*, 9 October 1875.
3. *JWM*, 4 September 1875, pp. 767. All dollars are Mexican Silver Dollars.
4. See Note 48, Ch. 6.
5. Shinoda Kozo, ed. *Bakumatsu Meiji Onna Hyakuwa* (Tokyo: Kadokawa Sensho, 1932) p. 27, and Ubukata Toshiro, *Meiji Taisho Kenbun* (Tokyo: Chuokoron Bunko, 1981), p. 20. Also see the copy of the family tree (keizu) in Tsuchiya Yoshio, Shibusawa Eichi (Tokyo, Yoshikawa Kobunsha, 1988] p. 278.
6. J. Roberts, *Mitsui: Three Centuries of Japanese Business* (New York, Weatherhill, 1991) p. 64.
7. Shinoda Kozo, ed. *Bakumatsu Meiji Onna Hyakuwa*, pp. 27-35. Prof. K. Ishii initially suggested this source.
8. *Ibid.*, p. 27.
9. *Ibid.*, p. 27.
10. 1 *ryo* – approximately the cost of amount of rice that one man could eat.
11. *Beikoku* is not as in the homonym, Beikoku, meaning United States. Bei=rice, *Koku*, as in kokumatsu, meaning grain.
12. Ubukata Toshiro, *Meiji Taishō Kenbun*, p. 19-20.
13. Sawada Akira, *Meiji Zaisei no Kisoteki Kenkyu* (Tokyo: Houbunkan, 1934) p. 79.

14. Ubukata Toshiro, *Meiji Taishō Kenbun*, p. 20-1.
15. Many have assumed the nickname derived from that fact that the firm's principal offices were located in Yokohama on lot number one. In reality, Yokohama lot #1 was the offices of Jardine Matheson & Co. Walsh Hall & Co.'s offices were actually located on Lot #2 but still retained the name.
16. George Hall and Francis (Frank) Hall are sometimes confused in treaty port histories.
17. F. G. Notehelfer, *Japan Through American Eyes: Journal of Francis Hall, Kanagawa and Yokohama, 1859-66* (Princeton: Princeton University Press, 1992) p. 37.
18. Norman Beecher and Nancy Bartram Beecher, *Fortunate Journey: Our Lives, Our Family, and Our Forebears* (Saline, MI: McNaughton & Gunn, 1993) p. 394.
19. *Ibid.*, p. 394.
20. F. G. Notehelfer, *Japan Through American Eyes*, p. 37.
21. *JWM*, 16 October 1875.
22. Nagai Minoru (ed.), *Jishyo Masuda Takashi-o den* (Tokyo: Chuo Koronshya, 1989) p.115.
23. *Ibid.*, p. 131.
24. *Ibid.*, p. 273.
25. Shinoda Kozo, ed., *Bakumatsu Meiji Onna Hyakuwa*, p. 34.
26. *Ibid.*, p. 35.
27. *JWM*, 4 September 1875.
28. Shinoda Kozo, ed., *Bakumatsu Meiji Onna Hyakuwa*, p.35.
29. *JWM*, 4 September 1875.
30. *JWM*, 4 September 1875.
31. Zin Coy and Sin Coy are all variations used by *JWM*.
32. *JWM*, 23 October 1875.
33. *JWM*, 16 October 1875.
34. Many thanks for Masaki Nakabayashi for this infomation. See article by S. Hara 'Shin Kin-yu no Sosetu' in *Yokohama shi-hi* (Yokohama: Yurindo-Yokohama, 1961) vol. 3, pp. 166-226.
35. *JWM*, 27 November 1875.
36. *JWM*, 27 November 1875.
37. *JWM*, 4 September 1875.
38. *JWM*, 4 September 1875.
39. *JWM*, 2 October 1875.
40. *JWM*, 11 September 1875.
41. The cheque referred to in this matter seems to be a type of promissory note that did not need to be cashed. The note, like currency notes, passed current in the treaty ports.
42. *JWM*, 9 October 1875.
43. *JWM*, 9 October 1875.
44. *JWM*, 4 September 1875.
45. *JWM*, 4 December 1875.
46. *JWM*, 4 December 1875.
47. *JWM*, 16 October 1875.
48. *JWM*, 16 October 1875.
49. *JWM*, 4 September 1875.
50. *JWM*, 16 October 1875.
51. *JWM*, 16 October 1875.
52. *JWM*, 23 October 1875.
53. *JWM*, 6 November 1875.
54. *JWM*, 23 October 1875.
55. *JWM*, 4 December 1875.
56. *JWM*, 13 November 1875.
57. *JWM*, 8 January 1876.
58. *JWM*, 8 January 1876.

59. *JWM*, 4 September 1875.
60. *JWM*, 16 October 1875.
61. *JWM*, 11 December 1875.
62. *JWM*, 16 October 1875.
63. *JWM*, 27 November 1875.
64. *JWM*, 27 November 1875.
65. *JWM*, 23 October 1875.
66. He reportedly absconded with $800. *JWM*, 13 November 1875.
67. *JWM*, 23 October 1875.
68. *JWM*, 27 November 1875.
69. *JWM*, 11 September 1875. and Nagai Minoru (ed.), *Jishyo Masuda Takashi-o den*, p.115.
70. 13 November 1875, *JWM* refers to the firm as E. Fischer & Co., although in the following issue, the firm is listed as E. Fisher.
71. S. Macaulay 'Non-Contractual Relations in Business: A Preliminary Study', *American Sociological Review*, 28 (1963) p. 57.

CHAPTER EIGHT: TOWARDS IMPLICATIONS AND THEORY

1. A. Greif, 'Reputation and Coalition in Medieval Trade: Evidence on the Maghribi Traders', *Journal of Economic History*, 49 (1989) pp. 857-882.
2. O. Williamson, *The Economic Institutions of Capitalism* (New York: Free Press, 1985), pp. 30-31.
3. Nagai Minoru (ed.), *Jisho Masuda Takashi-o den* (Tokyo: Chuo Koronsha, 1989), pp. 88-89.
4. S. Macaulay 'Non-Contractual Relations in Business: A Preliminary Study', *American Sociological Review*, 28 (1963), pp. 55-69.
5. *Ibid.*, p. 59.
6. *Ibid.*, p. 58.
7. Chicken, Prisoner's Dilemma and the War of the Sexes are all names of interactive choice scenarios used in game theory.
8. H. Beale and T. Dugdale, 'Contracts Between Businessmen: Planning and the Use of Contractual Remedies' *The British Journal of Law and Society* 2 (1975) pp. 45-60, and R. Lewis, 'Contracts Between Businessmen: Reform of the Law of Firm Offers and an Empirical Study of Tendering Practices in the Building Industry' *Journal of Law and Society* 9 (Winter 1982) pp 153-175.
9. O. Williamson, *The Economic Institutions of Capitalism*, p. 21.
10. S. Macaulay 'Non-Contractual Relations in Business: A Preliminary Study', p. 57.
11. F. R. Eldridge, *Oriental Trade Methods* (New York: D. Appleton and Company, 1923) pp. 5-9.
12. *Ibid.*, pp. 31-33.
13. *Ibid.*, p. 34.
14. See for example, Nakamura Hajime's characterization of the Japanese as 'non-logical' in 'Basic Features of the Legal, Political, and Economic Thought of Japan', and 'Consciousness of the Individual and the Universal Among the Japanese' C. A. Moore, ed. *The Japanese Mind: Essentials of Japanese Philosophy and Culture* (Honolulu: East-West Center Press, 1967).
15. J. H. Wigmore, 'Materials for the Study of Private Law in Japan', *TASJ* (Supp), 20 (1892), Introduction to part I, pp. 3-4.
16. J. Okada to editor, *London and China Express*, 25 January 1884. Also see J. E. Hoare, *Japan's Treaty Ports and Foreign Settlements: The Uninvited Guests, 1859-1899* (Kent: The Japan Library, 1994), pp. 28-29.
17. Alcock to Vyse 24 September 1859, in Great Britain, Public Record Office. Foreign Office Papers, *General Correspondence, Japan* (F.O. Series 46, reel 4).
18. J. E. Hoare, *Japan's Treaty Ports and Foreign Settlements*, p. 28.
19. *Ibid.*, p. 28.

20. Janet T. Landa, *Trust, Ethnicity, and Identity: Beyond the New Institutional Economics of Ethnic Trading Networks, Contract law, and Gift-exchange* (Ann Arbor: University of Michigan Press, 1996), p. 104.
21. R. Ellickson, *Order Without Law; How Neighbors Settle Disputes* (Cambridge: Harvard University Press, 1991), p. 184.
22. E. McKendrick, *Contract Law*, p. 7.
23. J. Kay, *Foundations of Corporate Success; How Business Strategies Add Value* (Oxford: Oxford University Press, 1993) p. 51.
24. P. S. Atiyah, *An Introduction to the Law of Contract* (Oxford: Oxford University Press, 1995) p. 35-6.
25. A 1847 Preface to Addison, *Treatise on the Law of Contract* in R. Lewis, 'Contracts Between Businessmen: Reform of the Law of Firm Offers and an Empirical Study of Tendering Practices in the Building Industry', *Journal of Law and Society* 9 (1982), p. 153.
26. *Ibid.*, pp. 161-6.
27. *Ibid.*, p. 163.

CONCLUSION: THE REPUBLIC OF COMMERCE

1. O. Williamson, 'Calculativeness, Trust, and Economic Organization', *Journal of Law and Economics*, 36 (1993), p. 471, and L. Huemer, *Trust in Business Relations, Economic Logic or Social Interaction?* (Umea: Borea Bokforlag, 1998), p. 17.
2. S. Johnson, J. McMillan, and C. Woodruff, 'Trust or Tort? Contract Enforcement in Transition', Unpublished draft, 2 November 1998, (Sloan School of Management, MIT and Graduate School of International Relations and Pacific Studies, UCSD) pp. 19-33.

SELECT BIBLIOGRAPHY

PRIMARY SOURCES

NEWSPAPERS AND MAGAZINES CONSULTED

The Daily Japan Herald. 1864-1867.
The Daily Japan Herald Extra. 1866.
L'Echo du Japon. 1870-85.
The Far East. 1866-7.
The Hiogo and Osaka Herald. 1868-75.
The Hiogo News. 1868-1898.
The Hiogo News Extra. 1870.
The Hiogo Shipping List. 1870.
The Japan Commercial News. 1863-5.
The Japan Daily Herald. 1874-81.
The Japan Express. 1862.
The Japan Gazette [Daily]. 1874-1886.
The Japan Gazette, Mail Summary and Shipping and Market Report. 1873-1874.
The Japan Gazette, A Fortnightly Summary of the Political, Commercial, Literary, and Social Events of Japan. 1881-1883.
The Japan Herald. 1861-1865.
The Japan Mail. 1870-1917.
The Japan Mail Extra (Hiogo News Issue) 1870.10.27.
The Japan Punch. 1862-1867.
The Japan Times. 1865-78.
The Japan Times Daily Advertiser. 1865-1866.
The Japan Times' Overland Mail. 1867-1869.
The Japan Weekly Mail; a Political, Commercial, and Literary Journal. 1870-1885.
The Nagasaki Express. 1870-74.

The Nagasaki Shipping List. 1869-70.

The Nagasaki Times and Shipping List. 1868-9.

DIRECTORIES

The China Directory. Hong Kong: Shortrede and Co., 1861-64.

The Japan Directory. 1872-1885.

BOOKS

'The Principal Trade Route of the Clipper Ships based on Admiralty Chart 1078': Permission of the Controller of the H. M. Stationary Office, [n.d.].

Alcock, Rutherford. *The Capital of the Tycoon: A Narrative of Three Years Residence in Japan.* 2 vols. New York: Harper and Brothers, 1863.

Baba, T. *The English in Japan; What a Japanese Thought and What He Thinks of Them.* London: Kegan Paul, Trench and Trubner, 1875.

Beasley, W. G., ed. *Select Documents on Japanese Foreign Policy. 1853-68.* Oxford: Oxford University Press, 1955.

Bird, Isabella. *Unbeaten Tracks in Japan.* London: John Murray, 1911.

Black, John R. *Young Japan.* 2 vols. Oxford: Oxford University Press, 1968.

Brooke, John M. *John M. Brooke's Pacific Cruise and Japanese Adventure.* Honolulu: University of Hawaii Press, 1986.

Chassiron, G. C. De. *Ambassade de France Au Japon.* Paris, 1861.

Edwards, O. *Residential Rhymes.* Tokyo: Hasegawa, n.d.

Eldridge, Frank R. *Trading with Asia.* New York: Appleton and Company, 1921.

Eldridge, Frank R. *Oriental Trade Methods.* New York: D. Appleton and Company, 1923.

Fontblanque, Edward B. de. *Niphon and Pe-che-li, or Two Years in Japan and Northern China.* London, 1862.

Fortune, Robert. *Yedo and Peking: A Narrative of a Journey to the Capitals of China and Japan.* London: John Murry, 1863.

Fraser, H. *A Diplomatist's Wife in Japan.* Vol. 2. London: Hutchinson, 1988.

Fukuzawa, Yukichi. *The Autobiography of Yukichi Fukuzawa.* Translated by Eiichi Kiyooka. New York: Columbia University Press, 1968.

Fukuzawa, Yukichi. *An Outline of a Theory of Civilization.* Translated by David A. Dilworth, G. Cameron Hurst. Tokyo: Sophia University, 1973.

Groos, A. 'Madame Butterfly: the Story Behind the Story'. *Madama Butterfly Program for the Welsh National Opera*, Cardiff: 1998.

Harris, Townsend. *The Complete Journal of Townsend Harris: First American Consul and Minister to Japan.* Garden City: Doubleday, Doran & Company, Inc. for New York Japan Society, 1930.

Heco, Joseph, and James Murdoch. *The Narrative of a Japanese: What He has Seen and The People He has Met in the Course of The Last Forty Years.* 2 vols. San Francisco: American-Japanese Publishing Association, n.d.

Heusken, Henry. *Japan Journal.* New Brunswick: Rutgers University Press, 1964.

Hodgson, C. P. *A Residence at Nagasaki and Hakodate.* London, 1861.

Katsu, Kokichi. *Misui's Story.* Translated by Teruko Craig. University of Arizona Press, 1988.

Morton-Cameron, W. H., ed. *Present Day Impressions of Japan.* London: The Globe Encylopedia Company, 1919.

Nagai, Minoru. *Jishyo Masuda Takashi-o den.* Tokyo: Chūō Kōronshya, 1989.

Nakano, Makiko. *Makiko's Diary; A Merchant Wife in 1910 Kyoto.* Translated by Kazuko Smith. Stanford: Stanford University Press, 1981.

Notehelfer, F. G., ed. *Japan Through American Eyes: The Journal of Francis Hall, Kanagawa and Yokohama 1859-1866.* Princeton: Princeton Univeristy Press, 1992.

Porter, Robert P. *Commerce and Industries of Japan:* Circular of Information of the National Association of Manufacturers of the United States of America, c. 1898.

Satow, Ernest. *A Diplomat in Japan.* London: Shelly, Service & Co. Ltd., 1921.

Shinoda, Kozo. *Bakumatsu Meiji onna hyaku wa.* Tokyo: Kadokawa Shoten, 1971.

Wakefield, C. C. *Future Trade in the Far East.* London: Whittaker & Co., 1896.

Whitney, Clara. *Clara's Diary: An American Girl in Meiji Japan.* Tokyo: Kodansha International, 1979.

Yokohama Kaikō Shiryōkan [Yokohama Archives of, ed. *Irustorashion nihon kankei kiji shu.* Yokohama: Yokohama Archives of History, 1986.

SECONDARY SOURCES

Adams, F. O. *A History of Japan.* London: H. S. King & Co., 1874.

Arias, Patricia. 'La Consolidacion de una Gran Empresa en un Contexto Regional de industrias Pequen-as: El Caso de Calzado Canada'. *Relaciones,* no. 3.

Barr, Pat. *The Coming of the Barbarians; A Story of Western Settlements in Japan 1853-1870.* London: Penguin Press, 1967.

Barr, Pat. *The Deer Cry Pavilion: a story of Westerners in Japan 1868-1905.* London: Macmillan Publishing, 1968.

Beasley, W. G. *Great Britain and the Opening of Japan.* London: Luzac, 1951.

Beasley, W. G. *The Meiji Restoration.* Stanford: Stanford University Press, 1972.

Beasley, W. G. *Japan Encounters the Barbarians; Japanese Travellers in America and Europe.* New Haven: Yale University Press, 1995.

Beecher, Norman, Beecher, Nancy Bartram. *Fortunate Journey: Our Lives, Our Family, and Our Forebears.* Saline, MI: McNaughton & Gunn, 1993.

Berry, Mary Elizabeth. 'Public Life in Authoritarian Japan'. *Daedalus* 127, no. 3 (1998): 133-165.

Blum, Paul C. *Yokohama in 1872, A Rambling Account of the Community in which the Asiatic Society of Japan was Founded.* Tokyo: The Asiatic Society of Japan, 1981.

Bolitho, H. *Treasures Among Men: the Fudai Daimyo in Tokugwa Japan.* New Haven: Yale University Press, 1974.

Booth, Martin. *Opium; A History.* New York: St. Martin's Press, 1996.

Brown, Philip C. 'Practical Constraints on Early Tokugawa Taxation: Annual Versus Fixed Assessments in Kaga Domain'. *Journal of Japanese Studies* 14, no. 2 (1988): 369-401.

Burks, Ardath W. 'Administratve Transition from Han to Ken: The Example of Okayama'. *Far Eastern Quarterly* 15, no. 3 (1956): 371-382.

Burks, Adrath W., ed. *The Modernizers; Overseas Students, Foreign Employees, and Meiji Japan*. London: Westview Press, 1985.

Burks, Ardath W. '[Review of] Japan's Treaty Ports and Foreign Settlments; The Uninvited Guests 1858-1899'. *Journal of Japanese Studies* 22, no. 2 (1996): 444-446.

Chang, Richard. 'The Chiasma Case'. *The Journal of Asian Studies* 34 (1975): 593-619.

Chang, Richard. *The Justice of the Western Consular Courts in Nineteeth-Century Japan*. London: Greenwood Press, 1984.

Cobbing, A. *The Japanese Discovery of Victorian Britain*. Surrey: Japan Library, 1998.

Cortazzi, H. 'The Pestilently Active Minister: Dr. Willis's Comments on Sir Harry Parkes'. *Monumenta Nipponica* 39 (1984): 147-161.

Cortazzi, Hugh. *Dr. Willis in Japan, 1862-1877: British Medical Pioneer*. London: Athlone Press, 1985.

Cortazzi, H., ed. *Mitford's Japan: The Memoirs and Recollections, 1866-1906, of Algernon Bertran Mitford, the first Lord Resdale*. London: Athlone Press., 1985.

Cortazzi, Hugh. 'Yokohama: Frontier Town 1859-1866'. *Asian Affairs* 17 (1986): 1-68.

Cortazzi, H. *Victorians in Japan: In and Around the Treaty Ports*. London: Athlone Press, 1987.

Craig, A. *Chōshū and the Meiji Restoration*. Cambridge: Harvard University Press, 1961.

Craig, Edwin O. Reischauer and Albert. *Tradition and Transformation: Japan*. Boston: Houghton Mifflin Company, 1989.

Crawcour, S. 'The Development of a Credit System in Seventeenth Century Japan'. *Journal of Economic History* 21, no. 3 (1961).

Crawcour, E. Sydney. 'The Tokugawa Heritage'. In *The State and Economic Enterprise in Japan*, ed. William W. Lockwood, 17-44. Princeton: Princeton University Press, 1965.

Daniels, Gordon. *Sir Harry Parks; British Representative in Japan 1865-83*. Surrey: Japan Library, 1996.

Davis, Winston. 'Parish Guilds and Political Culture in Village Japan'. *Journal of Asian Studies* 36, no. November (1976): 25-36.

De Becker, J. E. *The Annotated Civil Code of Japan*. London: Butterworth and Co., 1909.

Dennett, T. *Americans in East Asia: A Critical Study of the policy of the United States with reference to China, Japan, and Korea*. New York: Macmillan and Company, 1941.

Duus, P. *The Rise of Modern Japan*. Stanford: Stanford University Press, 1976.

Ericson, Mark David. 'The Tokugawa Bakufu and Leon Roches'. Ph.D. diss., University of Hawaii, 1978.

Fox, Grace. *Britain and Japan; 1859-1882*. Oxford: Oxford University Press, 1969.

Francks, Penelope. *Japanese Economic Development; Theory and Practice*. London: Routledge, 1992.

Gluck, Carol. *Japan's Modern Myths*. Princeton: Princeton University Press, 1985.

Griffis, W. E. *The Mikado's Empire*. New York: Harper Brothers, 1913.

Hale, J. O. 'The Myth of the Reluctant Litigant'. *Journal of Japanese Studies* 4 (1978): 359-390.

Hall, John Whitney. 'The Castle Town and Japan's Modern Urbanization'. *Far Eastern Quarterly* 15, no. 1 (Nov) (1955): 37-56.

Hara, S. 'Shin Kin-yu no Sōsetu'. In *Yokohama shi-hi*, 3. Yokohama: Yurindo-Yokohama, 1961.

Hartoonian, H. *Toward Restoration*. Berkeley: University of California Press, 1970.

Hauser, William B. *Economic Institutional Change in Tokugawa Japan: Osaka and the Kinai Cotton Trade*. New York: Cambridge University Press, 1974.

Henderson, Dan Fenno. *Conciliation and Japanese Law; Tokugawa and Modern*. Vol. 1. Tokyo: Tokyo Univeristy Press, 1965.

Henderson, D. F. *International Encyclopedia of Comparative Law*. Vol. 7. Boston: Martinius Nijhoff Publisher, 1973.

Henderson, Dan Fenno. "'Contracts" in Tokugawa Villages'. *Journal of Japanese Studies* 1, no. 1 (1974): 51-81.

Henderson, D. F. *Village Contracts in Tokuugawa Japan*. Seattle: University of Washington Press, 1975.

Hoare, J. E. *Japan's Treaty Ports and Foreign Settlements: The Uninvited Guests, 1858-1899*. Surrey: Japan Library, 1994.

Hoare, J. E., ed. *Britain and Japan, Biographical Portraits*. Vol. 3. Surrey: Japan Library, 1999.

Hoare, J. E. *Embassies in the East: The story of the British Embassies in Japan, China, and Korea, from 1859 to present*. Surrey: Curzon Press, 1999.

Honjo, E. *The Social and Economic History of Japan*. New York: Russel, 1965.

Howell, David L. 'Territoriality and Collective Identity in Tokugawa Japan'. *Daedalus* 127, no. 3 (1998): 105-132.

Hunter, Janet. 'Labour in the Japanese Silk industry in the 1870's: the Tomioka Nikki of Wada Ei'. In *Europe Interprets Japan*, ed. Gordon Daniels. Tenterden, Kent: Paul Norbury Publications, 1984.

Hyde, Francis E. *Far Eastern Trade 1860-1914*. London: Adam and Charles Black, 1973.

Imai, Kenichi, and Komiya, Ryutaro eds. *Business Enterprise in Japan: Views of Leading Japanese Economists*. Translated by Dore, Ronald, Whittaker, Hugh. Cambridge: MIT Press, 1994.

Ishii, Kanji. *Kindai Nihon to Igirisu Shihon: Jyarudin Maseson shyokai o chushin ni*. Tokyo: University of Tokyo Press, 1984.

Iwamura, H. 'Kobe chuzai Eikokoku taishika saibamkiryoku hoyaku, 1871 Kugatsu yori 1872 jyu ichi gatsu made no kiryoku', [Japanese translation of Documents of British (sic) consular court at Kobe, From September 1871 to November 1871]. Osaka Keizai HokaDaigaku Ho Gakkai 16 (1987).

Jansen, M. *Sakamoto Ryōma and the Meiji Restoration*. Princeton: Princeton University Press, 1961.

Jansen, Marius B., ed. *The Cambridge History of Japan*. Vol. 5. Cambridge: Cambridge University Press, 1993.

Jeater, Diana. 'A Dying Practice? African Arbitration and Native Commisioners' Courts in Southern Rhodesia, 1898-1914'. Unpublished (1999).

John, Nicholas, ed. *Madam Butterfly; Opera Guide 26*, Opera Guide. London: John Calder (Publishers) Ltd., 1990.

Kalland, Arne. 'A Credit Institution in Tokugawa Japan: the Ura-tamegin Fund of Chikuzen Province'. In *Europe Interprets Japan*, ed. Gordon Daniels. Tenterden, Kent: Paul Norbury Publications, 1984.

Kawada, Solomon B. Levine and Hisashi. *Human Resources in Japanese Industrial Development*. Princeton: Princeton University Press, 1980.

Kawashima, Takeyoshi. 'The Legal Consciousness of Contract in Japan'. *Law in Japan: An Annual* 7, no. 1 (1974): 1-21.

Keene, D. *The Japanese Discovery of Europe, 1770-1830.* Stanford: Stanford University Press, 1969.

Kinmonth, Earl H. *The Self-Made Man in Meiji Japanese Thought; from Samurai to Salary Man.* Berkeley: University of California Press, 1981.

Kiritani, Elizabeth. *Vanishing Japan; Traditions, Crafts, and Culture.* Tokyo: Charles E. Tuttle, Inc., 1995.

Kusuya, Shigetoshi. *Bakumatsu Oshu Kenbun Roku.* Tokyo: Shinjinbutsu Oraisha, 1992.

LaFeber, Walter. *The Clash; U.S.-Japanese Relations throughout History.* New York: W. W. Norton & Company, 1997.

Lockwood, W. *The Economic Developement of Japan; Growth and Structural Change 1863-1938.* Princeton New Jersey, Princeton University Press, 1954.

Lockwood, Sephen Chapman. *Augustine Heard and Company, 1858-1862; American Merchants in China* Harvard East Asian Mongraphs. Cambridge: Harvard University Press, 1971.

Lunt, Carrol. *Some Builders of Treaty Port China; In Two Parts.* Whittier, CA: Everett Stockton Trade Press.

Matsumoto, Junichi. *Yokohama no atta Fransu no Yubinkyoku.* Tokyo: Harashobou, 1994.

McMaster, J. 'The Japanese Gold Rush of 1859'. *Journal of Asian Studies* 19 (1960).

McMaster, J. 'British Trade and Traders in Japan: 1859-69'. Ph.D. diss., University of London, 1962.

Medzini, Meron. 'French Policy in Japan During the Closing Years of the Tokugawa Regime'. Ph.D. diss., Harvard Univerity, 1964.

Medzini, Meron. *French Policy in Japan During the Closing Years of the Tokugawa Regime.* Cambridge: Harvard University Press, 1971.

Minami, Ryoshin. *The Economic Development of Japan; A Quantitative Study.* London: Macmillan Press Ltd., 1994.

Morris, Morris David. 'The Problem of the Peasant Agriculturist in Meiji Japan, 1873-1885'. *Far Eastern Quarterly* 15, no. 3 (1956): 357-370.

Morris-Suzuki, Tessa. *A History of Japanese Economic Thought.* London: Routledge/Nissan Institute for Japanese Studies, 1989.

Nakamura, Hajime. 'Basic Features of the Legal, Political, and Economic Thought of Japan'. In *1967*, ed. Charles Moore, 141-163. Honolulu: University of Hawaii Press, 1967.

Nakamura, H. 'Basic Feature of the Legal, Political, and Economic Thought of Japan'. In *The Japanese Mind ; Essentials of Japanese Philosophy and Culture*, ed. Charles A. Moore. Honolulu: East-West Center Press, 1991.

Nakaoka, San-eki. 'Japanese Research on the Mixed Courts of Egypt in the Earlier Part if the Meiji Period in Connection with the Revision of the 1858 Treaties'. *Jōchi Ajiagaku* 6 (1988): 11-47.

Nishikawa, Takeomi. *Bakumatsu Meiji no Kokusai shijo to Nihon: Kito Boueki to Yokohama.* Tokyo: Yuzankaku Shuppan, 1997.

Ooms, Herman. *Tokugawa Village Practice: Class, Status, Power, Law.* Berkeley: University of California Press, 1996.

Paske-Smith, M. *Western Barbarians in Japan and Formosa in Tokugawa Days 1603-1868.*

Kobe: Tanaka Printing Co., 1930.

Puccini, Giacomo. 'Madama Butterfly'. Cardiff: Welsh National Opera, 1998.

Putney, Albert H. *Business, Commerce, and Finance; Foreign Laws*. Chicago: Cree Publishing Company, 1910.

Ramseyer, J. Mark. 'The Costs of the Consensual Myth: Antitrust Enforcement and Institutional Barriers to Litigation in Japan'. *Yale Law Journal* 94, no. 3 January (1985): 604-645.

Ramseyer, J. Mark. *Odd Markets in Japanese History*. Cambridge: Cambridge University Press, 1997.

Reischauer, Haru Matsukata. *Samurai and Silk; A Japanese and American Heritage*. Cambridge: Harvard University Press, 1986.

Roberts, John G. *Mistui: Three Centuries of Japanese Business*. New York: Weatherhill, 1991.

Rozman, Gilbert, Marius B. Jansen. *Japan in Transition from Tokugawa to Meiji*. Princeton: Princeton University Press, 1986.

'Rule Britannia'. *Law Institute Journal* 67, no. 12 (1993): 1198-99.

Sargent, G. W. *The Japanese Family Storehouse*. New York: Cambridge University Press, 1958.

Seidensticker, Edward. *Low City, High City; Tokyo from Edo to the Earthquake*. Cambridge: Harvard University Press, 1991.

Shibusawa, E. *The Autobiography of Shibusawa Eichii: From Peasant to Entrepreneur*. Translated by T. Craig. Vol. University of Tokyo Press. Tokyo, 1994.

Shinbo, Hiroshi. *Kinsei no Bukka to Kaeizai hatten: zenkogyoka shakai e no suryoteki sekkin*. Tokyo: Toyo Keizai Shinpōsha, 1978.

Skene-Smith, N. 'Materials on Japanese Social and Economic History: Tokugawa Japan (1)'. *Transactions of the Asiatic Society of Japan*. Second Series, Vol. 14, June 1937.

Smith, Thomas C. *The Agrarian Origins of Modern Japan*. Stanford: Stanford University Press, 1959.

Spalding, William F. *Eastern Exchange Currency and Finance*. London: Sir Isaac Pitman and Sons Ltd., 1918.

Statler, Oliver. *Shimoda Story*. Honolulu: University of Hawaii Press, 1986.

Steenstrup, Carl. *A History of Law in Japan until 1868*. New York: E. J. Brill, 1991.

Sugiyama, Shiya. *Meiji Ishin to Igirisu Shōnin, Tomasu Guroba no Shōgai*. Tokyo: Iwanami Shoten, 1993.

Takayanago, Shinzo. 'Wakai shugi ni tatsu Saiban'. *Chūō Kōron* 56, no. 4 (1941).

The Kanagawa Prefectural Government. *The History of Kanagawa*. Yokohama: The Kanagawa Prefectural Government, 1985.

Toby, Ronald. *State and Diplomacy in Early Modern Japan; Asia and the Development of the Tokugawa Bakufu*. Stanford: Stanford University Press, 1991.

Torbert, D. F. Henderson and P. M. 'Traditional Contract Law in Japan and China'. In *International Encyclopedia of Comparative Law*, 8. Boston: Martinius Nijhoff Publisher.

Totman, C. *The Collapse of the Tokugawa Bakufu, 1862-1868*. Honolulu: University of Hawaii Press, 1980.

Totman, Conrad. *Japan Before Perry*. Berkeley: University of California Press, 1981.

Tsuchiya, Takao. 'An Economic History of Japan'. *The Transactions of the Asiatic Society of Japan* 15 (Second Series) (1937): 1-269.

Tsuchiya, Yoshio. *Shibusawa Eichi*. Tokyo: Yoshikawa Kobunsha, 1988.

Ubukata, Toshiro. *Meiji Taishō Kenbun*: Chūōkōron Bunko, 1981.

Ware, Edith E. *Business and Politics in the Far East*. New Haven: Yale University Press, 1932.

Waswo, A. *Modern Japanese Society, 1868-1994*. Oxford: Oxford University Press, 1996.

Waters, Neil L. 'The Second Transition: Early to Mid Meiji in Kanagawa Prefecture'. *The Journal for Asian Studies* 49, no. 2 (1990): 305-322.

Westney, D. Eleanor. *Imitation and Innovation: the transfer of Western organizational patterns to Meiji Japan*. Cambridge: Harvard University Press, 1987.

Wigmore, John Henry. 'Private Law in Old Japan'. *The Transactions of the Asiatic Society of Japan* 20, no. Dec. (1892).

Wildes, Harry Emerson. *Aliens in the East*. Philadelphia: University of Pennsylvania Press, 1937.

Williams, Harold S. *Shades of the past; or, Indiscreet tales of Japan*. Tokyo: Charles E. Tuttle Company, 1959.

Williams, Harold S. *Foreigners in Mikadoland*. Rutland: Charles E. Tuttle Company, 1972.

Williams, Harold S. *Tales of the Foreign Settlements in Japan*. Rutland: Charles E. Tuttle Company, 1986.

Yamamura, Kozo. 'From Coins to Rice: Hypotheses on the Kandaka and Kokudaka Systems'. *Journal of Japanese Studies* 14, no. 2 (1988): 341-367.

Yen-P'ing, Hao. *The Comprador in Nineteenth Century China: Bridge between East and West*. Cambridge: Harvard University Press, 1970.

Yokohama Kaikō Shiryōkan. 'Yokohama ni atta seiyo: Bakumatsu no gaikokuji kyoryuchi'. *Tamakusu* 5 (1987): 1-56.

Yokohama Kaikō Shiryōkan. *Shiyou ga kataru Yokohama no hyakunen: Bakumatsu kara Showa Shoki made*. Yokohama: Yokohama Kaikō Shiryōkan, 1991.

Yokohama Kaikō Shiryōkan. *Yokohama Chukagai [Yokohama's Chinatown]*. Yokohama: Yokohama Archives of History, 1994.

Yokohama Kaikō Shiryōkan. *Sekai manyukatachi no nippon: Nikki to ryokoki to gaido bukku*. Yokohama: Yokohama Kaikō Shiryōkan, 1996.

Yokohama Kaikō Shiryōkan. *Yokohama Eifutsu chutongun to gaikokujin kyoryuchi*. Tokyo: Tokyo do Shupan, 1999.

Yokohama Kaikō Shiryōkan and Yokohama Kindai shi Kenkyukai. *Yokohama no Kindai*. Tokyo: Nihon Keizai Hyoronsha, 1997.

Yokohama Shishi Ko. 11 vols. Yokohama: Yokohama Shiyakusho, 1931-1933.

Yokoyama, Toshio. *Japan and the Victorian Mind: A Study of Stereotyped Images of a Nation 1850-80*. London: The Macmillan Press Ltd., 1987.

Yonemura, Anne. *Yokohama Prints from the Nineteenth Century*. Washington, D.C.: Smithsonian Institution Press, 1990.

Yumoto, Kouichi. *Meiji Jibutsu Kigen Jiten*. Tokyo: Kashiwa Shobou, 1996.

ECONOMIC AND LEGAL THEORY

The New Palgrave: A Dictionary of Economics. Vol. 2, ed. John Eatwell. London: The Macmillan Press Limited, 1987.

Aoki, Masahiko. 'Toward an Economic Model of the Japanese Firm'. *Journal of Economic Literature* 28, no. March (1990): 1-27.

Arias, Patricia. 'La Consolidacion de una Gran Empresa en un Contexto Regional de industrias Pequeñas: El Caso de Calzado Canadá'. *Relaciones* 3: 171-253.

Atiyah, P. S. *The Rise and Fall of Freedom of Contract*. Oxford: Oxford University Press, 1979.

Atiyah, P. S. *Essays on Contract*. Oxford: Oxford University Press, 1986.

Atiyah, P. S. 'Common Law'. In *The Invisible Hand*, ed. J. Eatwell, M. Milgate, and P. Newman, 70-78. New York: Macmillan Press Limited, 1989.

Atiyah, P. S. *An Introduction to the Law of Contract*. 5th ed. Oxford: Oxford University Press, 1995.

Ayres, Ian, and Robert Gertner. 'Filling in Incomplete Contracts: An Economic Theory of Default Rules'. *The Yale Law Journal* 99, no. 1 October (1989): 87-130.

Barney, Jay B., and Mark H. Hansen. 'Trustworthiness as a Source of Competitive Advantage'. *Strategic Management Journal* 15 (1994): 175-190.

Barton, John H. 'The Economic Basis of Damages for Breach of Contract'. *Journal of Legal Studies* 277, no. 1 (1972): 277-304.

Beale, Hugh, and Tony Dugdale. 'Contracts Between Businessmen: Planning and the Use of Contractual Remedies'. *The British Journal of Law and Society* 2, no. 1 (1975): 45-60.

Bolton, Philippe Aghion and Patrick. 'Contracts as a Barrier to Entry'. *American Economic Review* 77, no. 3 (1987): 388-401.

Campbell, David, and Susan Clay. *Long Term Contracting: A Bibliography and Review of Literature*. Oxford: Centre for Socio-legal Studies, 1995.

Cheung, Steven N. S. 'Transaction Costs, Risk Aversion, and the Choice of Contractual Arrangements'. *Journal of Law and Economics* 23, no. 12 (1969): 23-42.

Chung, Tai-Yeong. 'Incomplete Contracts, Specific Inverstments, and Risk Sharing'. *Review of Economic Studies* 58 (1991): 1031-1042.

Coase, R. *The Firm, the Market, and the Law*. Chicago: University of Chicago Press, 1988.

Craswell, Richard. 'Efficiency and Rational Bargaining in Contractual Settings'. *Harvard Journal of Law and Public Policy* 15, no. 3 (1992): 805-837.

Davis, John. *Exchange*. Buckingham: Open University Press, 1992.

Eatwell, John, Murry Milgate, and Peter Newman, eds. *Allocation, Information, and Markets*, The New Palgrave. London: W. W. Norton, 198s. *Contract as Promi Milgate, and Peter Newman, eds. The Invisible Hand*, The New Palgrave. London: W. W. Norton, 1989.

Eggertsson, Thràinn. *Economic Behavior and Institutions*. Cambridge: Cambridge University Press, 1990.

Ellickson, Robert C. 'Of Coase and Cattle: Dispute Resolution Among Neighbors in Shasta County'. *The Stanford Law Review* 38, no. 2 Feb (1986): 623-687.

Ellickson, Robert C. 'A Critique of Economic and Sociological Theories of Social Control'. *Journal of Legal Studies* 16, no. January (1987): 67-99.

Ellickson, Robert C. *Order Without Law; How Neighbors Settle Disputes*. Cambridge: Harvard University Press, 1991.

Fried, Charles. *Contract as Promise*. Cambridge, MA: Harvard University Press, 1981.

Friedman, D. 'Law and Economics'. In *The Invisible Hand*, ed. J. Eatwell, M. Milgate, and P. Newman, 99-104. New York: Macmillan Press Limited, 1989.

Friedman, Lawrence M. 'Law, Lawyers, and Popualar Culture'. *The Yale Law Journal* 98, no. 8 June (1989): 1579-1606.

Friedman, Lawrence. *The Republic of Choice*. Cambridge: Harvard University Press, 1990.

Fuchs, Victor R. (ed). *Policy Issues and Research Oppurtunities in Industrial Organization: Fiftieth Anniversary Colloqium III*. New York: Columbia University Press, 1972.

Fukuyama, Francis. *Trust: The Social Virtues and the Creation of Prosperity*. London: Penguin Group, 1995.

Gilmore, Grant. *The Death of Contract*. Columbus: Ohio State University Press, 1974.

Granovetter, Marc. 'Economic Action and Social Structure: The Problem of Embeddedness'. *American Journal of Sociology* 91, no. 3 (1985): 481-510.

Greenhouse, Carol J. 'Just in Time: Temporality and the Cultural Legitimation of Law'. *The Yale Law Journal* 98, no. 8 June (1987): 1631-1651.

Greif, Avner. 'Reputation and Coalitions in Medieval Trade: Evidence on the Maghribi Traders'. *Journal of Economic History* 49 (1989).

Greif, Avner. 'Institutions and International Trade: Lessons from the Commercial Revolution'. *American Economic Review* 82 (1992).

Greif, Avner. 'Cultural Beliefs and the Organization of Society: A Historical and Theoretical Reflection on Collectivist and Individualist Societies'. *The Journal of Political Economy* 102 (1994).

Greif, Avner, Paul Milgrom, and Barry R. Weingast. 'Coordination, Commitment, and Enforcement: The Case of the Merchants Guilds'. *Journal of Political Economy* 102 (1994).

Heap, Shaun Hargreaves, Martin Hollis, Bruce Lyons, Robert Sugden, and Albert Weale. *The Theory of Choice: A critical guide*. Oxford: Blackwell Publishers, 1994.

Ivamy, E. R. Hardy. *Mozley and Whiteley's Law Dictionary*. 11th ed. London: Butterworths and Co. (Publishers) Ltd., 1993.

Karsten, Peter. '"Bottomed on Justice": A Reappraisal of Critical Legal Studies Scholarship Concerning Breaches of Labor Contracts of Quitting or Firing in Britain and the U.S., 1630-1880'. *The American Journal of Legal History* 34, no. 3 July (1990): 209-261.

Kay, John. *Foundations of Corporate Success; How Business Strategies Add Value*. Oxford: Oxford University Press, 1993.

Klein, G. L. Priest and B. 'The Selection of Disputes for Litigation'. *Journal of Legal Studies* (1984).

Kronman, Anthony, and Richard Posner. *The Economics of Contract Law*. Boston: Little, Brown and Company, 1979.

Landa, Janet Tai. *Trust, Ethnicity, and Identity; Beyond the New Institutional Economics of Ethnic Trading Networks, Contract Law, and Gift Exchange*. Ann Arbor: The University of Michigan Press, 1996.

Lewis, Richard. 'Contracts Between Businessmen: Reform of the Law of Firm Offers and an Empirical Study of Tendering Practices in the Building Industry'. *Jour-*

nal of Law and Society 9, no. 2 (Winter1982): 153-175.

Liebermann, Yehoshua. 'Economic Effciency and Making of the Law: The Case of Transction Costs in Jewish Law'. *Journal of Legal Studies* 15, no. June (1986): 387-404.

Llewellyn, K. N. *The Bramble Bush: On Our Law and Its Study,* 1960.

Macaulay, Stewart. 'Non-contractual Relations in Business: A Preliminary Study'. *American Sociological Review* 28, no. 1 (1963): 55-69.

Macaulay, Stewart. 'Elegant Models, Emperical Pictures and the Complexities of Contract'. *Law and Society Review* 11, no. 3 (1977): 509-528.

Macaulay, Stewart. 'Popular Legal Culture: An Introduction'. *The Yale Law Journal* 98, no. 8 June (1989): 1545-1558.

Masten, Scott E., and Keith J. Crocker. 'Efficient Adaption in Long-Term Contracts: Take-or-Pay Provisions for Natural Gas'. *The American Economic Review* 75, no. 5 (1985): 1083-1093.

McKendrick, Ewan. *Contract Law.* 2nd ed. Macmillan Professional Masters, ed. Marise Cremona. London: Macmillan Press Ltd., 1994.

Mnookin, Robert H., and Lewis Kornhauser. 'Bargaining in the Shadow of the Law: The Case of Divorce'. *The Yale Law Journal* 88, no. 5 April (1979): 950-997.

Nader, Laura. 'Disputing Without the Force of Law'. *The Yale Law Journal* 88, no. 5 April (1979): 998-1021.

Offer, Avner. 'Between the Gift and the Market: The Economy of Regard'. *History Review* 50, no. 3 (1997).

Ostrum, Elinor. *Governing the Commons.* Cambridge: Cambridge University Press, 1990.

Posner, R. *The Economics of Justice.* Cambridge: Harvard Univerity Press, 1983.

Prichard, J. Robert S. 'A Systemic Approach to Comparative Law: The Effect of Cost, Fee, and Financing Rules on the Development of the Substantive Law'. *Journal of Legal Studies* 17, no. June (1988): 451-473.

Priest, George L., and Benjamin Klein. 'The Selection of Disputes for Litigation'. *Journal of Legal Studies* 13, no. January (1984): 1-55.

Richards, Paul. *Law of Contract.* London: Pitman Publishing, 1995.

Said, Edward. *Orientalism.* New York: Vintage Books, 1994.

Schultz, Franklin M. 'The Firm Offer Puzzle: A Study of Business Practice in the Contruction Industry'. *The University of Chicago Press* 19 (1952): 237-285.

Treitel, G. H. *An Outline of the Law of Contract.* 5th ed. London: Butterworth, 1995.

Trilcock, Michael J. *The Limits of Freedom of Contract.* Cambridge: Harvard University Press, 1993.

Varoufakis, Shaun P. Hargreaves Heap and Yanis. *GameTheory; A Critical Introduction.* London: Routledge, 1995.

Williamson, Oliver E. *The Economic Institutions of Capitalism: Firm, Markets, Relational Contracting.* New York: Macmillan, Inc., 1985.

Wittman, Donald. 'Is the Selection of Cases for Trial Biased?'. *Journal of Legal Studies* 15, no. January (1985): 185-243.

Wittman, Donald. 'Dispute Resolution, Bargaining, and the Selection of Cases for Trial: A Study of the Generation of Biased and Unbiased Data'. *Journal of Legal Studies* 17, no. June (1988): 313-352.

INDEX

For Product Safety Concerns and Information please contact our EU
representative GPSR@taylorandfrancis.com Taylor & Francis Verlag GmbH,
Kaufingerstraße 24, 80331 München, Germany

Printed and bound by CPI Group (UK) Ltd, Croydon, CR0 4YY
08/05/2025
01864357-0002